WHITE CITY

Donald James Wheal

WHITE CITY

C̄

Century · London

Published by Century 2007

2 4 6 8 10 9 7 5 3 1

First published in Great Britain in 2007 by
Century
Random House, 20 Vauxhall Bridge Road,
London SW1V 2SA

www.randomhouse.co.uk

Addresses for companies within The Random House Group Limited can be found at:
www.randomhouse.co.uk/offices.htm

The Random House Group Limited Reg. No. 954009

A CIP catalogue record for this book
is available from the British Library

ISBN 9781846050855

The Random House Group Limited makes every effort to ensure that the papers used in its
books are made from trees that have been legally sourced from well-managed and credibly
certified forests. Our paper procurement policy can be found at:
www.randomhouse.co.uk/paper.htm

Typeset by SX Composing DTP, Rayleigh, Essex
Printed and bound in Great Britain by
Clays Ltd, St Ives plc

CONTENTS

From World's End to White City

In 1944 my family were bombed out of the World's End, Chelsea. I had lived in this warm, dirty, rundown part of London all my life, as had my parents and their parents, so that the web of family was held on threads that stretched back deep into the nineteenth century. The bombing of the World's End abruptly ended this continuity. After a few months' stay near Windsor we moved back to a clean but bleak London suburb called White City.

This is a book about adolescence, and therefore a book with themes uncomfortably intermingled. It's about first sex and first love. But it's also about emerging from one world where we knew only war against the Hitler tyranny into another where we were gradually exposed to evidence of the equal, sometimes even darker, villainy of Joseph Stalin.

Victory over Nazi Germany brought an end to the dangers we had all survived but no end to the privations of wartime. There was a widespread housing shortage in the bombed cities; class distinctions seemed as strong as ever; and for many there was still a war to continue in the Far East.

But as a family war had enabled us to take, indeed forced upon us, a first step that my father had long planned, a move away from the

World's End and the limitations of our pre-war background to an increasingly affluent life in the years that followed. Yet there remained the strange pull which continued to be exerted upon all of us by that warmer, more crowded, but more sparsely provided existence of our World's End past.

From World's End to White City is dedicated to my parents, Robert and Phyllis Wheal. It was, after all, their journey.

ONE

World's End

One Saturday evening in the winter of 1930 two young working people left the 22 bus at World's End, Chelsea, and walked down Blantyre Street to the river. The tide was on the turn lapping a wide, glistening mud bank pock-marked with pieces of broken machinery and peppered by the tracks of rats and sea birds. It was the second evening the couple had been out together and they had already put flirtatious banter behind them. Leaning on the embankment wall with the shouts and Saturday night songs of the King's Arms pub behind them, watching the navigation lights of the coalers heading up-river for Lots Road Power Station, she asked him what he really wanted out of life.

He didn't hesitate. 'I want to marry you and have two sons.'

'Then,' she said, completely unruffled, 'I'll have to see what I can do.' She lifted her eyebrows, smiling. 'Anything else while we're about it?'

'Yes. I want us to get out of the World's End. Find our own place. Bring the boys up somewhere different. Somewhere where a Saturday night in the King's Arms . . .' he tipped his head towards the pub behind them where his mother and her friends were carousing '. . . isn't all they have to look forward to each week.'

'Our own place?' Nobody she knew owned their own place. 'And where will the money come from for that?'

'I don't know yet. Will you leave that to me?'

'I'll have to,' she said. 'After all, I'm going to be busy with the two boys.'

My parents had known each other, in the way most local children in the World's End knew each other, for most of their lives. In their late-teenage years they used to go to the same youth club and had begun occasionally to dance together on music nights before my father formally asked my mother to go to the pictures with him. I think the first film they saw together was *The Jazz Singer*. He was a plumber by trade, a strongly built young man of no more than average height, but determined, direct in his approach to his world's challenges. She was an unusually tall young woman for the time, just twenty years old, who attracted a lot of interest among the local boys. My father often tactlessly outspoken, my mother a natural diplomat, they were either a totally ill matched or a perfectly balanced pair.

My brother and I were lucky.

In the thirties and wartime forties when I grew up there, World's End was an area of mostly mean streets showered by dust and grit from the four chimneys of the coal-burning Lots Road Power Station. King's Road linked us to Sloane Square and Belgravia at the other end of Chelsea, a mile away, or a world away, however you chose to look at it.

Although it was part of one of London's richest boroughs, World's End's cheap purpose-built tenements, though only fifty years old, were already mouldering with damp and often enough rat-ridden. In the tenements bathrooms were unknown, lavatories were one between every two or three flats, and the common front door was left permanently open. Haphazardly among these slums were streets of houses which still retained a suggestion of their own Victorian elegance, unpainted, broken-windowed and crowded with several families as many of them were. They pointed back to a more prosperous period in the history of the area.

On Saturday evenings, the hub of the World's End, the 'island' as we called it, throbbed with life. On summer nights there would often be accordion music and dancing outside the World's End pub from which the area took its name. A sizeable crowd would be gathered outside Thwaite's, the brightly gas-lit butcher's where the Saturday night meat auction took place. With no refrigeration the butchers were obliged to sell off the week's unsold cuts in an auction conducted with less than Sotheby's decorum. Mr Thwaite, the butcher, would be standing in blood-stained apron and straw boater on a heavy chopping table he had dragged out of the shop. Pieces of dripping, unwrapped meat were waved about above the heads of men and women jostling and pushing for a better view. There were more scuffles than actual fights. My maternal grandmother, Eliza Toop, looked after my younger brother Kit and myself while my mother worked in a local shop and would often be charged with buying the Sunday joint. She was a tall woman, good with her elbows, and I fancy usually got the joint she was aiming for.

On really exciting nights in the late 1930s there were big political meetings at World's End. Union Jacks and party flags flying, Oswald Mosley and William Joyce (the man later notorious as Lord Haw-Haw) would march down King's Road at the head of a chanting column of Blackshirts. It was a short, convenient march from Mosley's headquarters in nearby Sloane Square. On Blackshirt nights the Communist Party would often filter through the side streets to confront the Fascists and my grandmother would hurry us back through the throbbing drums and the surging, menacing crowd before the serious fighting broke out.

Once or twice we were caught in the fray. Mounted police would be fighting to control the crowds and my grandmother, leg of lamb wrapped in bloodied paper in one pocket, twist of snuff and a bottle in the other, would guide my brother and me among the bucketloads of flying marbles hurled by Fascist and Communist alike underneath the police horses' hooves in an attempt to make them lose their footing.

One night she'd overstayed at the pub and we found a grim line of Blackshirts blocking our path. 'Not this way, lady,' one of the thugs said, arms crossed, truncheon visible on his belt.

Eliza drew herself up. 'I got these two boys to get home – and I'm going to get them home.' She pointed past him.

'Not this way you're not.'

'Listen, face-ache. This is King's Road, the king's highway. You going to stand aside or you want me to welt you one round the chops?' My grandmother brought her hand up, fist clenched. Kit and I were wide-eyed. 'And we'll bite his legs,' Kit said.

The prospect of struggling with a woman and two small boys didn't fit the Blackshirt's self-image. 'All right, lady,' he muttered. 'Just this once.' He looked round furtively and backed away to let us through.

I was really excited. 'Would you have hit him if he'd said no?'

'Oh, I would have landed him one all right, Dee,' she said. And laughed. 'Then I would have grabbed you and Kit and run like mad up the other meeting.'

'Up the other meeting' was a now long-lost term for as far away from the scene of trouble as possible.

In its nineteenth-century past the World's End had been an area of prosperous prostitution centred around the open-air cafés and dance-rooms of the notorious Cremorne Pleasure Gardens which ran from King's Road down to the river where the power station now stands. After the gardens were closed, the houses of ill repute lingered on along Lamont Road, Blantyre Street and Seaton Street for another generation or two. By the time I was growing up there in the 1930s this source of income was no longer significant in the local economy, though I suspect casual or occasional prostitution was a last resort of more working-class women in the fifty years before the outbreak of the Second World War than is generally recognised. Indeed, my own grandmother, perhaps inspired by the sights of her girlhood, had been on the fringe of this life for much of her youth, working as a 'waitress' in places like Dirty Dick's in Spitalfields. The morality of such matters looks different when it's a straight choice between the workhouse with inevitable separation from your child and doing what you can to keep a roof over your family's head.

In these pre-war years our immediate family consisted of my mother and father, my brother and myself, and my maternal grandmother, Eliza. On my father's side too we had grandparents living in the World's End: Henry James Wheal, my quiet, sharp-eyed grandfather, a First World War conscientious objector (derided as a 'conchie') who had, in fact, survived four years of the mud and shells of the Flanders battlefields as a volunteer ambulance driver; and his wife Minnie, approaching fifty years old at this time, a hard, aggressive woman. There were also a number of uncles and aunts and a clutch of cousins. We were much closer to my mother's side of the family: her sister, our Aunt May, and her six children lived a few yards from us. My grandmother Eliza, ever broke, overgenerous, and full of wildly inappropriate stories about her early life, felt part of our family. Not so my other grandmother, my father's mother Minnie. I have no idea how she met my grandfather, still less why he married her. Since moving to World's End just before 1900 she had ruled her family and a good many other families in her street. She was squarely built, loud, and from the age of about twenty-eight, toothlessly ugly. Notorious for physically intervening in other families' disputes, egged on by her dropsical side-kick Mrs Bashford, or Ma Bash as she was known, my grandmother Minnie was prepared to fight men as well as women if the cause, as *she* judged it, was right.

My grandfather, Henry James, would show deep disapproval

when Minnie came home recounting her latest triumph outside the King's Arms.

'You'll get your head knocked off one of these days,' he'd tell her. 'And if I'm there, I'll stand by and let it happen.'

''Course you would,' she'd say casually. 'Too much of a bloody conchie to do anything else.'

From the time I was born we lived in one room in Seaton Street behind the World's End pub. The house had once been a brothel like so many others in the street, but had since sunk low. The gas stove, lavatory and sink were on the floor below. But my mother already had her sights locked on to a very different form of accommodation.

In the twenties and thirties Chelsea was being cleaned up. Patches of poverty-stricken Victorian dwellings around Sloane Square were erased and people resettled in the blocks built by charitable institutions like the Peabody, Lewis and Guinness Trusts. These blocks were titled Dwellings or Buildings, to distinguish them from the blocks of expensive flats with more fancy names which were also being erected, often on the sites of the demolished property.

Developers undoubtedly saw that the World's End, with its riverside industry, its wharves and flour mills, huge power station, brewing and small metal-working businesses, was not a practical proposition for clearance. I believe the Guinness Trust was responding to the evictions which were taking place in other parts of Chelsea when it leased an unused nursery site (once part of Cremorne Gardens) on the King's Road. The decision was reached to construct upon it, for displaced or under-housed residents of Chelsea, four low-rise, five-storey, walk-up blocks of tenements.

A Chelsea girl has described how her family first saw Guinness Trust going up and the excitement when they realised these were not flats but Buildings, and thus affordable at a pinch. The day the Buildings were opened for occupation was an event. Of course no one could afford the hire of a van. Instead, a convoy of pony-drawn carts and costermongers' barrows piled high with chairs, brass beds and mattresses, swaying like a camel train, made its way down King's Road.

The new tenement blocks were designed to be a cheaper version of the established Guinness style of working-class dwellings, having fewer frills and amenities (white-tiled entrances for easy cleaning, gaslight only, no electricity, no bathroom and an outside 'balcony' lavatory), so that the sporadically employed journeymen tradesmen, and low-paid workers generally, could afford the very modest rents. Shortly after my younger brother was born, my mother, father, our newly widowed grandmother Eliza, Kit and myself moved into a one-bedroomed flat at number 3, Guinness Trust Buildings, Chelsea, London SW10.

TWO

Return to Royal Windsor

I told the story of the bombing of this poorer part of Chelsea and the tragedy at Guinness Trust Buildings in my last book, *World's End*. The Luftwaffe raid on London during the night of 23 February 1944 had Chelsea Power Station at Lots Road as its principal target. The power station survived but bombs were scattered across World's End. The morning following the raid we were homeless, refugees with bulging suitcases and faces blackened by soot blast. We were not alone. Hundreds of people in Guinness Trust Buildings, along King's Road and in the streets around Lots Road Power Station, were sifting through the wreckage for their few remaining possessions, wondering where they would sleep that night. Hundreds of others were lying injured in hospitals throughout Chelsea. The bodies of a further seventy-seven men, women and children, some school friends of ours, almost all nodding acquaintances at the very least, filled makeshift mortuaries like the line of coal sheds at Guinness Trust. Many, disfigured by blast and burning, were still being identified. A few, nobody knew how many, some still living, some dead, remained buried under the rubble.

At just after nine o'clock the air raid warning sounded, unusual in daylight for that period of the war. Looking up, we saw two single-engine aircraft flying east–west at a great height. Puffs of white anti-aircraft fire exploded around them as they dived steeply. Two Focke Wolf 190 fast reconnaissance aircraft were photographing the untouched Chelsea Power Station, the real target of last night, and the devastated blocks of Guinness Trust Buildings.

I was still several months off my thirteenth birthday, Kit a little younger; my mother and father a few years into their thirties. Now we were leaving World's End, Chelsea, leaving the tight network of streets where all four of us were born and where our grandparents, and some of our great-grandparents, had lived since Dickens' time. It was an area and a way of life that my brother and I loved as children. It offered freedom, plentiful friends, bombed houses to explore, the excitements of the muddy foreshore of the Thames . . .

For my parents, it was different. They were aware of the stigma attached at that time to being from the World's End and, in particular, to living in Guinness Trust. They were determined it was not going to attach to my brother and myself. Certainly, for my mother, there was also some regret at leaving the warmth and familiarity which comes from having lived in one place all your life; for my father, whose memories of the World's End were harsher, a move away from it was part of his young life's ambition. Ultimately I believe they were both ready to go.

Yet on the morning of 24 February 1944 there was no time to balance anticipation with regret. Our thoughts were all for the catastrophe around us. We had escaped from our flat by night but as we returned from where we had fled, we could see by shocking daylight what had really happened in the smoke and chaos of the night's air raid: fires still burning, our part of King's Road totally demolished, half Guinness Trust Buildings torn down, and random pockets of damage in the streets all around us. On that morning it was clear to us all we could no longer live in the World's End.

Whichever way you looked at it, it was the beginning of a new life for us. Better or worse than the old, we still couldn't guess.

Our first refuge was with my mother's sister, our Aunt May, who had taken her large family from the World's End at the beginning of the war and was now billeted in the disused wing of a rectory a few miles outside Windsor. I'm not aware of any of us suffering any psychological ill-effects after the World's End bombing, though I recognise that we did not lose any of our family or ourselves suffer any injuries. As ever we received a warm welcome from my aunt and her family who were collectively known as the Easts. Indeed we received a warm welcome from everybody except the Vicar of Braywood.

Selfish and lazy, the Reverend Daniels, Vicar of Braywood, looked with disdain at Kit's soot-embedded face and myself, dust-covered from rummaging through the remains of our flat. 'Out of the question,' he said when my mother's sister asked if we could rent two unused rooms in the wing of the rectory. 'Storage. I've plans to move some of the church draperies to a dryer place. Those two rooms will be ideal.'

'My sister's family have just been bombed out,' my aunt told him. 'They've nowhere to live.'

'Then she'll need to see the local billeting officer in Windsor. I can't sacrifice any more space than I have already. No one could deny that I've done my bit.'

He went further. At first he made it clear that he would not welcome us staying with my aunt even for the time my mother needed to apply for new ration books, prove we were entitled to an emergency set of clothing coupons and arrange somewhere for us to stay. In the end we were allowed a few days but no longer. Charity was simply not a word in the Reverend Daniels' vocabulary.

But these were also days of intense excitement. Nobody could miss the vast preparations being made in southern England for the invasion of Europe. Everywhere there were marching soldiers – British, American, Canadian, Polish; everywhere tented camps had sprung up; on every road huge convoys of military vehicles thundered by, day and night.

In that week we stayed at Braywood there were American soldiers to be talked to in their camp on the hillside in front of the vicarage. Their arrival one evening about a month earlier had seriously upset the vicar's equilibrium. The Reverend Daniels had become accustomed to seeing the hillside as part of his personal fiefdom where he liked to walk his red setter, Rajah. When a US armoured reconnaissance unit arrived with signed orders to pitch camp in front of the vicarage, Reverend Daniels, the clergyman who had refused shelter even to a dozen scouts rained out of their tents, was beside himself with wrath. Protesting impotently, he watched a village of khaki tents erected across the hillside in front of the vicarage: supply tents, cookhouse tents, bell tents, mess tents . . . Telephone wires looped down to the road; American and regimental flags fluttered from improvised flagpoles. The syncopated beat of Tommy Dorsey and Glenn Miller issued from camp loudspeakers . . .

This arrival of the Americans was a source of great pleasure to us. The latest stories of their clashes with the vicar were exchanged with relish. I can concede that the vicar had some cause for complaint – from a moral viewpoint. The girls lurking in the bushes beside the drive were certainly there to offer more than tea and sympathy, although his complaints seemed to centre more on the volume of the music than any other nuisance. My mother and Aunt May, never women to take unconsidered pleasure in anyone else's discomfiture, simply could not stop laughing every time they watched Daniels, cassock fluttering, marching down the hillside to deliver yet another futile protest to the imperturbably polite Texan colonel who commanded the unit.

THREE

At Joe and Jinny's

But the vicar had spoken. So once again it fell to my mother to find us somewhere to live. She faced a really difficult choice. She might have tried to find somewhere with a few creature comforts, that's to say with electricity and perhaps an indoor plumbed lavatory. Or equally she might have thought that to return to people we knew, even in conditions that were far from perfect, would be better for all of us.

The point was that this was not our first stay in the area. We had been evacuated to Windsor at the end of the first London Blitz and already knew one couple here. We had stayed several months with Joe the Poacher and his wife Jinny, champion Brussels sprout picker, world's worst cook, and the kindest-hearted gypsy woman you could hope to find.

I can still see Joe walking down the lane: broad, weighty, cap pulled to one side like one of the Dead End Kids, red face grinning with pleasure at seeing us all again. He walked as always when he came back from a poach, hands pushed deep in trouser pockets, elbows steadying the shotgun hinged to fit in the special poacher's pocket my mother had sewn into his jacket when we were last here; perhaps a trail of blood dripping from where he'd hooked a big hare into the back of his belt.

And Jinny at home, small, dark-skinned, black-eyed, in the rear room of the two-up, two-down cottage, the back-house or 'backus' as we all knew it, her nut-brown hands and arms smeared with blood as she tore the skins from the backs of yesterday's half-dozen rabbits which Joe had snared with the help of his ferrets.

Joe and Jinny were probably in their late thirties, although I doubt whether either of them would have been quite sure of their age. Joe was quick, cunning, sly and generous. Unless you lived with him, as we did, it would have been difficult to tell that he was unable to read or write. Jinny had probably spent a year or two in school somewhere and could write a letter with her own colourful phonetic spelling, Elizabethan in tone. Asked where they were born, Joe would vaguely claim Langley in Buckinghamshire though I believe that was simply the farm on which he and Jinny had first met. Neither of them ever once mentioned parents and perhaps had never known any. Neither seemed to have a past.

Uncomfortable, even unsavoury, as Water Oakley Cottages were, my mother decided the advantages of living with old friends prevailed. By the end of March 1944 we were reinstated in the upstairs two rooms of Joe and Jinny's farmworker's cottage.

The cottages, a row of five, still stand, empty now and about to be demolished, on the Windsor Road not far from the village of Bray. Unknown to us then, Bray Film Studios, where I subsequently often worked, stood on the river bank a hundred yards away at the end of our lane. I realised now that Joe and Jinny were unable to tell us that we lived cheek by jowl with a film studio because they were totally unaware of what a film studio was, having never seen a film in their lives. Kit and I were left to imagine that the studio was the secret headquarters of some covert wartime activity because there were occasionally guards on the gate. This was, in fact, because the studio shared an entrance drive with the abandoned stately home next door, where Winston Churchill had temporarily installed General de Gaulle, exiled from London perhaps as punishment for some display of Gallic arrogance. The crumbling riverside mansion known as Oakley Court was the post-war HQ for Hammer Horror films, a humorous coincidence that I'm sure Churchill would have enjoyed. From our tree house in the copse beside the cottages we had often seen a big official car leave the driveway, a long-necked unknown man in foreign uniform sitting alone in the back.

But our world was not one of high politics. It revolved around the row of cottages and farmworker inhabitants, every man, woman and child there looking up to Joe as rat-catcher, weather-man, poacher, unofficial farm manager, and commentator on the probable course of the war. George and Lizzie Soden lived on one side, diminutive Dimple Soden and his large wife Mollie on the other. Bert Latham, with his wife and two daughters, Doris and Hazel, lived one cottage further down. Leading a pair of heavy-shouldered cart-horses drilling, harrowing or rolling the land, Bert, at five foot tall, had to reach above his head for the bridle.

I came to see that Joe had changed since our last stay at Water Oakley. Now, for instance, he wore under his jacket a dark green US Army sweater, badly holed at both elbows but a sweater at least which he had never possessed before. He would also, on occasion, pull out a packet of Lucky Strike and offer them to anyone he was talking to, though he never smoked himself. Most remarkable was the fact that he had begun to move his lips when he stared at the *Daily Mirror* headlines. Kit and I both noticed that he had begun to get their meaning with new accuracy.

Jinny was touchingly and perhaps indiscreetly proud of these developments. 'It's they there Yanks,' she said. 'Joe's friend the Colonel, he bin and told Joe to go on a course they have up at Hollyport. Lots of they young Yanks can't read properly. 'Course Joe can, but he's been a bit lazy with his reading these last few years.'

My mother, perfectly straight-faced, said she'd never guessed. Good for Joe if he were polishing up his reading.

'They Yanks are different,' Jinny said. 'They don't take no for an answer, you know. They just laugh and say "move your bum", though they use a different word for it.' Her eyes sparkled. 'Joe said he's going to take me to Lunnon after the war. See the sights. And we'll come and see you and the boys. We'll bring a couple'a rabbits with us and a bit of old Drakey's pork fat to fry them in.'

My mother smiled. 'When we find a house, you'll be the first on the list, Jin.'

Our world was one of a great deal of warmth and friendliness but it was also one in which the fifth sense was predominant. Coming from the World's End, we were not unfamiliar with noxious industrial smells. Our school was rammed up against Chelsea Power Station. The coal dust and tang of burning in the air was only matched by the outpouring from the gas works. But country smells are different. The bluebell glade offered no challenge to the cottages' stench of over-flowing rust-bucket privies, the hideous reek of Joe's caged ferrets, the nauseating sweet-sour smell of a cupboardful of dead rabbits, or perhaps worst of all the high stink of three-hour-long cooked cabbage, Jinny's *specialité de la maison*.

Yet we felt lucky. We had survived the bombing. Every time my father came to Windsor for a weekend (he worked as a porter in Whitelands House, a very upmarket block of flats just short of Sloane Square) he brought with him news of other families, other school friends, who had died or been injured at Guinness Trust. We felt lucky, too, to be with people like Joe and Jinny who had become something more than friends, more, as they were to remain, part of the same family. But we had lost the anchor that the World's End had always provided.

I remember the weekend my father came down and told us that he had just discovered that La-di-dah had been killed the same night we were bombed. He was the madly eccentric newspaper seller, small, emaciated, epileptic, invariably dressed in a flat cap and a reach-me-down overlong raincoat, who scuttled about the 'island' at the heart

of the World's End. He was known as La-di-dah from the garbled
way he screeched his wares: '*News, Star, Standard!*' La-di-dah was
his version of one of the cries of old London. I knew no one in the
World's End who ever called him by another name.

When we were younger we were all (without good reason) a little
afraid of him. Later, 'La-di's 'ad a fit again,' from some passer-by
was enough to get a dozen callous, thrill-seeking kids racing down
Dartrey Road to see for themselves. Kit and I would certainly be
among them.

News of his death was yet another reminder of the permanent
change that had taken place in our own lives. Playing down by the
river at the bottom of the lane, Kit and I talked about it in a desultory
way.

''S funny about La-di.'

'I didn't think he'd be killed,' Kit said.

'Nor did I.'

We were trying to lure a duck close enough to be captured for
dinner. We'd never succeeded yet.

'I wonder who'll be there when we go back?' I said. 'Who'll be
selling papers.'

Tears welled up in Kit's eyes. For a while we forgot about the
duck. Perhaps he was thinking, like me, of the last time we had seen
our flat, the morning after the raid. We'd picked our way through the
suddenly unfamiliar rooms, silenced by the thought that all this
destruction had taken place around us yet the four of us scrambled
from it uninjured. We stared at shattered walls, window frames
ripped from their setting, broken furniture, doors torn off hinges,
menacing splinters of glass lying thick on the lino floor. Smoke
drifted through it from fires still burning in the King's Road.
Outside, I watched my school friend, Ted Simon, picking his way
over a huge mound of rubble. He was holding high a badly bent cage
with a dusty yellow canary, still alive, fluttering about inside.

The duck bobbed on the calm surface of the Thames. We didn't feel like murder any longer. 'Let's go back home,' Kit said. 'I mean, back to Joe and Jinny's.'

We stood on the river bank and gulped at each other. We no longer had a place we could talk about as home. We still used the word, and it still referred to number 3, Guinness Trust Buildings. But it was like talking of the dead. They are both with you and irretrievably lost to you at the same time.

My father, as I now see him, was a dominant personality. But except perhaps in his desire to execute a decision immediately, to 'get cracking', he was not overbearing. He would not, in any case, have succeeded in being overbearing with my mother, who exuded a quiet authority which impressed all, even those far better educated than herself. She was tall and, as I later began to understand, good-looking, but there was more to her than that. This is hard to say since it seems so obviously partial: she was not educated – like everybody of that World's End generation she had left school at thirteen or fourteen – but I never met anyone who knew her who was not impressed by her good sense and balanced view of the people and the world immediately around her.

Together they made a formidable marital team. Different as they were, Kit and I never once saw an argument between them. Talents they certainly had, but they lived in an age which wasted such talent in the working class with an insouciant profligacy. My mother's talent for diplomacy was to be confined to her family, friends, and to schmoozing the authorities into improving our lot. Against all competition she had got us our flat at Guinness Trust before the war; in 1939 she had talked herself into a job as an LCC auxiliary in order to stay with Kit and myself when we were evacuated. She had effectively taken command of our group of children in the chaos of the early days when we had lost touch with the headmaster and the rest of the school. My father's talent for organisation, more abrasive but decidedly effective, was expended on rising from stoker to manager of Whitelands House, the large and expensive block of flats in Sloane Square where he had first worked as a journeyman plumber in 1937.

Whitelands occupied an important place in our lives. Its tenants and their wealthy way of life were the subject of endless talk and a good deal of laughter between our parents. Whitelands was where we slept in the heat and coke dust of the huge furnace-room during the 1940 blitz. It was where we stumbled to the night we were ourselves bombed in 1944. It was the source of good things from a variety of tenants, from German U-boat captain's boots to, one Christmas, mysterious hard, cold green peas, frozen peas from an American tenant, the first we had seen in our lives. By 1944 my father had long emerged from the boiler room where he had begun as stoker, though he continued for many more years to stoke its great furnaces if the regular stoker were absent. He had been promoted first to porter in about 1942 and was by now second porter among the six or so (unfit for military service) who still serviced the one hundred flats.

Kit at this time was an eleven year old, still wrapped in dreams of sporting success from which he was never quite to emerge until he did National Service and shaped the commanding personality which would eventually make him a significant success in business, the chairman of leading British, German and French companies.

I personally had emerged from the World's End a twelve-year-old boy with a hyperactive imagination. Much of this had been inherited from my grandmother Eliza with her stories of her childhood and early life. She had died just four months before we were bombed, a last link with a Victorian world of sentimental song and unsentimental story where poverty made up the trappings and not the point of the tale. From my father came the lesson that you had best learn to fight your own battles. My mother's philosophy made for a sturdy sense of independence but was not competitive. My father's was. He once told Kit that he believed he would have been a rich man 'if it hadn't been for your mother'. There was, however, Kit says, no regret in his voice.

The winter had turned from mild to a cutting cold. There was thin snow on the ground and ice on the puddles of urine and excrement leaking from the outside bucket lavatories. At least it meant that the little girl in the next-door cottage was no longer playing in it.

Kit and I found plenty of things to grumble about. As the temperature dropped, our bedroom froze. All three of us slept on the floor and there weren't enough blankets to go round. We loved Jinny but we hated her food. We missed World's End.

For my mother more than Kit and me, life was impossibly difficult. The water supply to the cottage was one communal tap, sometimes frozen, situated in the backus. There was no water and no electricity on our floor of the cottage, although in my mother's earlier victory she had confronted the local authorities and the farmer landlord and succeeded in her request for an electricity supply. A single electric light was provided for the ground-floor front room. There was no gas to cook with. Water was heated on the iron stove in the front room, which was also Joe and Jinny's bedroom. Our wash basin was a bowl with a splash of warm water in it from the kettle if there was any left to cut the cold. A pee in the night was into a bucket on the landing. A bath was, of course, unknown to anybody who lived in Water Oakley Cottages, and remained unknown to Joe and Jinny all their lives.

My mother was at this time constantly on the go, putting our life together again. Then came a further blow. Kit and I had passed a certain bureaucratic marker since we were last living in Windsor in 1941. My mother was thus no longer recognised as having small children and therefore became eligible for conscription.

Less than a month after the bombing of Guinness she was issued with call-up papers for work on the land as a farm labourer. Somehow she took this cheerfully, joking with Joe and Jinny about how well equipped she was for land-work. They and others at the cottages, like our neighbours Dimple Soden and Mollie, certainly helped her all they could. But it was bitterly hard work in this raw weather, digging out potatoes, shredding Brussels sprouts from the vine, bagging them up in heavy, mud-sodden sacks and lugging them to the distant tractor points in the big Emmet fields.

When he came down the weekend after she had started, my father took my mother off to the pub alone. They seemed to us to be away a long time. When they came back he gave a brisk nod of his head, meaning that he wanted to speak to Kit and me upstairs in the bedroom. My mother said: 'Go easy on them. It's not their fault.' We didn't like the sound of that.

Upstairs, my father forcibly pointed out to Kit and me how much rested on our mother's shoulders these days, and how much any casual grumbling by us could increase the weight on her. She bore enough already, trying to organise schools, new ration books, replacement Identity Cards lost in the bombing, finding furniture for these two rooms here at Joe and Jinny's where there were no beds or blankets . . . None of it was easy for her, three months since her mother had died, and to cap it all now, she had to spend most of her day in the fields while we sat in warm classrooms. 'Stone the crows!' he said. 'You boys have it easy, and don't forget it.'

The message was more than clear: pitch in and help. Get out in the fields and help your mother when you're back from school, and no complaints about your own lot.

FOUR

The Future

After my father's robust lecture Kit and I tried to keep our grumbles from my mother but she was aware that in one area we were both deeply unsettled, not by the experiences at Guinness Trust or even the uprooting involved but most particularly by the fact that we would now be going to different schools. In fact, it was worse than that. These were not different schools that backed on to each other as at World's End where we could shout to each other across the dividing fence, but buildings five miles apart. Kit was to go back to Braywood, the village school we'd both attended when we were first evacuated to Water Oakley Cottages, and I to Windsor itself, to the grandly named local grammar, Windsor County Boys' School.

At Braywood Kit was faced with the familiar taunts and attempts at bullying from the local boys. But he wasn't prepared to put up with them. We had grown up in my father's credo that there was nothing to be expected but misery at school for anyone who was not prepared to fight the bully. In London we had practised with him since we were quite literally toddlers, swinging ill-aimed punches and receiving a poke, none too gentle, in the ribs to show us that no fight was all one-sided. In our teens, much to my mother's horror, we would take turns to fight my father bare-fisted but under strict rules

– no punching above the throat. Not the sort of upbringing that would be much approved of today. But as children we were also taught to be fervently anti-bullies and to regard all bullying as cowardly. The result so far had been a happy school life for us both in a culture where bullying was rife. When Kit arrived at Braywood there were by then a few more Londoners at the school than there had been during our previous stay. He quickly became the Londoners' champion and he and his friend Freddie Coco organised them into a highly effective defence group. It did nothing to improve the town versus country atmosphere at Braywood – but it did a lot to improve Kit's time there.

At Windsor County there were no bullying problems, or at least none that I encountered from the boys. My problems were of a very different order. First, it was made clear to me that boys should arrive on time at nine o'clock. A minute or two late and you were punished. When I first heard this I was deeply shocked. What sort of a school was this? In London, I had attended the West London Emergency Secondary School for Boys where it was pretty much accepted that a high proportion of the pupils would be late, especially after a night of heavy raids in the area. So, at Windsor, a five-mile bike ride in the mornings tested my unpractised punctuality to the limit.

Secondly, I quickly realised how far behind I was academically. The West London Emergency Secondary School for Boys was a makeshift amalgamation of the remnants of six West London grammar schools that had been evacuated at the beginning of the war. Those boys who had stayed behind had been jostled together in one emergency establishment housed in Sloane School, World's End. We spent much of our time there playing cards in the shelter and calling out to the girls next door in Carlyle School. From time to time we'd indulged in a very modest amount of school work. To my horror I found the boys at Windsor were under the whip from nine to four. Homework was given, and even expected to be completed! I made nervous and very tentative enquiries about progress in History and French, my strongest subjects as I thought. There was, I knew, no point in asking about Maths or Physics. A boy named Grant-Smith (there were quite a few of these double names), or Granny Smith as he was known (a rural joke I never got until years later), told me that in History they were studying Magna Carta – some of it in Latin. I had heard of Magna Carta – but in Latin!

And they were doing the Future, he said, in French. I stared at him in astonishment. 'If you know the future,' Granny Smith said loftily, 'there are so many more things you can do.'

'Well . . .' I said hesitantly. '. . . there must be.'

I knew that I had not understood but I wasn't at all sure what it was I hadn't understood. My grandmother had regularly used tea-leaves to tell our fortunes, but if we were to be studying the Future, why do it in French? My father, who would certainly have found some answer, was in London. Tentatively I asked Joe. 'They there Frenchies,' he said, 'they don't really have a future till we kick out they Jerries.' Could it be anything to do with that?

My mother, as full of practical common sense as she was, had nevertheless not much grasp of the concept of the Future Tense (as the problem finally revealed itself to be) of the French language. My dear old grandmother Eliza, when she was still with us, always claimed she could parlay-voo with the best of 'em but I had by now come to the conclusion that her knowledge of French was confined to that old First War song: '*Mademoiselle from Armenteers, parlay-voo?*' There was, apparently, no help to hand. But some degree of salvation, sartorial salvation as it happened, was not far around the corner.

In my first minutes at Windsor County I had identified my most alarming problem as being the school uniform. At the West London Emergency Secondary School we'd had six different ones. Uniformity was, in the nature of things, out of the question. Even tidiness was difficult to impose. We pleaded shortage of clothes coupons, we pleaded mothers on war work unable to spare the time for repairs to torn pockets. Some boys (sometimes genuinely, but in any case with not too much relevance) pleaded narrow escapes from the bombing that week. Our masters just shrugged. They were mostly long past retirement age, recalled to replace staff serving in the forces and waiting patiently for the imminent end. Not their own but the imminent end, or so it seemed in early 1944, of the war.

At Windsor it was totally different. Turn-out was something the masters were very keen on. The school uniform was grey shorts until the age of fourteen, green school jacket with red piping and school badge sewn on breast pocket, green cap with roundels of red tape. Every boy came to school looking like an immaculate Just William. In screeching contrast I had presented myself on my first day perfectly turned out, or so I imagined, in the only clothes I had: these were items supplied by the Lord Mayor of London's Air Raid Relief Fund and carried a red satin label on the inside jacket pocket to attest to the fact. I doubt if the Lord Mayor of London had in fact much to do with the selection of the clothes, all donated via the unending generosity of the American people. There was nothing second-hand about the clothing but, not surprisingly, my particular outfit caused a stir among boys and staff. I was dressed for my first day in a wide-shouldered, dark grey, generously orange-checked Californian cashmere jacket and palest zoot-suit gabardine trousers. Hair flopping over the eyes, I felt I only needed a clarinet to step up with the band and swing to 'American Patrol'.

I received a few odd looks from other boys as I made my way to the second-form classroom, nothing too intimidating, but in the classroom I met for the first time the cold eyes of my new form master. I introduced myself.

He drew himself up straight-backed. 'What are you wearing, boy?'

I looked down at my jacket and trousers. The questions of bullying schoolmasters always have simple answers. But I knew that to respond, 'A jacket and trousers, sir,' would be unwise.

I stumbled over my reply: 'I, sir . . . Well, sir . . . It's all I've got, sir.'

'At Windsor County we have a school uniform. In case it has escaped your notice, boy, it is forest green in colour. With red piping to the jacket.' He spoke like that. He was the English master, after all. He leaned forward to inspect me. 'I see no forest green. I see no red piping.'

I looked down at my jacket. Truth was, I didn't either, but then I didn't expect to. He obviously did.

He raised his eyebrows, inviting an explanation. When I clearly had none to offer, he began again. 'Where did this come from?'

'It's from the Lord Mayor, sir,' I stuttered.

'The Lord Mayor's Show?' he enquired silkily, infinitely pleased with his *bon mot* and the burst of laughter from the class.

'The Lord Mayor's Fund, sir.' I was getting angry now. Bullies come in all shapes and sizes. But this one I couldn't challenge to a fight in the playground.

Everybody knew what the Lord Mayor's Air Raid Relief Fund was. Everybody in London anyway. As I explained in deliberate detail our recent difficulties and the origin of my outfit, he wrapped his gown closer round him and frowned in an exasperated, superior manner. A cockney oik in tasteless American hand-me-downs, I suppose he was thinking. Today I wonder if resentment of American wealth and generosity was already eroding his self-confidence, as it has so many others' since? Had he stood with American soldiers in Windsor pubs, watching while they freely bought drinks for the locals, and decided they were paid too much for their contribution to victory? Was he thinking that he would never know what it was like to wear clothes of the quality (if not necessarily the style) of my cashmere jacket, and certainly never be well off enough to donate brand new jackets to charity?

Who knows? He looked down at his register, bored with the game. His last words to me were a brisk instruction to get myself a school blazer as soon as clothing coupons allowed.

Festina lente would have been my motto if I'd known the Latin for hurrying slowly. I did as commanded but by then I had come to love my American outfit. And it was not without its impact on some of the other boys. My cashmere jacket and wide pale grey trousers had the same effect on them as had, earlier in the war, the U-boat captain's ankle boots my father had acquired for me when I'd grown out of my old shoes and we had no coupons for new ones.

And not without importance to my acquisition of status at the school was the fact that I was now the only boy in the second form at Windsor County wearing long trousers. Our form master had by now given up making comments about my clothes as I dragged out the trusty clothing coupons excuse. To my classmates, I also had the distinction of having been bombed out by the Luftwaffe. I had even let it be known that I sometimes wore captured U-boat captain's soft leather ankle boots. When I felt like it, I added casually.

Life became more tolerable as I was seen as something of an early well-dressed rebel-without-a-cause.

FIVE

Shirley

My American outfit had opened up other vistas, too. There was a girl we used to play with down at Monkey Island Lane during our earlier stay at Water Oakley, a bold, red-haired tomboy a year or two older than me, named Shirley. For a few months in 1941 when Kit and I had attended Braywood School, the one big classroom all ages were taught in together meant I saw her every day, observed the cheeky way she could behave to our teacher, Mr Snow, or Gaffer Snow as he was known. One day we were all jostling in the entrance to the classroom when Shirley let out a really loud scream. We all turned to look at her. 'Eric Knight just pinched my bum,' she shouted, outraged.

Knight, a burly boy and something of a bully, reddened and moved away from her. He held his hands wide. 'I didn't, I wouldn't touch her. Wouldn't want to.'

'Just carry on. Take your places.' Gaffer Snow hustled us in.

Eric Knight shoved his face at Shirley. 'I didn't touch you, see?'

Undaunted, Shirley turned on him. 'Then if it wasn't you, it must have been Mr Snow. Is that right, sir?'

Knight ducked as if she'd hurled a missile. The Gaffer flinched. Charges of sexual harassment were unknown then but Mr Snow's pale face went even paler. He looked down at his charges. 'T-take your places,' he stuttered. 'And see me at break, Knight. I won't have this behaviour towards the girls.'

With a none-too-secret smile Shirley walked demurely to her desk.

By the time we returned to Windsor I think the taunting of Eric Knight and a few balancing games we'd played together on a log down by the river were the only facts I would have recalled about her. If I'd had any reason to try to recall Shirley herself, I wouldn't have got further than her readiness to answer back at school and her vibrant auburn hair.

She lived with her farm-labourer parents just outside the village, about a mile down the road from Water Oakley. I remember seeing her again shortly after we arrived for the second time. She got off the bus from Windsor, hair flowing, fourteen maybe just touching fifteen, a big girl, the sort of girl I was very much beginning to notice nowadays.

She had seen me, I'd no doubt about that. Even recognised me. Her lipsticked lip curled for a moment then she looked the other way and crossed the road, swinging her handbag. But as she passed, barely turning her head towards me, she said: 'Flash jacket.'

I couldn't think what to say. She was ten steps past me before I got out the words. 'American,' I called out to the back of her bobbing auburn head. 'It's American.'

She didn't stop, just continued walking over to where two older girls were standing on the street. Within moments they were laughing together, one of them, a girl of about sixteen, occasionally turning and making it clear that they were laughing at me.

It was late May. By now there was no other subject of conversation up and down the country in barracks, pubs, clubs, schools and hospitals, but *invasion*. It was like 1940 but this time we weren't talking about the Germans invading *us*. Our armies, British, American, Canadian and Polish, were poised to invade *them*. Where exactly on the coast of France we didn't know. The choice was wide: the Pas de Calais, Normandy, Brittany or even the Bay of Biscay. More important than where, however, was when, and on that we speculated endlessly. It was the time of Laurence Olivier's patriotic rendition on film of Shakespeare's *Henry V*. Snatches of his speeches were recited throughout the country:

> And gentlemen in England now abed
> Shall think themselves accursed they were not here,
> And hold their manhoods cheap whiles any speaks
> That fought with us upon St Crispin's Day

It was stirring stuff on the eve of our return to France where the German Army had totally defeated us in 1940. There had been significant victories throughout late 1942 and 1943 in North Africa and Italy, in the air and at sea. But we were impatient for a land victory in France. Churchill was impatient. I was impatient.

Invasion activity was all around us. Army trucks rumbled through the night; American signals specialists, mostly black, worked at the top of telephone poles to keep the overloaded system operating. Joe went out, sniffed the air and said, 'Weather looks rough.'

This was deeply worrying. It meant no invasion of Europe this week. Did Joe agree?

'Mebbe so, Raz D.' He often, mysteriously, prefaced my initial with this Arab honorific. Kit similarly was usually Raz K.

'Tell you what,' said Joe, who had developed a close if unlikely relationship with a very upright West Point colonel at the Hare and Hounds, 'you watch out for they Yankees to leave Hollyport.'

Hollyport was the huge American army camp just down the road to Maidenhead. 'Leave?' My heart fluttered with alarm. 'They're not going home?'

He shook his head as if he were privy to the precise time and place of the invasion. 'The day they Yankees be gone, the next morning you'll have your invasion.'

'Did the Colonel tell you they were in the first wave?' I probed. We all knew terms like 'first wave' by now.

'Not a word,' he said with a big red-faced grin. 'You arse too many questions, Raz D, you know that?'

'Did he say where his beaches were? The Germans would like to know that. Did he tell you, Joe? I won't tell a soul.'

Joe grinned. 'Me and the ole Colonel just talks about how you outwit they there hares, doan we, Raz D? We leave it to the bright boys in Lunnon to outwit they Germans.'

Another talent wasted. He should have been in MI5.

Poachers have a special tight-lipped quality. People knew instinctively that they could trust Joe. I wonder now how much he really knew about the exact date the Americans were to move down to the assembly areas on the south coast. I think it quite possible it was more than he revealed.

These six months in the country were, for me, a watershed in a dozen ways, but most particularly in the way that I saw, the way I thought about, the opposite sex. In the blackout I had played touch and kiss games with the girls from Guinness Trust. There'd been excitement then, especially when I became aware that the girl I most favoured was allowing herself to be caught in the game, not running off into the darkness as speedily as she might have. I'd certainly felt excitement then, but as much as anything else, curiosity. It seemed to me that I could understand well enough why I should be interested in kissing her, I liked feeling her squirm and laugh in my arms. But I couldn't really understand why she wanted to be caught, why she should be interested in kissing *me*.

When we went to the country after the bombing I had already started my journey through puberty. I believe that some boys step largely oblivious across the threshold into male adulthood, noticing the changes taking place in their bodies but not so much those taking place in their minds. Fernfoils of pale pubic hair and a slightly hoarser voice had been with me some little while. But now it seemed I was developing a different cast of mind as well. I spent much more time alone, usually riding my bike down to the village. In the newsagent's there, Maggie Mole's, I would buy a comic and hang around covertly looking at the covers of *Woman* and *Woman's Own*, studying the bright-eyed young housewives depicted there.

In my ignorance and uncertainty, I found such changes alarming. Hitherto I'd always been clear, in the way my mother was, about what was right and wrong. But suddenly I seemed to be harbouring two sets of moral values. Suddenly there was something at least as powerful as the wish to do the right thing. There was, ill-defined as it might have been, desire. Or rather, lust.

At this time it centred on Shirley. Despite the humiliation of my last meeting with her, I wanted to talk to her again. At just fifteen she was already shapely. Since first seeing her get off the bus I'd tried to speak to her two or three times. I couldn't say I liked her, she had an acid tongue, but I liked looking at her. I used to look out for her when I was down in the village, even timing my visits to Maggie Mole's to coincide with the bus that brought her from her work in Windsor. She knew I was interested. I could tell that by the way she swung her bag, and her hips, as she passed me. Sometimes she'd stop to say a few words in a flip, jeering manner, sometimes she ignored me totally.

But one day she confirmed her liking for my cashmere jacket.

'Where d'you get 'un then?'

'London.'

'Soft, annit?' laying a hand on my arm. ''S different.'

'I told you, it's from America.'

'That's true, that is? Come all the way from America?' Her face lit up. 'Ah, that's it then.'

The next few times I saw her she'd always mention the jacket. If I was wearing a pullover instead, she'd stop. 'Where is it then?'

'The jacket? At home.'

'You ought to wear it all the time. I told you, it's really flash.'

In fact tragedy struck for me no more than a few days later. It was a hot day at the end of May and I had taken off my cashmere jacket and strapped it to the rack above the back wheel of my bike. I arrived home to find that it had slipped off. I jumped back on the bicycle and rode all the way to Windsor again but there was no sign of my cashmere jacket from the Lord Mayor's Fund.

When I next saw Shirley I was wearing a second-hand Windsor County green and red-edged blazer. A size too small.

She stopped and stared at me. 'Where is it then, that there Yankee jacket?'

I shrugged uncomfortably.

'What you be wearing *that* for?' She plucked contemptuously at my blazer.

'I have to. For school. Windsor County,' I added, hoping against hope that it might impress her.

Her lip curled and she walked on, swinging her handbag.

To me this was a catastrophe, much worse than the loss of a coat. My cashmere jacket was a disguise. In a rural world of open identities, school colours, known faces, I was beginning to need anonymity. I think now of this need for anonymity as one of the most important stages in puberty. The need to be alone and unknown is probably the deciding factor. If a child (a boy at least) is denied the opportunity to order even part of his own world, it will redirect his development. It will force him to return to his own mind to seek, in fantasy, that autonomy of action he craves. Paradoxically, if he's not allowed to be alone, the danger is that he will become a loner.

The jacket was gone but I still had the pale grey trousers. Worn with a white open-necked shirt, I thought they had a sporty air. Man of the world *en relaxe*. I would have to get Shirley's reaction.

I rode down to the village a couple of times that week without seeing her get off the bus. The third day I was in good time, well placed outside Maggie Mole's when the bus rolled in. She was not among the three or four villagers who alighted. I was about to turn back when I saw her auburn hair in the front seat. I wanted to drop my bike, run along beside the bus, rap on the window, warn her that she was dreaming, that she was going to miss her stop. But there was no time. When the bus drew away I cycled after it.

I was soon far behind the square-ended green bus. There were few stops before Maidenhead and in minutes it had disappeared altogether along the twisting country road, arched over with the new leaf of early-summer trees. I dawdled along, thinking I wasn't going to ride all the way into Maidenhead. Perhaps, I thought, I'd go to Hollyport to watch the Americans playing baseball instead.

As I approached the camp I saw an American soldier at the gate talking to two girls. It was impossible to miss Shirley's bright hair. Or the tight white sweater and the bow of bright lipstick. The other girl was someone I vaguely knew as an older friend of hers. I can remember nothing of what she was wearing. I was looking at Shirley. In that white sweater she looked like Betty Grable.

I was consumed by love. Or something.

A jeep came through the camp gates. The GI driver stopped. The soldier talking to Shirley and her friend swung himself into the front, the two girls got into the back. With a lot of whooping from the two GIs, the four of them drove off together.

I felt half a dozen emotions, a sort of sickness too. Suddenly, I now knew so much more about Shirley, I knew about her secret life. How much I really knew I wasn't sure. I knew in theory what some girls were supposed to allow American soldiers to do to them for cigarettes or money. I had seen the condoms on grassy banks at bus stops, although I didn't imagine that Shirley went that far. I felt sick with unrequited lust.

I cycled down to the village early one Saturday evening as spring was turning to summer. Time has entirely obliterated any memory of

who I was with, perhaps I was alone. Or perhaps it was the shocking
nature of what happened in the village street that obliterated all the
surrounding detail.

As I passed the bottom of Monkey Island Lane I saw a small group
of people outside Maggie Mole's. Another few yards and I heard
voices, a man's and a girl's. Shirley was struggling with her father
outside Maggie Mole's shop. She wore lipstick and powder, her
white Betty Grable sweater and a wide belt, I remember, bright red
like her lipstick. Her father was a small, wiry man. His cap was off,
lying a few yards away on the pavement, the few strands of hair
normally brushed across his crown now hanging down by his temple.
The bus to Windsor was approaching.

'I'm not letting you on that bus,' he was shouting as he tried to
take a grip on her arm with one hand.

'I'll go where I like,' Shirley was shouting back, pushing at him
fiercely. 'You got no rights on me.'

'You going with that there Martha girl,' he said, his voice muffled
now, but still loud enough for the small group of people around them
to hear. 'I know what you're doing.'

He loosed his grip on one arm and Shirley was big and strong
enough to take advantage. The bus was drawing up at the village stop
now, a few yards from them. She dragged the other arm free and
pushed him squarely in the chest. Turning, she ran. In a desperate
attempt to stop her, he snatched at the side of her white sweater. It
flew clear of the restraint of the belt, stretching as she pulled away.
With his free hand he was hitting her across the back of the head.

'Let go my sweater,' she screamed. 'Stop that . . . stop hitting me!'

'Prostituting for they Yanks,' he shouted, purple with rage and
humiliation. 'You and that Martha, 'arlots, common prostitutes, the
pair of you!'

I saw it coming. She had turned and leaned back to gain an arm's
length between them. Then she slapped him hard, high on his cheek.
He reeled back, releasing his grip on the sweater. The bus was just

pulling away behind Shirley but she twisted back quickly, ran two or three steps in her heels, leapt for the platform and was gone.

People stood silently watching her father as he stared after the disappearing bus. Then he walked slowly and bent to retrieve his cap. Pushing his hair back over his bald head, he fitted his cap over it. By the time it was back on his head the onlookers were drifting away.

'And you get going,' he turned on me. 'Go on, before I give you one.'

Within days, it seemed, I heard them all talking about Shirley.

'Youse heard she goes with they Yankees?'

'If you're short of fags,' Dimple Soden from the cottage next door said, 'ask that there Shirley. She'll sell you a packet.'

'*Give* you a packet, more like.' I didn't understand the men's laughter at the time.

And from the women: 'A bad lot, that one. Always said she'd turn out a bad lot, din't I?'

'Hangs around Windsor station with the pro-fessionals now, waiting for when they Yanks fall off the train from Lunnon.'

'You hear about how her dad chased her down the street? I saw that. Yelling out that she were a common pro-fessional, he was.'

No end of people claimed to have seen the whole thing.

I met Shirley in the village a week or so later. Did she know I had seen the fight with her dad? I wondered. If she had it didn't seem to trouble her. Shirley was her usual self. She wasn't jeering. She just asked me when we were going back to London.

'Soon as we can find a flat,' I said. 'They're not easy to find in London.'

'Can't be,' she said. 'I heard about all that bombing.'

'We were bombed,' I said.

'Yeah?' Her thoughts were clearly somewhere else. She swung her bag idly around. 'I'd like to go to Lunnon myself. Never been. What's it like?'

'Well . . .' I was at a complete loss, mouth dry with anxiety to say something she'd like to hear. I shrugged as if I used to be up in Piccadilly every night. 'You know, there's always something going on.'

'I bet.'

'Plenty,' I said. Unspecified delights.

She nodded. 'Lunnon's big, annit? Like twice as big as Windsor. Or more?'

'Twenty times at least.'

'Never. Where did you live in Lunnon, then? Anywhere near Rainbow Corner?'

'Rainbow Corner, the Yanks' club?'

'You been there?' she asked.

I shrugged in a way that might have meant yes. 'We're not far from there.' Well, we used to be just a 22 bus ride away, though I'd never actually been to Piccadilly. 'Why d'you want to know?'

'Somebody asked me if I wanted to go there, that's all. Dancing.'

'A Yank? Was it a Yank who asked you?'

She laughed. 'Girlfriend of mine. Don't know no Yanks, me.'

'Round Piccadilly it can get rough,' I said. 'Blackout and all. You're better off here.'

She flicked her hair. 'It's all right for you, from Lunnon. But who'd want to live in a dump like this for the rest of their lives?'

I could see I'd given her all the answer she wanted. I felt grown up talking to a girl like that, a girl wearing platform heels and make-up, a girl whose own father had called her a prostitute. Whatever I knew in theory about the transaction involved between prostitute and client, I never allowed myself to apply it to Shirley. I had heard girls say that they Yanks were always wanting to feel your top, and even offering cigarettes or those small bottles of whisky for it. I knew the mechanics of the sexual act but I never imagined Shirley allowed that up against a wall behind Windsor Station in the blackout. But, of course, she did.

I didn't share in the condemnation that surrounded her. My own secret desires predisposed me to her defence. I also knew that the father who publicly called her a prostitute had never been reluctant to take his belt to her. I knew, too, that she lived in the sort of squalor we were familiar with at Water Oakley. I wasn't too surprised that young clean-cut GIs 'feeling your top' seemed to offer a road out.

A week or two later the village gossip was that Shirley had left home (thrown out more like, the women said) and had gone to live in London. When we finally arrived back there I used to scan passing groups of girls hoping to see her among them. Or I did for a week or so.

SIX

The Longest Day

By the beginning of June Kit and I had taken to leaping out of bed to go down to the front room (Joe and Jinny's bedroom) to catch the early news. They were already in the fields. My mother, as a conscripted farm worker, was allowed an extra half-hour to get our breakfast. We held our breaths for the announcement of the invasion. Now the roads outside Water Oakley Cottages were crammed with marching American troops, and long convoys guided by Snowdrops (white-helmeted American Military Police) rumbled past. We knew from the number of units around us that our area between Maidenhead and Windsor was an American staging point. Each day we cycled up to the Hollyport camp but there seemed to be no change there. Baseball games flourished on the huge dusty diamond in the centre of the hundreds of neatly aligned bell-tents. A half-dozen girls waited with exaggerated nonchalance at the gate.

Then, on perhaps 3 or 4 June, we arrived back from school to the rumour that the Americans had gone. No one seemed to be sure. Joe and Jinny were still away in the fields. Dimple Soden said unconvincingly that 'he'd heard tell of somethin' like that'.

Kit and I looked at each other. We had heard the rumbling of heavy trucks passing the cottages before we went to sleep. But there was nothing too unusual in that. That morning as my mother gave us breakfast she had said the trucks seemed to be going through most of the night. Yanks on the move, we thought. But it never occurred to us that they were *our* Yanks.

We jumped on our bikes and rode down to the crossroads at Monkey Island Lane then on through Fifield. Hollyport was a desolate sight: a great yellowed field of churned earth and flattened grass on which was laid a grid of dust roads. The prefabricated sentry post had been demolished. Scattered condom packets around the unguarded gate, Wrigley's Chewing Gum wrappers, and a few shocked girls in heavy make-up were all that was left of 20,000 men, their equipment and vehicles, all now packed up and heading for the South Coast. Then, as we rode back to Water Oakley, in the skies above, aircraft, hundreds of aircraft, British and American, passing in massed squadron formations overhead. Kit and I stopped our bikes by the roadside. For a few moments we stared up at the sky, then looking at one another excitement bubbled up like brook water. We jumped on our bikes. Beating our rumps with one hand, we 'Yippee-ed' our way back home with the news. We could not be more than days, hours even, from the cross-Channel invasion.

The real news burst upon us on 6 June. Allied troops had landed on the coast of France. Of the five beach-heads (three Anglo-Canadian and two American), landings on four had gone according to plan. The fifth beach, code-named Omaha, was yet to gain its tragic reputation. Kit was smiling smugly throughout the day. He had won the sweepstake that my mother had organised along the cottages. The kitty was five shillings. He had never in his life had so much money.

Six days later, early-shift workers living just beyond the railway bridge at Grave Road, Bethnal Green, in the East End of London, had pulled back the blackout curtains to hear the sound of a curiously loud motorbike. Even more odd was the fact that the bike seemed to be sailing through the lightening sky above. When the noise ceased abruptly people turned back to the task in hand: shaving, tea-making, rousing others for work. The explosion that followed a moment or two later was sharper, fiercer, than any of the bombs the East End already knew well. It was an explosion with a blast-force powerful enough to render 266 people homeless and an as yet unknown number dead or injured. Three days later, after several dozen such bombs had been loosed at London, the Home Secretary announced that the capital was under attack from pilotless planes. The information he gave was sparse but south-east England soon got to know that Grave Road had suffered from the first of Hitler's Revenge Weapons, the V-1, a ton of high-grade explosive in a stubby-winged black robot aircraft with a cheap air-thrust rear-mounted engine that sounded uncommonly like a motorbike on its last legs.

Londoners called the new weapon the flying bomb, the buzz-bomb or the doodlebug – and tried to live with it.

At Windsor we began to receive intimations that this would be harder than it had seemed. A housing consultant for London Underground named Harry, another improbable friend of Joe's, an RAF ex-squadron leader type, worked in London and came back to his wife Molly in Windsor at weekends. She told my mother that London Underground properties (for housing their workers) were being damaged faster now than at any time since the height of the Blitz. Londoners, Harry said, were getting weary. Fast as the V-1 sites along the Channel coast were being cleared by the Canadians, the Germans developed new launch sites in forests and even succeeded in launching from the underbelly of the Heinkel 111 bomber.

My first sight of a V-1 was one afternoon just before the beginning of the summer holidays. Cycling back to Water Oakley from school, I was aware of a motorbike engine somewhere behind me. I looked back and saw that the noise was in the sky, coming from a small, low-flying, black plane with a flame (I thought it was an engine on fire) streaking from its tailplane. It came over Windsor Castle and the engine cut. The plane glided over my head towards Dedworth, a mile or so outside the town. It tipped, hurtled down at an angle and hit the base of a timber yard factory chimney. The explosion was terrifying. I had stopped my bike. Staring in astonishment, I watched the chimney cut clean off at its base. Then it toppled, slowly it seemed to me, and disappeared behind the line of rooftops.

I turned my bike and rode up towards Dedworth. When I arrived people were standing about in the streets, women mostly, talking quietly and shaking their heads. There were one or two ambulances and wardens but no Heavy Rescue people. The damage to houses seemed light, damage that might have been created by a freak storm. Then as I turned a corner I saw the factory yard. Buildings had been laid low by the fall of the chimney. A little further over some of the houses, red-brick, metal-windowed, tile-roofed, had been wrecked but were still standing. A fat man in overalls came running past and stopped, looked at me and said: 'Here, they say there's a baby up there in the bedroom. You want to lend a hand, son?'

As I dropped my bike and followed him, I cast a nervous glance behind me. There seemed to be only the two of us.

'They thought they got everybody out,' he shouted as he ran. 'But someone's reported hearing a baby crying in number sixteen.'

'Where's its mother?' I caught up with him and jogged along beside him.

'Unconscious,' he puffed. 'They took her off to the Aid Station.'

We stopped before the house. The outer wall facing the street had collapsed so that the bedroom floor-joists had no support on that side. They sagged, stripped by blast of their ceiling plaster, the laths exposed. This much we could see from outside.

We looked at it, neither at all happy about going in. We listened. Nothing. No baby crying. I hoped he'd say, That's it. No baby there. But he didn't. He turned to me, adjusting the metal clips on his overalls. 'OK, son?'

I nodded. I felt suddenly cold and hot – like having 'flu.

'Sure?'

I nodded again, one eye on a piece of brick which had toppled from the rear wall and was sliding down the hanging bedroom floor. He edged through the doorway, walking across the flattened front door. I followed him in.

The dust had settled. I was looking at the ceiling above our heads and the sloping, unsupported joists. If we ducked under them we could see the staircase. It was missing almost everything, banister rail, several stairs. Shards of glass glittered on the stair carpet.

I could sense his uncertainty. 'What d'you think?' he said.

Perhaps he was waiting for me to say that I thought we should wait for the Heavy Rescue Unit to arrive. Then it came to me that I'd been in far more bombed houses than he had. In fact, I was an expert at climbing around obstacles, testing the strength of a joist or the solidity of a staircase. Bombed houses were where we used to play every Saturday in London. This was no different, just a bit more recent. Here, we were going to have to jump from the upper usable step of the staircase to the shaky floor level about three feet below and hope it held. I looked first at the unsupported joists, then at my overweight companion. My guess was that if I stayed at the foot of the stairs, he could easily bring the whole lot down on my head. 'I'll go first,' I volunteered. He thought it was courage that inspired me.

There was no baby. There was a cot in one of the rooms and some baby clothes spread across the undulating carpet, but there was no baby. When I clambered back to the staircase a woman was standing just inside the doorway, the baby's aunt, telling us the child was safe with his grandmother.

We all got out of the house. The woman talked, at least part of the time, directly to me. The senior warden came over and did the same, telling us there had miraculously been no deaths or serious injuries. I was covered with dust and feeling good. I enjoyed being a bit of a hero.

★

Back in Water Oakley, where the summer stench was more intolerable than ever, my mother had news. Harry, the London Underground housing manager, had somehow contrived to get a house allocated to us. A whole three-bedroomed house, and by its description very similar to the one the fat man and I had searched for the baby. A whole house for just the four of us.

'Is it in London?' Kit and I asked anxiously.

'Of course it is,' my mother said. 'It's a place called White City.'

White City? Anyway, London. We were going home.

SEVEN

White City

When we left World's End, Chelsea, I had only heard of White City as a dog track, as remote as Harringay or New Cross. But then ignorance of place other than their own was an aspect of most London children's life. Before the war ended I had never been to Piccadilly, never seen Buckingham Palace or the Houses of Parliament, although they were all fifteen minutes away (in those traffic-free days) on the 11 or 22 buses that ran down the King's Road. We knew our own pockets of London well – but a mile or so away, Bayswater, Brixton, Victoria, Notting Hill Gate were no more than names we saw on the front of buses. Indeed, for many of my very early years I had thought 'abroad' was anywhere across the other side of the Thames, Battersea in particular. This was reasonable enough because all the men I knew talked of abroad, with a jerk of the raised thumb, as 'over the water'. Battersea therefore occupied an uneasy place in my young thoughts. I used to stare suspiciously across the river when my grandmother took Kit and myself for a walk along the embankment, steeling myself for the moment when the Kaiser, probably concealed behind the chimneys of the Morgan Crucible Works, led his inevitable dash across Battersea Bridge to seize the World's End, understandably his primary London objective.

White City Stadium, which gave the area of our new home what fame it had, was on a four hundred yard strip of double carriageway called Westway, not to be confused with the modern elevated section. The houses in the small roads off Westway, of which our crescent, Primula Street, was one, were divided by strips of grass. No pubs, it's true, no shops, no street corner paper sellers, no whelk stall on Sunday morning. But well-kept grass between each block of houses.

White City Stadium had, I later discovered, been built for the London Olympics of 1908. The concurrent Franco-British Industrial Exhibition was housed in an elaborate area of man-made lakes, gardens, exhibition stands and halls finished in gleaming white stucco which covered what is now the White City Estate. When I first learnt this, I was intrigued to realise that we had moved from World's End, home of the notorious ladies of Cremorne Gardens, to White City, site of another pleasure garden and the work-place, at least during the Franco-British Exhibition, of a further large gathering of ladies of the night.

Even so the area seemed strange to us. I suppose the homogeneity of the buildings was most depressing. Every red-brick, Crittal-windowed two storey house along Westway and right up Western Avenue to Alperton and Park Royal had been built in the seven or eight years straddling the twenties and early thirties. We were living on the edge of Metroland. But what was striking was that nothing and nowhere around seemed as homely as the grime and variety of the World's End, except perhaps the Victorian Wormwood Scrubs Prison peering across the railway line into our new bedroom windows.

Bleakly suburban as our new district seemed, we nevertheless walked around our empty house in wonder. I felt acute excitement at the idea of having a bedroom I wasn't sharing with Kit and my grandmother. Kit, I know, felt the same. I've no doubt now that my parents felt equally blessed. Single, my mother had slept all her life with her mother or elder sister May, often with both together. At his childhood home, my father had had his sleeping place under the kitchen sink. Married, they had never had a room to themselves since Kit and I were born.

Today, it's impossible to convey the pure lift it gave us to have a bathroom. Almost absurd now to think that young boys could be moved by a bathroom. But I can remember Kit and myself standing in the doorway, the sun slanting through the window on to the white bath. I can remember the fresh smell of soap or soap powder from the last occupants, and the cold thrill that ran down my spine. Neither of us spoke but I would have bet money we were both thinking of Joe and Jinny's place and, for all the affection and gratitude we felt towards them, promising ourselves we would never be forced to live like that again.

There was a garden outside with red Underground trains running along the embankment at the end. In the middle of the garden was an Anderson shelter, a hump of earth planted with a few dahlias. Most gardens along the railway line had one, perhaps constructed by London Underground for their workers. They were certainly solid. The base, sunk about three feet into the ground, was lined with six inches of concrete. Into this was set a curving roof of galvanised steel, the whole covered with a foot or two of earth. A small opening, three foot high and two foot wide, was the entrance, easy enough for teenage boys, much more difficult for adults to clamber into. I think at this stage of our inspection we did little more than glance at the camel's hump that occupied most of the lawn. We were more interested in the fact that across the Central Line railway that ran along the end of the garden was the main gate of Wormwood Scrubs Prison, sombre and menacing even in the sunlight.

This was our new home. We were breathless with excitement, all four of us I think. But where was it? Where *did* we live? In the Borough of Hammersmith my father told us, but neither completely

Shepherd's Bush nor East Acton. That sounded, even felt to me, to be on the very lip of the world. The district, he said, was known as White City from the bright white concrete stadium. Someday the BBC and the now notorious White City flats would mean that every West Londoner knew the area. But in World's End we were aware of living somewhere that went back for centuries. My grandmother alone told enough stories about her childhood when Cremorne Gardens attracted all the young toffs and the ladies of the town. I knew, in no great detail I admit, but I knew it all the same, that at World's End we lived no distance from writers and painters. My other grandmother, the ever aggressive Minnie, and her side-kick Ma Bash used to clean for J. B. Manson, the Director of the Tate Gallery, at his house on King's Road, just opposite Oakley Street. My mother had inherited the job from her. Painters and sculptors from Augustus John to Henry Moore came to tea there. It's hard to say how and it could simply be the references we heard at school and on the wireless to Chelsea artists, writers, Chelsea Pensioners or Chelsea's football team, but much of our attachment to the World's End was undoubtedly that sense of living in a long-established, well-known part of London.

White City, by contrast, had no history. It was a sports stadium. A brick housing estate built just before the war. It was the beginning of a long road leading out to unexciting places like Park Royal and Hangar Lane. In 1944 when we laboriously explained our new whereabouts to our old school friends from the World's End, they came close to wondering aloud whether we were in danger of falling off the edge. Snobbery does not begin at Sloane Square.

My mother nevertheless set out to get to know our immediate neighbours. She could always sense when a little good public relations were necessary. What story she told them to account for the fact that we, none of whom worked for the Underground, were renting a London Underground house, I don't know. But her way of just getting to the heart of people was remarkable. In no time Mrs

Fribbins next-door was smiling at us over the back fence. Later, in a crisis when she decided she must leave her husband, it was my mother she turned to for advice, support and diplomacy. When young Mrs Sandom on the other side suffered a fatal heart attack, it was my mother and Kit who carried her body down the stairs in the middle of the night so that her young son would not see it.

In furnishing the new house my father's formidable energy came into play. Enough carpet to lay on the stairs, a bedroom or two, and wall-to-wall in the sitting room, a pair of comfortable armchairs, a variety of cupboards and a kitchen table, all came from Whitelands House where he had been storing them in the boiler room against the day, which he never doubted would arrive, when we moved from the World's End. Where did they originally come from? God knows. The carpet had been thick with dust from where he had kept it hidden under the piles of coke in the boiler room. But he had somehow manhandled it into the Whitelands service lift and up to the roof of the building where he, Kit and myself hurled buckets of soapy water at it and scrubbed it with bristle brooms. In the feeble London summer of 1944 we waited for it to dry, watching for the next shower as anxiously as we watched for the next flying bomb. We knew our carpet lay on Whitelands' roof, poised perilously between drying and rotting.

It was touch and go. Finally a great damp pink roll was conveyed by Mayfair laundry van for half a crown to the driver and before long we had wall-to-wall carpet. Coming from a linoleum-only flat and Joe and Jinny's paraffin-cleaned, cracked lino, carpet was an incredible luxury, albeit a luxury with a vague unluxurious damp smell of down-in-the-forest mulch for the first month or two.

There was also a bombed families furniture grant of, I think, £145. This provided our beds and curtaining. Blackout material, I seem to remember, was available off-ration. In fact we had passed the period when a blackout was necessary. The *Operation Steinbock* Blitz of early 1944 was pretty much the last time German bombers, apart from the occasional hit and run, penetrated as far as London. Our problem now was the psychologically menacing pilotless V-1.

Kit and I might have chosen to go to Clement Danes, the grammar school backing on to Wormwood Scrubs, a few minutes' walk from where we now lived. In fact we both preferred to make the journey of nearly an hour back to World's End, to the West London Emergency Secondary School for Boys – or Sloane School as we all called it.

For me it would be a return to old friends, to Kit it would be his first term in a new school but there were plenty of boys from the World's End he already knew. It meant a long bus ride each morning, to Shepherd's Bush by 105, from there to World's End by 11, but I think we both had no doubts it was worth it. We've only talked about it more recently but it seems we were equally reluctant to cut all ties with World's End. If we chose Sloane School we would be returning to a place of familiar warmth that White City never offered. I'm sure it's true that Kit and I missed World's End more than either of our parents. Going back to school there would mean a daily walk down Hortensia Road from the corner of which you could see the part-collapsed and empty shells of Guinness Trust Buildings where we had once lived. On what had been our side of the road two blocks of Guinness Trust were completely collapsed; the two others were marked 'Danger' and scheduled for repair. The World's End pub had survived but that summer there were no couples dancing outside to an accordion. There was no La-di on the island to run frantically between the conveniences in his long raincoat, but another colourful figure had taken over his role as World's End newspaperman. Henry Nichols, former potman at the notorious Weatherby on the corner of Slaidburn Street, was a cheerful soul whose working clothes were made distinctive by a battered black top hat which was to be seen decorated with rosettes and blue and white ribbons on the days Chelsea were playing at home.

But there was no denying the air of desolation that marked the

World's End. Chelsea Council had acted firmly in requisitioning empty flats and houses in the expensive part of the borough. The family of Kit's friend Ronnie Howes were now living in luxury in half a house in Markham Square. John Cheeseley's family, who had lived opposite us, were comfortably established in Old Church Street. Many of the survivors of the Guinness Trust bombing would finally move back to the rebuilt blocks on the old site, but when we returned to Sloane in the late summer of 1944 it hadn't yet happened, the community was scattered. The dangerous buildings had been demolished but dozens of houses stood like cardboard cartons, roofless, huge holes torn in the walls where there had once been windows. And the area smelt different. The power station still dominated, it's true, but along the streets when it rained you could smell nothing but charred beams and joists, or the wet dust of a million crushed bricks and tiles.

Once at school we spent a great deal of time in the cloakrooms which had been strengthened to provide shelters. These would certainly not have saved the lives of all the masters and boys in the case of a direct hit but lottery was what everybody in London lived with during the days of the V-1. Between seventy and two hundred flying bombs daily were now being launched at the city. Explosions punctuated our days.

On clear days and even nights a good proportion of the V-1s launched were shot down by flak or fighters; on misty mornings or foggy nights the majority would probably get through, although even then much reduced in number by RAF 11 Group with its crack 456 Australian night-fighter squadron. It meant that alerts were sounded day and night until finally they became almost meaningless and largely ignored. At school it was different. Air raid warnings had to be observed and the shuffle of gabbling, grubby boys, three abreast down the two staircases and into the cloakrooms, seemed to take up much of our day. Once there we sat tightly packed on wooden benches. Card games were renewed from where they'd been left off twenty minutes before. Comics were swapped from boy to boy and then from form to form, tall tales were told about girls from the school next door and pin-ups from *Lilliput* or *Picturegoer* were passed around for sale. Teachers read, chatted among themselves or went out for a smoke. Sometimes they intercepted a pin-up and stared at it wistfully before handing it back.

We did less work than we had done in any period since the Blitz. A little history of the Industrial Revolution; for English, a reading of Micah Clarke; virtually no Latin and very little French. Certainly I don't remember that we in the third form ever glimpsed much of the Future. But some understanding of the world at war was something to which even a young boy could aspire. It was quite crude as understanding goes but it served. What gave it total relevance, of course, was the fact that some of it was happening to us. We knew that advances along the north European coastlines meant fewer flying bombs. The number of miles advanced per day occupied the headlines so that every schoolboy was aware of progress towards quiet nights and the final defeat of Hitler. We concentrated on battles, mostly won at this time, or at least, like Arnhem, failure depicted as victory. With glee we studied newspaper maps illustrating the developing stranglehold on Germany. There was also the July Bomb Plot on Hitler's life which had set the adrenalin pumping. I don't recall knowing too many details at the time and perhaps they were masked by censorship but I did know that it was an army plot. The fabled loyalty of the German Army was cracking, was the message that got through to us, although again this might have been the work of the Ministry of Information. At the time we didn't realise that there was still the best part of a year to go.

Finally, through my father, there was an awareness of something else: that the fighting in the last months or year had been directed by Churchill, FDR and Stalin, each with one careful eye cocked on the post-war future. There were, from my friend Ted Simon, powerful echoes of his mother's Communist view of Russia's likely role in the new world. I think almost everybody at that time, at least those in the less privileged sections of society, believed that the Russian influence would be both significant and beneficial. My father had doubts. He believed Russia would try to make good her vast war losses with the same disregard for Germany's ability to pay that the French had shown at the end of the First World War. 'No way,' one of the Whitelands tenants had said, 'to secure a stable Europe.'

When I look back I find myself impressed by my father's insatiable curiosity. As a porter standing in the entrance hall of Whitelands House or taking tenants up in the lift, he seized every opportunity to ask questions. If it was an American Admiral he would ask about the war in the Pacific; a Frenchman would be questioned about Marshal Pétain and the Vichy government; a Polish diplomat would be quizzed about the post-war Polish frontiers. Some of this filtered down to me. There was by the last year of the war such an extraordinary variety of tenants and visitors to Whitelands that there was a form of contemporary education to be gained just by standing on porterage duty in the hall. My father took full advantage of it.

Some of the other boys took a mild interest in questions of the future which would soon confront us directly, but at this stage none of us could look beyond the defeat of Germany. By now, after six years, war was really all we could remember. It had to end for our new life to begin, even for new thoughts to germinate.

At the West London Emergency the days were tolerable, even in some ways enjoyable. We felt that we (with Adolf's help) were putting one over, not on the masters but on the school system itself, as we spent our days playing cards in the cloakrooms.

The nights, however, were different. When a V-1 chugged across the night sky in your direction there was no companionate bravado to warm the chilling blood. When the engine cut and you heard the V-1, as you sometimes did, singing across the rooftops, your breathing stopped until, perhaps only fifty foot above your head now, it swished over and exploded with a great powerful crack on the houses of some other unfortunates a few streets over.

In August, at the height of the V-1 attack, Churchill told Parliament that 180,000 houses had so far been totally destroyed and 800,000 damaged by the new weapon. On 7 September Duncan Sandys, junior air minister, made a statement to the press in a somewhat different tone.

'Except for a few last shots,' the minister in charge of the Revenge Weapon problem told us, 'the Battle for London is over.'

This was good news.

EIGHT

Rocket Science

On the same day that Duncan Sandys made his reassuring statement, across the North Sea in Holland an SS unit was clearing all Dutch civilians from a suburb in the Hague. Muted blue lighting was set up in the main square. During the night a special convoy of unusually long, tarpaulin-covered trucks arrived. They carried the new Revenge Weapon, the V-2, forty-five-foot long, loaded with one ton of high explosive, and set to pass into the stratosphere and descend on London at over three times the speed of sound. Far too fast to be shot down by anti-aircraft fire, untouchable by even the most modern mark of Spitfire. During that morning Hitler's second Revenge Weapon was hoisted vertical, to rest on its launch pad in the Dutch suburban square.

Where we lived at White City is under a mile, as the crow flies, from Staveley Road, Chiswick. By just before 6.40 p.m. on 8 September 1944 the first rocket thrust into the sky above Holland. Travelling at 3,000 m.p.h. it burst through the atmosphere, turned an arc in space and hurtled down towards London. It was in the air for less than four minutes.

In White City we were just about to have tea, our evening meal. That night it was late because my father had been delayed in

Chelsea. The sequence of events was an almost simultaneous flash and thunderous explosion, not sharp like the V-1's, more muffled but menacingly powerful. I looked at my mother. Her face was set. Kit looked towards the ceiling. My father was standing in the kitchen doorway.

'I didn't hear the engine cut,' my mother said.

My father said nothing.

I think we all knew this was something different even before the next stage, a totally strange, deep rumble which seemed to start at the point of the explosion and move round the horizon for perhaps ten or fifteen seconds. We had been listening to the first stratospheric rocket attack in history.

At the time we had no real idea what had happened. We went out into the street. A pall of smoke and crushed debris rose above the roofline not far from us, a low distorted mushroom cloud that someone was to describe later as resembling the figure of a monk, hunched in a dark cowl, slowly drifting across the rooftops. There were other people on the street, women in what had become the classic Londoner's pose, arms folded in front of them. A few words were exchanged, a final stare and shake of the head, before they went back in. The men and boys remained to exchange opinions. Nobody believed this was a flying bomb. The explosion was different, more muffled. And then that sinister rumble. What the dickens was that? the men asked themselves.

The government, in order to give German scientists no information on which to adjust their target settings, made no public announcement. The local press carried a story about a gas main explosion in Staveley Road. My father smiled and waggled his head when the gas main story was repeated by our neighbours. I asked him why he was waggling his head. Civilians, after years of aerial bombing, are not stupid. He told me that a lot of people were talking about a *flying* gas main. I didn't understand. 'Flying gas main? How can you have a flying gas main!'

'At last,' he said. 'The penny's dropped.'

But I still didn't get it.

'Let's say you can bet your life it's not some secret weapon developed by the Gaslight and Coke Company,' he said.

'What then?'

'One of these new German secret weapons Lord Haw Haw boasts about, perhaps?'

I was exasperated. 'Do you know what it is?'

He shook his head. 'I don't, Dee. Nor does anybody else outside the government. But you can be sure we're not going to like it.'

How right he was.

Our life as a family now took on a truly bizarre quality. V-1s were still falling nightly. Rockets were rumbling round the horizon, not many, perhaps an average of ten a day, but the unfathomable peculiarities of the sound barrier meant that a rocket explosion could seem close-by to someone up to six miles away. There were no sirens any more that could alert us to this danger, though of course the siren system continued to give constant warnings, day and night, of the approach of flying bombs.

By now we were all beginning to feel seriously short of sleep. We weren't alone, of course. The whole of London looked tired. Fatigue was visible in the faces of people on buses, women in food queues, and boys at school where it was not uncommon to see someone fall asleep at his desk. They were usually left sleeping by all but the more sadistic of the staff. Few boys were like my closest friend in these years, Norman Chapman, the possessor of completely sustainable (or at least readily renewable) energy sources.

The rockets were a novelty but the V-1s still had their moments, frightening or plainly weird. Everyone had their personal blast stories, of banknotes blown helter-skelter down the high street or crated geese released in their hundreds. Ours was milk. One night on the length of railway line that separated us from Wormwood Scrubs Prison our blast story was delivered when a flying bomb came down, derailing a lengthy milk train. Huge steel containers were split open by the blast or burst as they toppled from their wagons to roll, gushing milk, down the embankment. Gallons of it washed in a white flood along the gutters past the prison. After a day or so the sourness in the air was almost unbearable.

Before we had been back in London long, the sleep problem became serious. We would sit opposite each other at the kitchen table in the evening, at the mercy of a sort of creeping narcolepsy. Something had to be done. The first decision was that while my father was on fire-watching duty at his job at Whitelands House, my mother, Kit and myself would sleep in one of the Underground stations. Lancaster Gate was chosen, just along the Central Line that ran past the back of our garden before plunging deep into the earth at Shepherd's Bush.

The new routine would begin as soon as Kit and I were back from school at about five o'clock. We'd do our scrap of homework, set to maintain the practice rather than to exercise us in any way. When my father arrived home at about six we had tea. This was always taken with the back door open, however cool the autumn evenings were becoming. The point of the open door was that we had discovered that we, unlike almost all other Londoners, had a special alarm system all our own. Or our own and that of about five hundred criminals in Wormwood Scrubs. After tea Kit and I would be on V-1 watch. While our parents took this rare opportunity to be alone together, we sat on the back step completing our homework and listening for warning signals from the prison.

These took the form of a loud klaxon placed somewhere above the Victorian prison gate. It was, we later learnt, directly connected to radar stations on the Kent coast and to V-1 watch stations in south-east London. One blast signalled a flying bomb approaching London, on course for White City, or more precisely Wormwood Scrubs. We would shout out to our parents and they might continue chatting or join us at the door. Inside the prison I understand that the warders would rouse the prisoners from their bunks and get them out on to the landings outside their cells.

Two blasts on the klaxon meant there was a V-1 directly on course for the prison which also meant directly on course for us. In the Scrubs the prisoners would be brought down from the top landings.

Three blasts, continuously replayed, conveyed a sense of extreme urgency: V-1 dead on course for the prison, less than ten miles distant. I suppose the prisoners were assembled somewhere relatively safe on the ground floor. For us that urgent three-blast klaxon meant a quick retreat to the Anderson shelter in the garden. There, we'd crouch in this (barely) underground block of damp concrete listening for the phut-phut of the pulse-jet engine of the flying bomb. Most times it would pass over without the engine cutting.

A sigh of relief would go up and a great deal of laborious clambering began as my parents got out of the Anderson. And they were young. I can't imagine a sixty-five-year-old man or woman getting in and out of that entrance hole.

This would be the beginning of the evening. In the interlude we might hear two or three rockets and speculate, with no real confidence, about where they had struck. At this point, the original Chiswick 'flying gas main' had been the closest we had been to the point of impact. Part two of our evening began with my father leaving as it began to get dark, by bus or bike for Chelsea, and my mother, Kit and I making for East Acton tube station from where we would take the train to our second home on the platform at Lancaster Gate.

Tired as we were by then, a nightly journey down to Lancaster Gate was hard work. Three suitcases contained blankets and a pillow each. The rushing air from the passing tube trains was notably dry so bottles of tap water were a necessary and weighty part of our equipment. Add a book or two for a final brief, hopeless scribble at

the ever-neglected homework and sandwiches for our late underground supper at perhaps ten o'clock, and you had a heavy enough
suitcase for a walk down Primula Street, under the railway tunnel
across DuCane Road, past the length of Wormwood Scrubs Prison
and through the side streets to East Acton station. We were not
alone. Other family groups, usually without men, would be making
their way to the station, small children struggling with what seemed
oversized suitcases of blankets, occasionally stopping to rest, mothers
casting apprehensive glances at the sky as they hurried them on
again.

Our places below were reserved for us in a system I no longer
remember. We were among 73,000 Londoners sleeping in the tube
at this time, occupying the same station every night.

Our train passed underground just after Wood Lane station (now
called White City), dropped deep to Shepherd's Bush, stopped at
Holland Park, Notting Hill Gate and Queensway, and delivered us
to Lancaster Gate. On busy nights we stepped into a Hieronymus
Bosch scene. Pallid arms and legs, toothless men, half-dressed old
women, were all around. The lights were blue and low. Some people
slept and snored, others read or shouted out to acquaintances. One
of our neighbours who always settled down early produced
something approaching a soap opera in his sleep. 'Elsie' was the star.

'Elsie told me,' he would yell, startling everybody around him.
People would rise on one elbow and lift their eyebrows at one
another in anticipation of another instalment.

'Elsie's off with Billy,' he would confide in a rising, slurred voice
to the fifty people wrapped in blankets around him. 'Slips round
Billy's place . . . first chance she gets.'

A belch would roll along the platform, carrying the sourness of
half-digested beer. 'Her dad won't have it, you know. Not with her
husband overseas and all. Oh, no.' He would rouse himself, still
muddled by drink. 'Put a stop to that, did Alf.' By now he was
wide awake. He'd rub his eyes, pass his hand over the few wisps of

grey hair on his bald head, shrug with what might have been embarrassment or, equally, indifference, then turn over and go back to sleep.

During the nights I was down there Elsie was 'off' with a good number of her neighbours. Her father Alf's attempts to keep her on the straight and narrow seemed peculiarly ineffective. Sometimes it seemed to me that our sleeping informant might well be Alf, having drunk himself into oblivion. Whoever Alf really was, preserving his daughter's virtue was clearly an uphill task.

Our sleep-talker was only one among many night-time performers tucked closely together with family or strangers. Most of them were wide awake, however, as they sang or mumbled through the night. They were never short of an audience. Sometimes, as we settled down for the night, a woman would start singing softly one of the popular songs of the day: 'Wish Me Luck As You Wave Me Goodbye', 'As Time Goes By', or 'A Nightingale Sang in Berkeley Square'. Other women might join in, all singing equally softly. I remember the undercurrent of sadness.

> *I may be right, I may be wrong*
> *But I'm perfectly willing to swear*
> *That when you turned and smiled at me,*
> *A nightingale sang in Berkeley Square.*

The preacher who paid us a visit every few nights might have got a better reception from the down platform which was considered to be a little more refined. On ours he was given short shrift. 'Put a sock in it,' someone would yell at the first blast of fire and brimstone – and, if enough dissenting voices joined in, the preacher would succumb, haughtily packing his Jesus Saves stand and stepping through the open doors of the next train as it pulled along the platform. 'At Marble Arch they'll listen,' he'd shout defiantly over his shoulder as the doors were closing. 'Marble Arch will not reject the Word of God.' And he'd bend to look down at us and wave his fist as the train pulled away to a great burst of laughter from the shelterers lying in their blankets.

Our neighbour-station in the other direction, Notting Hill Gate, had introduced the idea of six people accommodated on six foot of platform, chain-link bunks stacked against the wall providing three places and three more allocated to sleepers rolled in blankets between the bunks and the edge of the platform. As late-comers to Lancaster Gate we slept on the platform a few feet from the incoming trains. The air was foetid and insufficient until another train arrived and dragged with it coolness from the tunnels. It made for disturbed nights. Women, I noticed, cried out often. Maybe they had succumbed to the same temptations as Elsie. Or perhaps they were just desperately worried about their husbands or boyfriends in Normandy or Italy, in Burma, in the skies over Germany or out on the Atlantic.

Kit and I slept on either side of my mother. On the other side of me there was an elderly woman with thinning grey hair. She would bid me goodnight before surreptitiously removing her teeth. I dreamed that one night her place would be taken by her granddaughter, a young woman who would be on leave from the WAAF, pretty and full-figured, whom I could charm with my pillow talk about aircraft recognition.

But for youngsters like us it wasn't all bad. During the evening Kit and I hopped the trains to go up to Marble Arch, the next station on the West End side. Taking orders for a mug of tea or a sandwich from the NAAFI canteen there, we would sometimes make as much as sixpence a night in tips.

Most fortunate about the choice of Lancaster Gate station for us was that the American Army had an Enlisted Men's Club pretty much directly above us. It made for a constant flow of GIs, dispensing gum and Hershey bars as they passed through on their way to Oxford Circus, Soho, and the huge American club at

Rainbow Corner. On an exceptionally good night one of the GIs would leave a copy of *Yank*, the soldier's magazine, which always carried at least one really worthwhile pin-up.

The American soldiers were particularly good with very small children (and, of course, with pretty girls, although there weren't too many of those on the platforms of Lancaster Gate). In Europe the mindset of automatic anti-Americanism had not yet set in. In London people certainly thought American soldiers too highly paid and that their access to luxury goods, particularly chocolate, whisky, cigarettes and nylon stockings, gave them an unfair advantage in competition with British soldiers. But there was as yet no institutional resentment. The great national sigh of relief when America entered the war had not yet expired. The ordinary American that British people met in the street, the pub, or on Lancaster Gate Underground, was a clean-cut, polite, friendly young man. I'm not painting an ideal world. There were fights in pubs, there were rowdy American soldiers. But in general the level of discipline and behaviour was high.

Of course the Americans weren't the only troops passing through Lancaster Gate. Canadians were regarded as being on the same level of friendliness as the Americans, as were Australians and New Zealanders. Among the non-English speakers, Londoners liked Norwegians, Dutch and Poles. They did not like the French.

This dislike was almost universal. It was not based on the machinations of de Gaulle in St James about which we knew nothing at the time. Churchill's *bon mot*, 'The heaviest cross I have to bear is the Cross of Lorraine,' was equally unknown to us. The English disliked the French for reasons that stretched deep into the historical past, from Agincourt to Waterloo – and had now reached forward into the present. They had collapsed ignominiously before the Wehrmacht in 1940. When France surrendered my grandmother had nodded knowingly. 'So much the better,' she said. 'No bloody foreigners to look after.' We had other complaints about the French:

they behaved in an unjustifiably haughty manner; they spoke French
– and they kept any chocolate bars they might have had strictly to
themselves.

Morning was not a pretty sight at Lancaster Gate. Even in the worst
conditions of awakening, there is usually the compensation of a
little daylight, a few streaks of dawn across the sky. Not in the
depths of Lancaster Gate tube. There were always a few early risers
stepping carefully over others in an attempt not to wake their
neighbours. But at about six-thirty, as if by common consent, the
denizens of Lancaster Gate rose, stretching and snorting, yawning
and coughing. A thousand arms and legs were pulled and pushed
through garments, some to remove the shirt they'd slept in, others
to get into warmer clothes in expectation of a chilly morning
'upstairs'. If I think about it now it was a seminal Second World
War scene, repeated in camps and bomb shelters all over Europe.
The chain-link wooden bunks, the overcrowding, the dim lights
and deep shadows, the grunts of concentration, the utter lack of
anything approaching privacy . . .

We would take the train back from the neighbouring tunnel,
sitting dirty and sleepy, not speaking too much except to wonder how
the night had been upstairs. Especially how the night had been
upstairs in Chelsea where my father was fire-watching. Then just
before Wood Lane station we would emerge from the tunnel, often
into brilliant sunshine, and the world would take on its normal shape
again. Perhaps a rocket or two rumbling round the horizon, before
tea and fried bread and dried egg for breakfast. Perhaps the chugging
and sharp crack of a distant flying bomb. My mother would always
go out to phone Whitelands House from the call box at the bottom
of the street to see my father was all right before she made her own
breakfast.

Then, for Kit and me, a quick wash before we went off to
school. And once there, of course, it was probably an early shuffle

into the cloakroom-shelters for a half-hearted attempt at a lesson quickly abandoned, a game of cards, and a few schoolboy boasts before the market-opening for the sale of any particularly saucy pin-ups.

NINE

The Ghost

At about this time it was decided that I should spend the nights in Chelsea with my father rather than make the evening journey down to Lancaster Gate with Kit and my mother. Technically my father was on fire-watching duty at Whitelands House. In fact, by this stage of the war there were no more German bombers over London to scatter the baskets of light, phosphorus-packed incendiary bombs which had done so much damage during the Blitz. Any fire now was likely to be the result of a V-1 or V-2 rocket explosion, an 'incident' which would bring the regular Fire Brigade on the scene immediately. In effect this meant the fire-watch system designed to smother small incendiary bombs was no longer needed. My father, however, had other reasons for needing to be in Chelsea every night.

These revolved around the recent difficulties with the law of the local World's End bookmaker, Alf Gordon. My father was well known to Alf, having worked for him on Saturday evenings for the last year as bookmaker's clerk at Stamford Bridge dog track. On occasion I had been called in to do some general running, checking nearby bookmakers' prices and when the regular man was ill, a few times even calling the odds as tick-tack man, a role requiring a sharp eye and familiarity with the hand signals then used at race tracks.

Alf's problems began when a new police inspector arrived on the World's End scene. It would be his responsibility to police the illegal practice of street bookmaking which was so large a part of local life and entertainment – and a large part of Alf's bookmaking business. The system was that Alf's two runners, Fatty the Yid and Darkie Evans, strolled through the streets of World's End collecting betting 'slips' which carried the scrawled details of the bet and inside which was wrapped the sixpence or shilling to be gambled. There would be a fairly regular twice daily visit to the King's Arms, the Riley Arms and the World's End pub itself. If a copper were seen to take an interest in them, Darkie, who would carry all the slips, would run like the wind for World's End Passage from where he had a choice of back doors to escape through. Fatty, who was incapable of running, would feign well-worn surprise at the extraordinary behaviour of his friend. It usually worked, though from time it ended in a chase down World's End Passage, and if an ambush had been prearranged, a fine for Darkie, which of course Alf took care of. Mostly the police didn't lean too hard. Fatty allowed himself to be found with the occasional betting slip in his pocket and the inspector at Chelsea Station was content his men were doing their bit. Everybody played by the rules. But a new inspector was an obvious problem. What would his rules be?

One evening, over a drink with the new inspector in the Chelsea Conservative Club opposite the old Chelsea Police Station, Alf thought he heard a discreet invitation. However it happened, Alf believed the new inspector was encouraging him to make a gesture. Alf therefore offered the inspector the occasional pony (£25) not to press too hard on his runners. The inspector agreed but refused to take the money from Alf there in the crowded pub. He'd meet him on Albert Bridge, he said, later that evening. A time was fixed for shortly after dark.

This was not something you sent one of your people to handle. In the blackout Alf Gordon ambled along the embankment to Albert

Bridge. He was, I suppose, a man of about forty-five, rather over-weight, wearing a suit and Homburg hat. Reaching the bridge, he crossed to a halfway point between the ornate Victorian suspension towers and leaned on the rail. Below him, no doubt, the moon metalled the dark water. As I tell it I realise I'm thinking of *The Third Man*, of Harry Lime. I can almost hear the zither music.

Then footsteps and the new inspector appears out of the darkness. Cigarettes and pleasantries are exchanged – and the handover of money effected. But barely has the pony been slipped into the inspector's inside pocket when there's a shout from the Battersea side of the bridge. Blue-masked torches bob towards them.

'You bastard!' Alf turns to run but there's another bobbing blue light on the Chelsea side. He is trapped like one of his own runners in World's End Passage. 'You bastard,' he says again.

'Just my job, Alf. You'll go down for this, you know. Bribing a police inspector.' He shakes his head sadly.

Most small bookmakers at this time started out with an illegal street bookmaking business before graduating to a licensed pitch at one of the big dog tracks. With Alf *hors de combat* there was a clear, if dangerous, opportunity for my father to take over the illicit part of the business, at least temporarily. Alf himself approved the idea; Fatty and Darkie said they'd be happy to work for my father.

My father talked to my mother. Even talked to Kit and myself. I had never seen him so apparently uncertain about a decision. Moving up from bookmaker's clerk, where you needed an extraordinary numerical dexterity but bore no part in the losses, to being the bookmaker and sole loss-taker, took courage. To operate in the World's End area where the local inspector was known not to turn a blind eye, involved serious risk. But I know now that the decision involved more than bookmaking, the infinite calculations of which my father loved. It was for him, more importantly, another step up a ladder he had set himself to climb.

He was clear-eyed about the risks involved. His savings (which were probably less than £150) could go on a couple of bad weeks. His job at Whitelands House would undoubtedly go too, if he were prosecuted.

'What do you really think?' he asked my mother.

She was silent for a moment. 'It's what you want to do,' she said. 'We're with you.'

He became an illegal street bookmaker.

The black-suited, huge-bellied Fatty the Yid and former lightweight boxer Darkie Evans were by that autumn of 1944 old friends of mine. Neither, since you ask, had any objection to the evident racial component of their names. Fatty was the man who had taught me tick-tack. He had a dry sense of humour, heavy lips, a judicious air, and the build of an overweight Peter Ustinov. Next to Darkie's lean brown face, Fatty's was heavy-jowled and ghastly white. His long black hair and shiny black suit, the jacket flapping open over his impressive belly, emphasised his pallor. Darkie Evans spoke little. His greeting to me would usually be a wink, a feint with his left hand and a mock right hook to my upper arm. Often enough this would end in a quick sparring match outside the World's End pub. I admired and enjoyed his speed, his ability to dodge and weave around me, landing light blows to the chest and arms. I enjoyed it even more on the very rare occasions I got a punch home.

My father would collect the bets each evening, calculate the winners and losers, and pay out through Fatty and Darkie. All this normally took place in a discreet corner of the World's End pub, the previously favoured Weatherby having been damaged in the February bombing. Sometimes Darkie or Fatty the Yid would be delayed at one of the pubs, perhaps at the King's Arms down by the river where my father's mother held court with Ma Bash. In that case I would be sent down to pick up the betting slips and deliver them back to where my father was calculating the odds. The winnings or losses would usually amount to a few pounds. I seem to remember that more often than not it was a few pounds of winnings, even after the two runners had been paid. This amounted to good money per week in the war years. Fatty said my father was a natural – and he himself had been in the street gambling business all his life.

By ten o'clock most nights we would be finished, the slips recorded, the winners paid out. A Sidney Greenstreet goodnight from Fatty ('I suppose you've got some unfortunate young lady lined up for tonight, have you, Dee?') and a cuff round the head from Darkie before they disappeared into the blackout. Then, for us, my father and I, the 11 bus up King's Road to Sloane Square, to my father's ostensible workplace at Whitelands House.

The one-time site of Mosley's British Union of Fascists' head-quarters, demolished in 1935 to give way to a block of expensive flats, Whitelands House was, from 1937, the first and only perma-nent employment my father ever had (short of a few months at the famous Thomas Crapper plumbing merchant's in King's Road). It was soon apparent to the management that he was an unusually efficient employee. By 1944 he was second porter and shortly afterwards head porter. This journey through the ranks had given him a rare opportunity as a working man to learn something of the habits, privileges, prejudices, strengths and weaknesses of the tenants, a class of which he'd had no previous knowledge.

Whitelands House was made up of a hundred rented flats whose tenants ranged through Generals and ambassadors at the smaller embassies to writers like Daphne Du Maurier. There were of course, in addition, the usual sprinkling of barristers, surgeons and wealthy unemployed. Backbench politicians in those days could not generally afford to live there.

The tenants were, in fact, a cracked mirror image of the immediately pre-war upper-class English. Many were notably civil and considerate. Others not. Frequently, in their shockingly bad manners to the porters who served them, they were typical of that dissolution of the sense of responsibility that had begun to undermine many of the upper-class before the war. They were, in their overbearing manner, far too often Randolph Churchills and Evelyn Waughs; the women, Nancy Mitfords (without the wit). I would repeat that there were numerous exceptions. My father liked and respected many, like General 'Boy' Browning who planned Arnhem or the daughter of John Galsworthy, but disliked or even despised others who seemed to believe they somehow deserved to live in a world where cleaning, sweeping, carrying parcels and opening lift doors was done by invisible hands. Even so late in the war there were still, among the tenantry, some proto-fascists who, narrowing their eyes to slits, just might have seen the shabby silver-braided black uniforms of the porters of Whitelands House as their own SS Praetorian Guard, inherited perhaps from the former Oswald Mosley Fascist headquarters which had occupied the site. They had only to open their eyes a little wider, of course, to see that porters like the scuttling Welsh Wally and lumbering Long Tom were unlikely recruits to any Praetorian Guard, and their true view of the residents was not the admiring deference they appeared to show. But opening their eyes to the social *bouleversement* of the last few years was a serious problem for some of the denizens of Whitelands House.

Nevertheless, as my mother was always quick to remind us, Whitelands served us well. It provided a job for my father, a cover for his more profitable bookmaking activities, as well as a barely furnished bedroom to sleep in when our former one-bedroomed flat in World's End got too crowded. It had provided us with an underground shelter in the furnace basement during the Blitz, and in the autumn of 1944 it was about to offer a new type of shelter, based on my father's calculations that the V-1, altogether more numerous and more alarming than the V-2, could not perform a vertical dive once its engine cut.

He had explained this in some detail, a map spread out on the table before him. 'The V-1 approaches from the Kent or Essex coast. Always from the south or east.'

'Yes.'

'That's why I've been sleeping in a room at Whitelands on the King's Road side, the north side of the building. Flying bombs have a fixed guidance system – if Whitelands gets hit it's bound to be on the river side.'

Seemed sensible.

He grimaced. 'That's what I thought. Except, I was wrong. Your uncle George was outside the King's Arms yesterday watching one come down. The engine cut as it crossed the river. He watched it glide towards King's Road when suddenly it banked and started diving straight at him. He said it chased him down to Lots Road Power Station.'

Neither Kit nor I liked Uncle George. Disbelief showed on our faces.

'The point is, it changed direction,' said my father who liked his prickly, sneering brother George no more than we did. 'This morning I went up on Whitelands roof. I saw two of them coming in. One cut and dived normally. The other cut and swung round so far as it dived that in fact it very nearly came in from the north.'

Which meant his room on the north side of the building was no longer as safe as he thought. 'So where do we sleep?' I asked him.

'Same place, but we've got to be quick about getting out if we hear one overhead.'

'We wouldn't have time,' I said, horrified. I was a heavy sleeper. I was thinking of all the times I'd have to struggle awake every night. He slept lightly, able to be fully awake in seconds. 'In any case, where would we go?'

'To the one place a flying bomb could never hit. However far it can glide.'

'Where's that?'

'The central well.'

Whitelands had been constructed, like many blocks of flats in the first half of the century, round a central light well. Corridors and some servants' rooms overlooked the well. My father's room was a twenty-yard sprint away from safety.

The logic seemed impeccable. V-1s did not cut and dive vertically. Crouched in the first-floor corridor overlooking the well, the depth of the building away from any explosion, we stood a good chance of being safe. If we could get there in time.

I had a lot of confidence in my father's wartime arrangements. He had bought huge catering tins of Spam before full rationing set in, rice and pepper the day after Pearl Harbour. He'd built a shelter in the bedroom at our flat in Guinness Trust. When he was the Whitelands stoker he'd found places for us to sleep in the furnace basements of Whitelands during fifty nights of bombing at the height of the Blitz. But any arrangement that depended on me waking and leaping out of bed within four to five seconds filled me not just with horror – but with serious doubt.

'There's one problem,' I said, hoping to undermine the whole scheme.

'What's that?'

'The Ghost.'

His lips twisted in frustration. 'Ah,' he said. 'Yes, the Ghost.'

The Ghost was a figure of some mystery, an older man to whom my father, by now head porter, had given a cleaning job at Whitelands. The mystery was, why. The Ghost was everything my father disliked: dirty, lazy, sly and usually drunk . . . At one point my mother hinted at some sort of distant relationship to my father, then seemed to withdraw the idea equally quickly.

His name was Albert, his surname never mentioned. He was probably in his fifties but drink had added a good ten years to his appearance. He was bent, with wispy grey hair and a lined face. As a cleaner and bin-man he didn't receive a silver-braided black uniform. He wore, as many workmen did in those days, a stained double-breasted suit, under it a shirt with a stud at the throat and no collar.

Bent forward as he was habitually, he would look up at you slyly with clear blue eyes. I, of course, always imagined that he was saying, 'I know something you don't.'

The Ghost plagued my father's existence. He could be drunk on cider at any time of the day or night. He would begin drinking in his room or in one of the staff lavatories and would disappear when he was needed for some task. At his most relaxed he would take his quart of cider and stroll down the carpeted corridors of the building, waving the Woodpecker bottle and mumbling incoherently to the tune of 'Nellie Dean'. He was not far, at this point, from collapsing to his knees or rolling over to pass out completely, still hugging his bottle. Then a call would come down to the porter's lodge from Captain Fitzgerald ('of the Guards' as he insisted on introducing himself) or perhaps Daphne Du Maurier, that there was an inert creature in the corridor outside their flat, and my father would go up and drag the Ghost down to his room to sober up, claiming to whichever tenant had complained that it was an outside intruder. The story just about stood up because few people living in Whitelands had ever seen the Ghost, whose nickname derived from the way he went about his duties (when sober), slipping from corridor to corridor, never presenting more than a grey, disappearing back.

The Ghost's room to which he was dragged was on the same corridor, indeed next door to my father's. This was our immediate problem.

In this narrow, cell-like room, my father and I slept in our shirts and underpants in the one single bed. In that first week at Whitelands there were Alerts every night as usual but only one evacuation of the room was attempted. I had heard nothing, neither air raid warning nor approaching V-1, when I was awakened by an elbow hitting my ribs with some force. I imagined my father was turning over in bed and turned over too. A second later the blankets were ripped from me, the elbow plunged deeper into my ribs. 'Run,' my father ordered. I got my feet down on to the floor and sat yawning as overhead the V-1 cut. 'Albert,' he yelled at the dividing wall, 'get down.' As he was shouting to Albert he was pulling me to the floor. We rolled under the bed. There was a long, long pause. The ensuing explosion was somewhere in Knightsbridge, Bayswater even.

At that moment the door opened and the Ghost stood in the doorway. He wore a long nightshirt and carried his bottle of cider in one hand. He was the porter in *Macbeth*. 'What was you shouting about?' he said.

We peered up at him from under the bed, then looked at each other, finding it impossible not to laugh. 'Up you get, son,' my father said finally. 'The next one may be closer.' He looked at Albert's nightshirt, at his wobbling legs. 'Stiffen the Prussian Guards!' he said. 'Leave that bottle here for the night and go and get some sleep.'

I suppose I got a little better at it, a little quicker. But the task of getting a drunken Ghost to his feet equalled the problem of getting me moving in the middle of the night. There would be shouting and mad scrambling, the Ghost being pushed or kicked down the corridor, the swirling stench of cider vomit, the three of us rolling in shirts and underpants on the thick Whitelands carpets. And the sick realisation that the V-1 had passed overhead seconds ago.

On the dozen nights we executed this mad routine, I never heard, after that first night, an engine cut above us. My father would wake at the approach of a V-1. As we scrambled for safety it would pass overhead with its chilling empty, popping sound to strike somewhere in North London. Three or four times I heard an uncomfortably close explosion but soon enough even my father, concerned as he was for my safety, had to recognise that this particular procedure was a dud.

All our antics really achieved was to forge a sort of bond between the Ghost and myself, though he volunteered almost nothing about himself. He would straighten up and salute from time to time, and claimed he had been in France during the First War. I suppose this was true. He was always telling me what a good father I had. To which I agreed. He liked to say that if I 'watched it', I'd be a chip off the old block.

I said I'd try.

Then one evening, when my father was busy downstairs in the hall, the Ghost brought me a present, putting it on the table and flitting away with a faint smile. I saw it immediately as further evidence of his eccentricity. He had 'given' me my father's 'John Bull' English Dictionary.

I showed it to my father when he came upstairs. 'Stone the crows!' he said quietly. It was one of his favourite exclamations. 'Stone the crows!', 'Stiffen the Prussian Guards!', 'Steady the Buffs!' and 'Snakes Alive!' all found their way into his daily vocabulary. He picked up the dictionary from the table. 'I got this for six Persil packets,' he said, as he often did when fondling his favourite book. He flicked it open and riffled through the pages. Then went back to the beginning. On the blank opposite the title page my father had many years ago drawn up a family tree in red ink. It didn't go back far and ended with the birth of my brother in 1933.

I saw him react and looked over his shoulder. There was an additional scribble on the page in black ink. I had no time to read it before he snapped the Dictionary closed. 'Bloody Ghost,' he said. He swore almost never. It was a measure of his anger.

He left the room before I could ask him what the Ghost had written. Afterwards he said it was nothing, just a scrawl spoiling the tree. When I next saw the book, at home in the White City, that page was missing.

I don't know how much I thought about what the Ghost had done. I stopped sleeping at Whitelands shortly after that and only saw the Ghost as he flitted about his bin-emptying duties. But more recently I've wondered about that scrawl across the page which wasn't really a scrawl as far as I had been able to see, more a written word or two.

My mother's half-hint of some relationship to explain my father's tolerance of the Ghost comes back to me now. A cousin of his was, I suppose, a distinct possibility. An elder brother was a grim thought but not out of the question, given my paternal grandmother Minnie's nature. Kit and I remember her chiefly for her cackling arrogance. A woman who terrorised her entire street by the sheer force of her conviction that she was always right. An illegitimate child when Minnie was sixteen or seventeen would have roughly fitted with the Ghost's age. Giving the child away would have definitely fitted with her hard view of the world, and determination never to be in the wrong. Against his will, she had organised a similar disposal of my uncle's illegitimate son when a magistrate, finding him guilty of the theft of some building materials, had sent him to sea in the Merchant Navy as an alternative to prison. Though I felt I could ask my father most things I found myself oddly reluctant to ask him if the Ghost was in fact his half-brother. His view of his mother was, I think, complicated. He believed strongly in family and family ties. Yet Minnie had on so many occasions betrayed her family by her reckless arrogance and utter conviction of rectitude. When she died I had no idea what my father really thought about her. He paid for her funeral and barely mentioned her thereafter.

I don't know what happened to Albert the Ghost. Our lives then were crowded with danger from the sky and from the police who might at any moment arrest my father for street bookmaking. Albert faded from view. When I next remember asking my father about him, he said, abruptly for him, 'Moved on.' And after a pause, 'High time.'

TEN

The Last Christmas

This was the strangest period of the war. On the one hand everybody in Britain was convinced that Germany was on the edge of defeat. In the east the Soviet Armies were rolling across Poland. Allied troops were at the Westwall, Germany's Siegfried Line. Yet civilians in London and other parts of the country were still under fierce robot attack from the air by the V-1s and V-2s. I suppose that we ourselves came closest to a direct hit when a rocket struck the White City flats behind the Stadium. It was perhaps a hundred yards away. The flash was blinding, the explosion terrifying, the rumble of sound surrounded you rather than crept away along the horizon. Kit and I went across to the flats on our way to school the next morning. We knew it was a V-2 but it was the first rocket crater we had ever seen, deep enough to engulf a London bus. Perhaps because its supersonic speed had driven the ton of high explosive deep into the ground, it had taken down fewer buildings than I expected, and the casualties were less than they might have been.

That rocket was certainly not the last to fall. There were many V-1s as well, some launched from aircraft right up to the last few days of the war. But after the White City flats I think we had the feeling that we really had turned the final corner, that by this Christmas or maybe a week or two after it would all be over. Nazi Germany, as Churchill would put it, would lay prostrate at our feet.

Meanwhile at school there had been what we considered a sinister development. We regarded ourselves as Sloane School, Chelsea. The West London Emergency School for Boys had never been a name that caught on. We played football as Sloane. We wore blue, Chelsea-like shirts. But the truth is that we were a rag-bag institution thrown together in the grim days of 1940. The real Sloane School had been evacuated throughout the war to a place called Addlestone in Surrey. The headmaster there was a significant and well-connected figure named Guy Boas. At least one of the school Governors, an amiable old gentleman named Bowes-Lyon, was related to the Queen. So indeed was Guy Boas' tall, straggly and myopic wife, Pussy.

In the autumn of 1944 Boas descended on us like the wolf on the fold. Before the war he had been one of the youngest and best-known headmasters of an inner-London grammar school. He was devoted to the theatre and had in the thirties developed a genuine Shakespearean tradition at the school. It was not unusual for him to have the *Times*, *Telegraph* and *Manchester Guardian* theatre critics at a school performance of *Hamlet* or *Cymbeline*. Indeed, there were photographs of scenes from Shakespeare, acted by the boys, hanging in all the school corridors. Philistines that we were, they had cut no ice with us. Guy Boas planned to change all that.

He returned to the school with one or two Addlestone masters for what I imagine he saw as a two-week-long reconnaissance. We felt his presence immediately. Speaking from the platform in hall, he said that he had observed several boys that morning slipping into school after the bell. Henceforth lateness would not be tolerated. Masters would be posted on the gate. We should be warned that every boy who was one minute late the following morning would be caned.

We didn't attempt to hide our outrage. Lateness for school was accepted as one of the perks of living in London during the war. Boys weren't on the whole very late. Ten, twenty minutes, a half hour if there had been a serious hold-up. But it was not good enough for Bo. Next morning the new guard took over on the gate. We latecomers straggled in, thirty, fifty . . . by 9.15 close to a hundred. Jostling in the playground finally, where we had been directed by the masters on the gate, were eighty-two miscreants.

We were lined up in alphabetical order and marched upstairs to the headmaster's study in batches of twenty-five. A name which begins with W is either good fortune or bad. There are no in-betweens. This time it was good fortune indeed. I arrived upstairs to find a wild-eyed, exhausted headmaster slumped against his desk. His black jacket was draped over his chair. His right hand which gripped the cane was wrapped in several handkerchiefs. Two broken canes were abandoned on the carpet.

He pushed himself up to his feet. His full red face was slick with sweat. Droplets glistened in his clipped moustache. His pinstripe trousers were crumpled, his waistcoat unbuttoned. He gestured to the first boy of our column to lean on the back of a chair placed in the middle of the room. The boy leaned over. I wondered why Boas had not recruited other masters, then I realised that this was a very personal contest. For the sake of the new Sloane School, he had to win.

Glassy-eyed, he advanced on the boy leaning over the chair. He gave him four cuts with the cane before stepping back to take a breath. His arm, I was happy to see, was shaking. It would not have been so easy for the ABCs at the head of the line.

'Next,' he croaked. And I stood up to the chair. My four of the best were painful but, afterwards, I wouldn't have wanted to be without them. I believe we all rather admired him, overweight and hypertensive as he probably was. I think that we, the boys, would not have wanted to abandon so significant a privilege as tolerated unpunctuality without a fight. He, in turn, would not have been happy for so significant a victory simply to have fallen into his lap. By the end of the morning both sides, headmaster and boys, could feel they had acquitted themselves honourably.

Some of the masters stayed on under the new regime. The ascetic Mr Nightingale, former Franciscan monk, brilliant mathematician for the mathematically gifted but confounder of the rest, was a recognisable eccentric. Towards the end of the first term he entered the classroom with his long, dipping Groucho Marx strides, cleaned the board by ripping a strip from his gown, stared alarmingly along the rows of boys in front of him and began to record on the blackboard predictions of our eventual salary level. 'Chapman, ten thousand a year man . . . Thomas, eight thousand . . . Roberts, based on a term's unsatisfactory effort, less than a thousand . . .' And making allowances for inflation, I don't think he did too badly. It was, in any case, a novel way of making an end-of-term report.

Mr Colon, heavy-shouldered and with a cat and mouse smile, who had miserably failed to teach us Latin but had clearly enjoyed flicking his fat forefinger painfully under our noses for any minor grammatical error, left at the end of the war. Harry Little, overweight, bow-legged but fast-moving, fast-talking and full of energy, would continue teaching his Commando French Course. In general this was popular with the boys, containing as it did an introduction to French life and art. For Harry that meant the life of the low apache clubs of Place Pigalle and the art of the Folies Bergère. Harry would lace his lessons with all sorts of tall stories from his past in Paris. He had been wounded as an infantry officer in the Great War and posted to a Paris hospital. He claimed that as he was recuperating he had been recruited by British Intelligence to sit at the boulevard cafés and night clubs and retail false military information to the street girls who approached him. If it were an exceptionally important piece of misinformation, he confessed, '. . . it would then behove me to accompany the young lady to her lodgings, to press the point home.'

He'd shake his head and add soulfully in his barely amended cockney accent, 'You boys can imagine how painful a patriotic duty that was to me. How potentially threatening to my cherished moral standards.'

And we'd all appreciate the joke though we didn't yet know too much about Harry's cherished moral standards, beyond the fact that it was a phrase that would come up often. There was, in the event, a good deal more to learn but for the moment we continued to enjoy him for his stories and his informality. 'Call me Harry,' he'd say. 'But not when old Bo's around. I have to watch myself or this new headmaster'll run me off the premises. Right then,' slapping his briefcase on the table, 'hand these papers out, my boy. Harry Little's Commando French Course, Part One, Question One . . . You, my boy, the Invisible Man there, crouching at the back,' his fingers clicked imperiously, 'let's have the answer. Quick about it. Before Adolf comes calling again.'

As the weeks shortened before Christmas Day things were improving all round. Fewer rockets and flying bombs. Everywhere German armies were retreating. There were now armies of four allies under Eisenhower's command. The British and Canadian army groups were fighting through Holland; US forces including Patton's Third Army had just taken the gateway city of Metz, while a French and American army group had captured Strasbourg and penned in a large German force at Colmar.

But we should have learnt by now that the Germans can never be relied upon to surrender. Ten days before Christmas, out of the freezing snow of the Ardennes, the Wehrmacht struck back. On 16 December eleven Panzer divisions overran six resting US divisions on a sixty-mile front and threatened to split the British and American forces in two.

In Britain it was a massive blow to morale. We had thought the war as good as won. Yet Americans were fighting in the snow and bitter cold of an Ardennes Christmas to prevent Hitler achieving a complete reversal of fortune on the Western front. We weren't at first to know that this was Hitler's last trump.

Then, as Christmas passed in London, and the US 101st Airborne's defence at Bastoigne catapulted the Battle of the Bulge into legend, we began to see that Germany was indeed defeated, that there was no prospect of Adolf Hitler holding out past the coming spring.

Yet there was still one more horror to be tasted before it was all over. In April 1945 British Army units reached Belsen in north-west Germany. Today its horrors are well known: the unburied mounds of dead, the pits full of bodies, the barely living stumbling aimlessly from wire to hut and back again. And the SS girls, shy, even giggly, with their infinitely brutal-looking Camp Commandant, Joseph Kramer . . . Belsen was a shock on the level of 9/11. A film, rapidly put together on Churchill's orders, was given wide distribution in local cinemas. People watched it in silence, stunned by the barbarism, by what appeared to be the deliberate murder of thousands.

In a rush we struggled to understand the full horror of what had been happening for five years in central Europe. That same month US troops liberated Buchenwald, and just outside Munich the far bigger camp at Dachau. The Russians had already taken Auschwitz and Sobibor, true extermination camps, but at this point we had little real information about them. The term 'Holocaust' had not yet been invented for the Nazi drive to exterminate Europe's 'subhumans', but even at my age, just short of fourteen, children, many children at least, realised that there was a new dimension to the Nazis we had been fighting and talking about and spitting at for so many years. Images of Joseph Kramer and his trio of SS women being marched away from Belsen stayed with many of us for life. The death camps, Auschwitz, Treblinka, Sobibor, when we learnt their full purpose, presented us with a baseplate for evil. The brief life there of man, woman and child offered a level of suffering imposed on humans by humans against which to measure all suffering. Humanity had no such measure before.

ELEVEN

Lord of Misrule

The lights came back on. Streetlights that we hadn't seen since I was a very young child and could only recall as a misty yellowed World's End memory. Now they seemed incredibly bright. Even more exciting were the uncurtained windows. You could walk down a street and see people inside, talking, dancing, making tea.

We spent VE night in the World's End. I'm not sure why but my memories of that evening are not sharply etched. There was a bonfire on the middle of the 'island' where La-di-dah once sold newspapers. There was port and lemon for the ladies, crisps and lemonade for the children, a grand knees-up along Blantyre Street and a conga line that went down to the river and back. For all the genuine joy, I think it was a subdued event. Women thought about their loved ones still away fighting in Burma or suffering in Japanese camps. There were memories, too, of the World's End bombing little more than a year ago and the sixty or seventy neighbours who had lost their lives. All the same it was victory, or at least Victory in Europe.

'Well, that's done for the Germans,' people said half-jokingly. 'What we got to look forward to now?'

We moved round from group to group, family to family. There were people we hadn't seen since the bombing, people who no longer lived in the World's End and had been allocated flats or houses, like the Cheeseleys who had lived opposite us in Guinness or Kit's football friend Ronnie Howes' family. But it seemed all had come back for the celebration. My father, as a street bookmaker, though still not having the standing of Alf Gordon was nevertheless treated as a figure of note. My mother seemed to be accorded a natural importance of her own. She knew everybody (from working since she was a girl in the local haberdashery) and was soon surrounded by friends she hadn't seen since the night of the bombing.

Various members of the Wheal family and the associated Bashfords were there. People arrived, talked a little with friends and moved on. Fatty the Yid and Darkie Evans were there, too, Darkie ever ready to duck and weave around me with his boxer's footwork, Fatty as usual unsettling me with remarks about the many girls I must be leading up the garden path.

If only . . .

We left quite early. We walked along the King's Road past the Guinness Trust Buildings where we had once lived. Of the four blocks, two had been virtually demolished, but by now the rubble had been removed, the ends of the building shored up with huge timbers. The buildings were gaunt, windowless, empty.

We talked about the last night we had lived here. About the plaster and chimney dust blasted into Kit's face, about the glass shards that had criss-crossed the room in their thousands and miraculously missed us all. It was hard to believe it was all over, but the street-lights, the gaslit windows and the sound of accordions and singing convinced me.

'I must admit,' my father said to my mother, 'for a long time I didn't think we'd make it.'

'I know,' she said.

'And you,' he said. 'What did you think, when it was really tough?'

'I thought we'd win,' she said. 'What else *could* we do?'

He smiled, pulled her to him and kissed her.

'What are you doing?' Kit said, embarrassed.

'I'm kissing your mother,' he said. 'I think you boys should, too. When you think of these last few years, she brought us through, you know. Kept us together.'

Young boys don't do gratitude. I'd never thought of it like that. My mother shook her head, denying my father's assessment, but Kit and I probably both had a lump in our throat as we gave her a quick, embarrassed hug.

That night, as a Victory treat, my father hailed a taxi to take us back to White City. For Kit and myself it was the first time we had ever been in one. I think it was the first time we had ever been in a car of any sort.

There were a few people in Hammersmith Broadway waving Union Jacks, and a couple of dozen dancing on Shepherd's Bush Green, but for the most part the city seemed quiet.

The next morning the newspapers showed hundreds of thousands of people in the West End and girls happily submitting to be kissed in Piccadilly. Front-page stories carried hints of unrestrained behaviour in the Royal Parks. I felt an intense ache, a longing. A terrible sense of missed opportunity.

Living in White City was like living in some sort of populated desert. Around us there was street after street all built of the same red brick, hundreds of similar semi-detached houses stretching in all directions. But at the same time I, and I think Kit and both our parents, still felt extraordinarily privileged to be living in a house at a time when London and all the bombed cities of Britain were suffering an acute housing shortage. Tens of thousands of people had been obliged to move into old Nissen huts vacated by the Army. Families were living in the German Prisoner-of-War camp on Wormwood Scrubs. Many hundreds were living in the Underground.

By now my mother had made 55 Primula Street more comfortable than anywhere we had lived before. It was a small house but the luxury of having our own rooms, a kitchen, sitting room, bathroom, offered a total contrast to our years in the World's End.

But my yearning for time alone had not diminished with our return to London. There were no more rockets or flying bombs so my father saw no reason why I shouldn't be freer to go out in the evening to see friends, or why I shouldn't go out on Saturdays or Sundays for what I thought of as my 'walking tests'. These were long walks (twenty miles was common), usually solitary, occasionally with Kit. I was drawn by the river. I would walk down to Hammersmith and see how far I could make it along the towpaths and riverside walks. By Chelsea embankment it was easier and I would walk east as far as I could go in the few hours I had, to the Tower, Shadwell, Limehouse and the Isle of Dogs. London, to me, has always been inextricably bound up with the river and for most of my life I have lived within a few hundred yards of it, in Chelsea, Battersea, Chelsea again, and finally now in Putney. Even (now I think of it) when we lived with Joe and Jinny at Windsor, we were less than a hundred yards from the river. A few years later, when I began my first (unpublished, unpublishable) novel, I called it *The River City*.

Walking soon became a regular part of my weekend, burning off energy and giving me the hours of anonymity and autonomy which I seemed to crave. At the same time the idea of staying away by myself for a night or two had gripped me. I began to plan and fantasise about the adventures I might have. Of course, there was an element of nervousness if not real fear, too. But I was thirteen, quite tall for my age and growing physically more confident all the time. I thought.

When I told my father I wanted to go camping by myself he was less than happy but it was so much a point of principle with him that if Kit or I wanted to push ourselves we should, that he didn't refuse.

I'll always admire the way my mother disguised her obvious anxiety about her thirteen year old going off by himself. But, although I couldn't explain it, spending a night alone was not a whim with me. I was anxious to the point of real need to get away on my own, to see how it would be to spend a night by myself in a field somewhere, to see how I handled the midnight bogeymen of childhood, to . . . even now I'm not sure what. Perhaps I was just checking to what extent I'd grown up.

Some weeks earlier my father had brought back from Whitelands an abandoned souvenir from one of the tenants, probably General Browning, a German one-man parachutist's tent. I planned to use that. On a Friday evening after school I packed my saddle bags with Heinz baked beans and Mulligatawny soup, an axe to cut firewood, a paraffin stove in case it rained, a couple of candles and a box of matches. Under the back of the saddle I rolled a blanket and the separate quarters of the tent and fixed them with the straps from an old pair of skates. Kit thought I was mad.

'Sooner you than me. How far are you going then?'

'I don't know. Haven't thought.'

'Windsor? Camp in one of old Emmet's fields? He'll chase you off with a shotgun.' He took aim and made two explosive sounds with his lips.

'Probably won't get that far anyway.'

I didn't. About ten or fifteen miles up Western Avenue a really disturbing thought struck me. I had brought everything for the night. Except one thing – a tin opener. I rode on to just before Uxbridge. To the right I could see fields and a twisting cart-track which it seemed might take me a half-mile or so from civilisation. I wasn't ready for much more.

I took the track. It was uneven and here and there puddled from the rain we'd had during the week. Close up the fields looked marshy. The lights of Uxbridge were perhaps a mile or so ahead. I rode on and chose a spot to pitch my tent. It was in a higher corner of the field, dryer than the surrounding area and just a few yards off the track.

Putting up the tent was not difficult but took time. When I was ready to raise the central pole it was already growing dark outside. And I still had to solve the problem of the tin opener. Without the use of one I would be eating dry bread for supper. My solution seems fanciful now, but in those days it was quite practical. I decided to unpack my saddle bags, stow them in the tent which was effectively camouflaged and almost invisible in the darkening corner of the field, then ride down to Uxbridge to find a soldier with one of those clasp knives with things on it for taking stones out of horses' hooves and, a good deal more useful, a tin opener attached. In my front basket I would carry back the baked beans and Heinz Mulligatawny (whatever that is), the tins held upright by the crumpled sheets of firelighting newspaper I had brought with me.

There was no trace of light in the sky as I set off. My bike had a headlamp which flickered fairly feebly in the lane but I made it down to the main road without much difficulty. From there into Uxbridge was no problem.

I found my soldier within five or ten minutes. He affably helped me open the tins, wished me the equivalent of *bon appetit* and within no time I was on my way back to camp. All was going well. Off the road it was now pitch dark. Five or six hundred yards down the lane I stopped, leaned the bike against a tree to fix my headlight to improve the angle of its beam on the uneven surface of the track. As I was bending over the lamp, I thought I heard a soft cackling somewhere behind me. Coughing maybe. Or a tree creaking. Nerves, I thought. Bound to have nerves. By yourself in the dark like this.

Then a soft footfall in a puddle. Plash. And a grunt.

So . . . somebody walking along the lane. Heading down into Uxbridge. Nothing alarming about that. At least, not necessarily. People in the country walked down dark lanes at night, I knew that.

They weren't all maniacs. But some of them could be. You only needed one. Hurriedly I got on my bike.

Almost before I began to pedal I saw him. In a sudden shaft of moonlight he was stumbling towards me, his arms flung wide. Stone the crows! He was blocking my path. Then suddenly he *screamed*, or maybe it was a croaking shout. I slowed, trying to turn back towards the main road, realised he'd be upon me by then, clawing me off the bike. There was nothing else for it. I turned the handlebars back again and pedalled straight at him. I could see him clearly now, a tramp, nearly bald, middle-aged, unshaven, drunk or mad. Both. All my nightmares.

To the left the lane appeared to meet a mound like a rising bank. I knew there was every chance of a ditch in front of it which would bring the bike and me down at the man's feet, but I had no choice. I wrenched the handle-bars. The front wheel shot into the darkness, bucked before me as it mounted the mound, and dropped two feet as I rollercoastered over the top to sail past the tramp and go speeding into the darkness.

My heart was beating, my legs shaking, as I drove the bike through slush and puddles. Behind me now I could hear the madman shouting. But I had got away from him.

I reached my marker tree, an elm with a big broken branch hanging white at the break. I rode past it in case the tramp was closer or more nimble than I thought. The tent was well concealed but it was no more than two or three hundred yards from where the man had appeared. I switched off the bike's frontlight and stood in the darkness listening. Not a sound. I delved into the basket. The newspaper was soaked with soup. I lifted the two tins out, leaned over a low point in the hedge and placed them on the grass. Then the bike.

Back at the tent I hid the bike in the bushes and crawled inside. My first move was to get out my axe and place it somewhere where I could easily reach for it in the dark. It was obviously too dangerous to light the primus stove. Through the camouflage material of the tent it would be possible to see a faint light. I stuck my head out and listened. Nothing. Perhaps the madman had gone on towards Uxbridge. I decided to call him a tramp in my own mind when I thought about him. 'Madman' was too scary.

I withdrew my head and lay back against the roll of groundsheet and blanket. My trousers were soaked from riding through the puddles. I was shivering, partly from cold, mostly from plain fear. Was he outside creeping towards the tent? I gripped the handle of the axe for comfort. This, I had to tell myself, was not going to be an easy night.

I could, of course, leave the tent and ride without lights down the lane, reach the road and make straight for home. I could. But then again, I couldn't. If I did that, and told them at home why, that'd be the end of my camping. Would they even believe my story of the madman in the moonlit lane? Kit would laugh, unbelievingly. My mother would just be looking for a chance to say comfortingly, 'Better leave it till next year,' or never. My father would say very little but I would know that he was disappointed. Would he believe my story? I think so. They say it's the East that can't bear to lose face.

I stuck my head out again and listened. There was a touch more moon but I could see very little and hear nothing. I pulled back into the tent and tried to pretend I was hungry. In the darkness I located a spoon and, careful not to make scraping sounds against the tins, I ate my soup and beans cold.

Well, what now? I had no watch but I guessed it was about ten or eleven o'clock. Time for bed. I rolled myself fully dressed in the blanket, keeping it loose in case I had to leap to my feet at a sound outside. I'd brought a comic to read by the light of my bike but that was far too risky. I checked outside again. The moon had slid from behind tumbled cloud. The fields looked grey and dead. Nothing moved. Good.

Back in the tent I rolled myself back in the blanket, clutching the axe. The worst was past. Don't dwell on the madman, the tramp, think about the girl at Windsor, Shirley. Think about if you met her again by chance catching an 11 bus at Shepherd's Bush.

She'd be dressed up, working in a shop on the Green.

'Shirley . . . you remember me?'

'Hey, of course I do. The one in that American jacket.'

'You remember the jacket, uh?'

'And who was wearing it.'

'Maybe I could buy you dinner one night? (American dialogue figured large in my fantasies – till then I'd never bought a girl as much as an ice-lolly.) Maybe take in a movie?'

'Sounds good to me.'

'Tonight?'

'You work fast.'

'I'll pick you up at seven.'

I drifted. I don't know how long I slept. It didn't seem long, if at all, when I awoke to hear a rustling outside the tent. Within yards.

I threw off the blanket, keyed up as I'd seldom been in my life. The axe in my right hand, I chose the side of the tent away from the entrance panel and slid my head under, cheek flat against the damp grass. The same dead moonlit fields. I listened hard, then heard it again. A rustling . . . Feet moving stealthily through grass? Could easily be. I could almost see the curved knife in the madman's hand, the dull glint of moonlight in his mad eyes. I strained into the darkness. I could make out trees and hedges that seemed to fade away from me as the moon was partly obscured. But nothing human.

Wriggling forward, I got half my body out, then my legs. I was in deep shadow. I was sure he thought I was still inside the tent. But where was he?

Very slowly I lifted my head. Then panic made me gasp. A dark figure was lying in the grass about thirty feet away. There was movement too. It looked as though the figure was slithering forward. I listened. A low grunt, undoubtedly a man.

I don't believe I was thinking too clearly. I was terrified and angry too. I was thirteen and the hormones were rising. I don't think I thought of running. I knew I had the advantage of surprise. And the axe. I took a deep breath and leapt to my feet. Racing across the short distance between us, I took one Indian leap, deadly Tomahawk poised above my head . . . and landed astride the back of an RAF man, trousers round his buttocks, a girl's face staring up at me, pop-eyed with fear. I just stopped the swing of the axe. The RAF man twisted his head to see me. He was equally terrified.

For a moment the couple lay paralysed on the man's uniform greatcoat. It was my chance to explain. I snatched at it.

'A tramp,' I said quickly. 'Did you see him?' I dropped my voice to a whisper. 'Bald,' I confided. 'Or almost. Completely mad.'

I had stepped back, no longer straddling my victims. The young woman was fumbling with her clothes, sobbing and glaring at me. 'Take me home, George. Now!'

'It's just a kid,' the RAF man said, the first words I can remember hearing from him. 'Just a bloody kid.'

'Make yourself decent, George. And just take me home.'

The idea of them leaving struck fear into me. I didn't want them to go. Any company was welcome. 'Please don't go.' I advanced on them again. 'You can stay all night. You'll be all right. I'm just over there – in the bushes.'

'Over there in the bushes! And he thinks we're staying here? He's off his bleedin' rocker,' the RAF man said. He was standing now, pulling up his trousers, preparing to come at me. But one glance at my axe was enough. 'Clear off,' he said feebly. 'You better clear off if you know what's good for you.'

I half turned to go. I wanted to prolong the contact. 'You sure you didn't see a tramp? Bald. In the lane. Mad.'

He glared at me. Then to the girl: 'Come on, love, we'll find somewhere else. There's only one mad bugger around here.'

It only took a little reflection the next morning to realise that he was right.

Three months passed, strange months when the German war had been won but we were not yet at peace. In Britain these months were dominated by the General Election that had been called for the end of July. The world saw it as a foregone conclusion, Winston Churchill would be returned as Prime Minister. Anything else was inconceivable. But, in fact, millions of those same British voters who saw, admired and even loved Churchill as a war leader, simply did not associate him with any particular party. Now they were being told to look on him not as the leader of Britain but of the Conservative Party. He himself seemed to be uncomfortable in the role and damaged his own chances by making some heavily party-political speeches. He and his party had not realised that the experience of the thirties and the experience of war itself had changed Britain. There was to be no return to the days of effortless neglect favoured by too many senior Conservatives. Sadly for Churchill and his party the real innovations of the war years, the Butler Education Act, the Bills for Family Allowances and a National Health Service, all initiated under his leadership, came too late in the war to fix in the mind of the electorate the image of Conservative-driven reform. Churchill lost by a landslide. With the war still unfinished, the Attlee government took over the governance of Britain and the founding of the National Health Service.

I was ignorantly fascinated by all these developments. For as long as I could remember I had followed the day-to-day developments of the war as a modern youngster might follow the fortunes of Manchester United. With that war, even in the Far East, moving towards a close, my interest turned to the politics of peace.

Then the first atomic bomb was dropped at Hiroshima; three days afterwards another at Nagasaki. A day later Japan agreed to surrender unconditionally.

The celebrations for VJ Day were different in spirit from those of VE night. Purely as celebrations of victory they were, in Britain, less deeply felt than the profound satisfaction we all experienced as Hitler's Germany crumpled in defeat. Of course, I exclude here all those who had family members in the Far East. But for most of the British people, whose war aims had been satisfied by the defeat of Germany and the death of Hitler, victory over Japan was a less emotional experience.

VJ Day was different. The diarist James Lees-Milne wrote of final victory after six years of war against Germany and Japan: 'I am strangely unmoved by this announcement. The world is left a victim of chaos, great uncertainty and heinous turpitude.' He was not an optimist. Anthony Heap saw simply 'thousands of weary-looking people wandering the streets or sprawling on the grass in the parks'. Sir Alexander Cadogan preferred to describe 'scores of thousands of morons wandering about'. They were of course the scores of thousands who, with our allies, had won the war. But it's true that throughout VJ Day the rejoicing was subdued.

Then with the coming of evening the mood seemed to change. The wealthier sort had already retired to private dinner parties at the Savoy or Dorchester; tens of thousands of others decided this was a night to stay at home. Looking back, I believe that as a celebration of a great allied victory what happened in London that night verged on the artificial. Perhaps it was in part because those newspaper hints of unrestrained behaviour in the parks on VE night had struck home: a working-class bacchanalia was to be the keynote of the night. The VE celebration had already tentatively pointed the way. For VJ night many older people decided to stay at home. During the festivities of May elderly people and parents with young children had been in evidence all over the West End. But VJ night was, by some curious common consent, appropriated by the young who still had no thought for the morrow. At thirteen, less than a month away from my fourteenth birthday, I considered myself one of them.

Leave passes had been issued to the forces in the United Kingdom, and the British-based forces of all nationalities included tens of thousands of young women as well as men. All headed for Piccadilly and the West End. The scene was set for a Night of Misrule.

Medieval England had a well-established tradition of Misrule. Quiet country towns or villages frequently had a night, perhaps occurring once every five years, when the law could be disregarded with impunity. I don't think murder would have gone unpunished. Householders would, however, have been expected to protect their own properties from theft. In a country town there might have been a bit of sheep rustling, but there's no doubt that a degree of sexual licence was what Misrule was chiefly about. For one night the lid was off. Hitch-hiking as a teenager in the late forties, I was present on such a night in a steel town in the North. A costumed Lord of Misrule misdirected the ceremonies. I saw no murders, only a few more fights than I imagine might have occurred in the pubs on a normal Saturday night. But the dancing was a story all its own. And women disappeared into alleys with men I could only believe were other than their husbands. Everybody drank huge amounts. We got a lift on a truck heading south the next morning long before the town had awakened and debts and grudges, if any could be remembered, were settled.

On VJ night this, I think, was the way many revellers looked on the festivities. I went with a few friends of about my age, but I had already decided that I would not be spending the evening with them. The newspaper stories about VJ night had got to me too.

I remember as we walked up Haymarket in the crowds that there were three young women in front of us. They stopped to look or point at something and we overtook them. They were about thirty, almost certainly married with husbands who had been away for a week, a month, several years. They were respectable women. If I'd known the term, or ever used it, I would have said lower-middle-class women. Most probably I thought they were quite posh, not Whitelands posh, but quite posh all the same. A man at a roughly constructed stall at the kerb was selling copies of a run-off account of the love life of Hitler. His sales pitch was to read aloud, his cockney voice affecting what he imagined was a German accent. It was pure pornography. The text was as crude as some of the schoolgirl essays I saw later in life (during my brief career as a teacher). Women giggled, men grinned before drifting on.

The three women in front picked up a few words as they approached. I thought, in fact I was convinced, they would walk past the man hustling the crumpled copies of Hitler's love life, with gaze averted. Noses turned up, even. And perhaps they would have if the man at the kerb had not produced a bunch of what I first took to be balloons then quickly realised, from the screams of delight of the women, were five hugely blown up condoms. As he began, like some licensed medieval jester, beating the women over the head with them, he quoted by heart the lewdest passages from the book.

They bought a copy. Walking up Haymarket, laughing, they read phrases aloud and handed the loose pages to one another. I had never seen a woman affected by the sort of verbal images that affected us as schoolboys. And if I'd imagined it was possible for a working-class girl to be affected, I had certainly never thought it possible for a middle-class wife.

The crowds thickened at Shaftesbury Avenue. They swirled into Piccadilly. Eros, the Lord of Misrule himself, was shuttered in his wartime green plywood enclosure in the middle of the Circus but that's where everybody headed. They knew he was there.

Accordion music came from every corner. Loudspeakers played from the tops of buildings. The occasional American soldier held his own audience with his trumpet or trombone. In the noise and dancing, in the singing and jiving, among the endless conga lines, not without deliberation I lost my three friends.

I had no plan, I simply craved anonymity. I wanted to behave as I wanted. I was alone amongst this vast crowd, mostly women it seemed to me, a crowd excited beyond the triumph of victory over Japan, a crowd reaching out to embrace strangers, a crowd throbbing with something I couldn't quite understand. Yet part of me understood because I felt it myself.

Darkness fell quickly. The streetlights glowed all the way down Piccadilly, past the Ritz to where fireworks were exploding in Green Park. I walked through the crowds. Sailors were kissing unprotesting girls who peeled off from one embrace into the arms of an American, Pole or Canadian until they reeled back, drunk with kissing, giggling among their girlfriends.

It seemed to me a chance that would never come my way again. A chance to kiss a grown woman, by which I meant a girl of at least seventeen. All around me they were throwing themselves into the arms of strangers, not all uniformed, men who were old enough to be their fathers, short, ugly men . . . Why not me? I chose a young-looking girl, seventeen or eighteen, who was holding back from one huge kissing group. She was dancing by herself, arms held high above her head, trying to start up a conga line. She smiled. I chose to think the smile was directed at me. I put my arms round her waist and she brought her body close to mine. I didn't understand that she was ready to dance but not to be kissed. She saw my juvenile intent as I lunged towards her. My mouth touched her lips.

She laughed. With one hand she pushed me full in the chest. I was unbalanced. I stepped back and tripped. Her friends gathered around me, laughing and pointing. 'At his age!' 'Cheeky bugger!'

I scrambled to my feet and snaked off through the crowd. When I had regained my anonymity I leaned against a wall, trembling, pouring with sweat. People streamed past me with barely a glance. I straightened up. I had done what I'd come here to do. I'd kissed a grown woman. Almost. I'd even perhaps brushed her breast.

*

When I look back I see my desire was motivated by fear of a sin of omission. What I couldn't resist was not the body of the young woman but the abandon of her dancing, the possibility that this was indeed an invitation and that I was going, through cowardice, to miss the opportunity presented.

In one so young this is hubris indeed. But I make the point because Harold Pinter has just publicly revealed that on this same night, a few dozen yards away, he was punched unconscious by a man whose girlfriend he had 'pinched'. I feel my transgression was of a different kind. But then I would, of course.

I had wandered down Piccadilly towards Green Park feeling a sense of achievement. I had not let this unique opportunity pass. I had taken advantage of the Night of Misrule. I had not let myself down. (Some, I recognise, would say differently.)

Just past the Ritz I turned into the park. There were a few lights on along the pathways. There were bursts of fireworks and long periods of darkness in the sky. A loudspeaker was playing popular songs from one of the speakers on a building across Piccadilly. Here in the park most people seemed to be in uniform. There were some WAAFs singing under a park light, not raucous singing, just low, melodious, one of the rather sad songs of the day. There was, as I remember, very little real drunkenness. A few Americans had bottles of whisky which they offered freely to the girls around them. A few British sailors were unsteady on their feet. But that was all.

When the fireworks died the park was dark beyond the dimly lit paths. People surged in groups towards me, some with arms linked, shouting greetings, some walking as if out for an evening stroll.

I turned off one of the paths and immediately saw that what I had imagined were a few people lying together in the grass were in fact numberless couples. I walked a few yards and lowered myself on to the grass among them. It was, to me, a sight I believed I would never again see in my life. A distant explosion of fireworks showed the whole ground level to be gently undulating. There must have been hundreds of couples copulating around me.

I think I sat there dazed. Not so much by what was happening in the park but by my experience in Piccadilly. I had kissed a grown woman. Perhaps even touched her breast.

Someone was picking their way through the couples in the grass. Whistles and trumpets were blowing from the balcony of the Ritz. By a peacock's tail of firework light I saw a woman coming towards me. She wore uniform but no hat, her jacket was open. She was waving some invisible something in her right hand. 'Who wants it?' she was asking. 'Who's for it?' An American voice.

She saw me sitting alone. 'Hey there. All alone on Victory night?'

She was close enough now. In the dim lamplight I could see she held up a small packet between thumb and index finger. A Durex packet. 'Can I interest you in a lovelorn American girl, honey? Received my Dear Jane just today. The bastard! Going to marry some rich Australian broad. Gives a whole different meaning to victory in the Pacific.'

I stood up.

She looked at me, finding it hard to focus. 'Hell, you're not much more than a kid.'

'No,' I said.

She hesitated, head to one side, an appraising smile on her face. 'Could be kinda fun.'

I said nothing. I wanted to turn and run. But I could feel another missed opportunity shaping up.

'You're shaking,' she said. 'Have a slug of this. Dutch courage.' She took a small bottle from inside her uniform jacket.

I shook my head. 'No, thank you.'

'OK.' She leaned forward. We were about the same height. I could feel the tears wet on her cheek. She kissed me, closed mouth but generously, on the lips. ''Bye, honey.'

I stood in the darkness while she turned away, walking with

exaggerated care, singing as she disappeared between the lights in the dimly lit pathway:

> *Maybe I'm right, and maybe I'm wrong*
> *And maybe you don't fucking care . . .*
> *But the night you took me in your arms . . .*

'A Nightingale Sang in Berkeley Square' was a great VJ night favourite.

TWELVE

Harry's Commando Paris Trip

From the day the German war ended Harry Little had his eyes set on France. As the summer holidays approached the 'onlie begetter' of the Commando French Course began to put out feelers, after his fashion. 'You, boy, you'd like to go to Paris, wouldn't you? All the sights. Harry Little's Commando Paris Trip. Don't let on to anybody yet.'

I assume he had made all the preparatory arrangements with the Foreign Office and the French Embassy a month before the Japanese surrender. Certainly he was recruiting before the end of the summer term. 'This'll be in the nature of a free trip, my boys. Or very nearly,' he'd add with that conspiratorial lift of the eyebrows we'd got to know well. It meant: Harry Little's up to something. It'll do you some good – and him even more.

'Tell your dads it won't cost more than a fiver each. Then just sign here on the dotted line, my boys . . .' And he'd bang his old briefcase down on the desk like a patent medicine hustler in the Far West. '. . . for the experience of a lifetime.'

At home at White City I could hardly wait for my father to get back from work. I was ready with all sorts of impractical proposals to help contribute to the five pounds – but they weren't necessary. My father agreed immediately. He thought it a great opportunity to see another country. Educational. A chance to learn some French. Perhaps he was aware how little we had been learning at school. In her restrained manner, my mother was horrified. 'It's a long way,' she said.

'Not when you look at it on the map. Not as far as from here to Cornwall.'

'And what will you do for food? Real food, I mean?'

'Mr Little says we'll take food with us.'

'I was wondering how he was doing it so cheap,' my father said mysteriously, as if he already knew something about Harry that I didn't.

'The war's hardly over. How can you be sure they've rounded up all the Germans? Wait till next year,' my mother urged.

But I was eager. More than eager. For all my remembered life there had been a line drawn down the middle of the English Channel. Beyond lay the forbidden land. Here be Germans. During the years of some of my earliest memories those German soldiers were preparing to come here. To march through Sloane Square, down King's Road and take possession of World's End. I'd seen them often enough in my waking dreams as they massed round the coffee stall outside the Ladies' Convenience. Had I not fought them through the ruins of the bombed apartments of Ashburnham Mansions and a dozen other shattered buildings?

Now the idea of leaving England, of seeing what was on 'the other side', was as exciting as it could get. I began to read anything I could see in my father's *News Chronicle* about France.

General de Gaulle was in power. I knew that from the newsreels of him walking down the Champs Elysées in a hail of bullets when Paris was liberated in August last year. Eastern France had only just been liberated and the Nazi-loving Vichy government under the oily, white-tied Laval and old Marshal Pétain had been chased out. The Marshal, commander in France's greatest First World War victory, ninety something by now, was going on trial for his life. I suppose that fact alone might have given me some measure of the turmoil of the France I was going to. I had one more fact, drawn from many a film featuring agents dropping by moonlight, the tumble of parachute silk, the sinister rustle of grass, the relief that it was a fellow agent waiting and not a German patrol. My incontrovertible fact was that the Resistance were the only Frenchmen who'd supported us, the only Frenchmen you could rely upon to fight Germans. That was about all I knew, or thought I knew, about France as it was today.

There was, of course, so much more to know, much of which was to concern me intimately when I was married to a Frenchwoman later in life. There were, centrally, the conflicting claims to power of Communists and Gaullists. There was the *épuration*, or purging, where untold thousands of Frenchmen were dragged from their homes and murdered by other Frenchmen. There was the massive emotional impact of the return through the Paris railway terminals of the *déportés*, the very few French and foreign Jewish survivors of the 75,000 who had been murdered in the camps, the 600,000 slave labourers, the numberless orphaned or abandoned children who had been barracked like soldiers all over France. My connection with France from here on would give me a link with each of these groups of survivors. But, as yet, I knew nothing of them.

I hurried to school the next morning to put my name down. Harry took me aside with a couple of other boys and gave us a list of necessary items.

'Write it down, my boys. One pound of sugar . . . on ration but I'm sure your mothers'll manage somehow. Four pounds of coffee beans, they're off ration so you'll have no trouble with them. Four bars of soap. Two bars of chocolate. One packet of tea . . . the nobs like tea in France . . . six tins of Nescafé . . . and fifty Players cigarettes. The system is we sell the goods, details arranged by Harry Little, and divide the spoils between you. As I promised you, my boys, it'll be the nearest thing to a free trip to Paris.'

For three days I lived in a French dreamland. I was fighting

Germans in the Paris Uprising. I was walking down the Champs Elysées with de Gaulle. I was looking out over Paris with the Tricolor fluttering in my face. Then the blow fell. Harry Little took me aside. He had a kindly, regretful expression on his face. 'Bad news, my boy,' he said. 'I'm oversubscribed. One too many for the group visa the French Embassy are letting me have.'

'Somebody's going to have to drop out?'

''Fraid so, my boy.'

'Not me, sir?'

'You're the youngest. First on the list for next year, though. Or even Christmas. Sorry, lad.'

'But . . .'

'Sorry, lad.'

But my father was not someone to take no for an answer. Not, at least, if there was any possibility at all that he could do something about it. I knew he'd try hard enough but what chance was there of him knowing someone in France after six years of war? What were the chances of anybody from the World's End knowing anybody in France anyway? I mooched around, trying to put a brave face on things.

The summer holiday began. Two days later my father bustled in. 'How do you fancy La Frette sur Seine?' he asked, taking out a piece of paper with an address written on it. 'La Frette sur Seine . . . That how you pronounce it?'

'What is it?'

'Near Paris, apparently. On the River Seine. River that runs through the capital. Sort of suburb. Or a village. They have villages there very close to the middle of Paris.'

I was beginning to get excited. 'And?'

'Someone I know . . .' he was as excited as I was '. . . her sister's just moved there. Very hard up at the moment. The sister says they'd probably like to take an English boy for a couple of weeks.'

Near Paris. It was too good to be true. Then a thought struck me. 'These people, can they speak English?'

'Well, the lady comes from Guildford so you're in there with a chance.'

'And the man?'

'He's French. Julien Lelong. Don't pronounce it Lee Long, make him sound like a Chinaman. It's sort of all one word his sister-in-law says – Lelong.'

'Does he speak English?'

'He was a submarine commander with the Free French here during the war, so his English is pretty good. Well . . . do you want to go?'

He'd done it again. I couldn't wait. Even my mother was mollified by the thought that there would be an Englishwoman doing the cooking.

My father was not an easy man for anybody to thank. It wasn't easy even for Kit and myself. Expressions of love or affection embarrassed him. Emotional communications passed from him through my mother. His was a world of practically expressed emotion. You did what you could for your family. You derived your pleasure, not from letters of thanks but from hearing from your son what it was like in France today. Or seeing your other son become captain of every football team he ever joined.

'There's a catch,' my father said as he watched me dance around in delight.

I stopped. 'What's that?'

'You'll have to become a smuggler.'

'What?'

'Sit down.'

I did. A smuggler!

'This Julien Lelong probably saved a few bob while he was over here. Submarine captain, after all.'

'Not a lot to spend it on under the water.'

'Exactly. Anyway he saved some before he went back to France and his wife's sister has it in a bank account here in London.'

'Why didn't he take it with him?'

'This is the bit I don't understand too well. But it seems the franc is losing its value all the time, don't know why. But that means as it gets weaker it's favourite to keep your money in pounds and only bring it into France when you need it.'

'And he needs it now?'

'He doesn't get paid a lot in France.'

'How much am I going to be taking?'

'A hundred pounds. Problem is, Dee, it's illegal to take that sort of money into France.'

I looked at him in alarm. A hundred pounds? I'd never seen that amount, not even at the dog track.

'You needn't tell your mother about this. All right?'

I nodded.

A smuggler. Then that's what I would have been with Harry Little, too. But a lone smuggler, this was different. At what age were you eligible for the guillotine over there?

THIRTEEN

Tickets, sans tickets?

Today it's nothing. I suppose we've never had such well-travelled children. But immediately after the war the journey to Paris for a thirteen year old was roughly equivalent to a journey to Afghanistan today. My parents and Kit saw me off from Victoria, my mother looking strained and apprehensive. The people getting on to the first-class carriages of the train all seemed to be bowler-hatted officials with briefcases as hand luggage or senior officers with red tabs on their lapels. (Regular troop trains, as I was to learn a few years later, passed from Harwich to the Hook of Holland.) My father had given me a brand new (in 1939) pale pigskin Gladstone bag with heavy brass fittings (purloined from Whitelands, no doubt). It seemed to me pure Sherlock Holmes and I was embarrassed even to carry it down the platform, but I didn't want to disappoint him.

'Watch out for anybody takes a fancy to your bag,' he warned.

I assured him I would, although I couldn't imagine any thief who'd want my Gladstone instead of the smart leatherette utility suitcases with the black tin handles most of the officers were carrying.

I found a second-class seat, put my case up on the netting rack, and waved to my mother who was pursing her lips and blinking in an effort to hold back the tears. I remember that, unusually, she was holding tight on to Kit's hand as if to say, 'You can't have them both.'

As the train pulled away I waved over-enthusiastically, but I was already thinking of France – and of the hundred pounds in big white five-pound notes bound in a bandage under my right sock.

Calais was a wreck. As we approached I could see the huge German concrete bunkers, part of the Fortress Europa that had been constructed to keep us out. Many of the three-foot-thick concrete lids had been blown apart. They are still like that today, though half-hidden in sand dunes and tufts of trailing grass. The town itself was battered, the station already being rebuilt. From the deck I could see dozens of workmen in blue overalls and black leather caps, the first Frenchmen I had seen on French soil. Along a harbour wall white-painted graffiti called for the hanging of Laval and Pétain. *Laval, Pétain à la lanterne.* Thin red distemper had been used by someone in an attempt to obliterate it. Another first, although this one I didn't appreciate, but it was, in fact, my first glimpse of the deep divide in French society.

Then, as we docked, the smells of a French port. Tobacco, acorn coffee, fish, the oily steam from the hissing locomotives . . .

In the long, open compartment of the train nobody took any notice of me. Nobody tried to steal my Gladstone bag. I shifted about on the wooden slatted seats. We were already nearly an hour late. Julien Lelong was to meet me in Paris. Say we missed each other?

My attention was caught by a line of cattle trucks marked '*40 hommes, 8 chevaux*' in the marshalling yards as we bumped slowly out of Calais Maritime. Forty men or eight horses! I had perhaps come upon my first trace of the German occupation. The cattle trucks could have been marked like that for the French Army at the beginning of the war, I suppose. Or were they trucks for deportees to

Germany? I was puzzling over this, unaware of anybody standing next to me, when: '*Jeune homme*,' a woman's voice said sternly. '*La douane.*'

I had no notion of what she was saying to me. She was short, heavy-breasted, and wearing a black skirt and some sort of uniform shirt. I tried to give her my ticket but she pushed it aside impatiently. '*Douane*,' she said. 'Customs.'

I'm sure I went pale. Ted Simon had told me all customs people were trained to look right through you. I don't know how he knew but, in that moment, I certainly believed him.

'*Passeport.*'

I fumbled it out and gave it to her.

'Why you here?'

'On the train?'

'In France,' she said heavily.

'Oh. Holiday. To learn French.'

'*Ta valise*,' the woman said, vaguely gesturing towards the Gladstone bag.

'It's called a Gladstone,' I said. 'After the Prime Minister.' I was trying to dissipate what I was convinced she must think was the bizarre quality of the bag. 'We have lots of them in England.'

She gestured for me to get it down.

I pulled it down from the luggage rack and put it on the seat.

'*Ouvre . . . ouvre.* Open . . . open.'

She searched it, pulling out a couple of books, socks and a sweater or two which she left trailing from the Gladstone. She'd obviously learned her trade during the Occupation. For a few moments she delved about in the bag, much of the time her eyes fixed on me. 'No foodstuffs?'

'A cheese sandwich.'

She picked it up, sniffed it and sneered. 'Coffee?'

What would I have said if I'd been on Harry's trip? 'No,' I said. 'No black-market coffee.'

She narrowed her eyes. 'Money?'

'No money, no.'

'Then how you live in Paris without money? You think it's free to the English and Americans, uh? For the price of the liberation? Perhaps you have cigarettes.'

'No, I'm too young to smoke.' I pulled my three pounds' worth of francs from my pocket. 'I have francs,' I said.

'English money. You have English money?'

'No.'

'I think, yes.'

I was trembling. Was this what Ted Simon meant?

'How much English pound you have?'

I desperately wanted to close my eyes to stop them watering.

'No English pound,' I said, suddenly aware that I was echoing her poor English.

'Give to me your coat.'

I took off my school blazer. She frowned suspiciously at the breast pocket. 'What is this?'

'My school badge.'

She lifted her eyes to the roof of the compartment. For a few moments she crunched and bent the Sloane badge backwards and forwards, no doubt hoping to hear the crackle of concealed five-pound notes. A second customs officer, male and wearing a cap, had come to lean on the back of the seat opposite. He grinned while the woman searched my jacket pockets and thrust her hands down the sleeves.

Disappointed, she tossed the coat on the wooden bench. It slid to the floor. She left it.

She gestured me forward with a snap of her fingers. 'Come.'

I stepped forward.

'Lift your arms.' She took me by the raised wrists and ran her hands down my arms and back up again. Then all over my chest. Then reached round to feel down my back. 'Open legs,' she said.

Taking a half-step backwards she dropped on to one knee and frisked me from the left ankle up to the groin. I'm not sure if I was more shocked at the intimacy or scared of what she'd find on my right ankle when she reached it. She plunged into my groin again.

'This part, she like,' her colleague said.

She dropped her hands down my right leg.

Laughing, the man at the door said something in French. She turned angrily towards him and her hands lost contact with my leg at the bottom of my calf, half an inch above the bandage and the twenty white five-pound notes.

They left and I fell back on the seat.

France!

Saint Lazare station was approached by a long cutting of soot-grimed grey brick covered with slogans, *Vive* something or *À bas* something else, mostly in the form of a series of indecipherable initials. The train had filled up with people after Calais Maritime. They were mostly small, poorly dressed men and women often carrying string bags of potatoes or leeks or sometimes a dead chicken, neck hanging down mournfully. The *News Chronicle* said that the wine ration was a litre a month but mysteriously a good many of the men in the train seemed to drink the best part of a litre on the journey from Calais. And why had my woman customs officer asked me if I had food when everybody else was so obviously bringing food in from the countryside?

As we left the train at Gare St Lazare a swarm of men hurried towards the passengers. They wore black leather caps, blue smocks and carried a hooked strap over one shoulder. Most of them lacked an arm or hobbled on a wooden leg. I was horrified when they tried to pull people's bags from their grasp, hook a heavy suitcase on to the strap and carry it for them. Passengers would struggle to reject their services. Most of the British were forced to submit.

I learnt later that these porters were the *mutilés de guerre*, the mutilated or wounded men of France's massive efforts in the 1914–18 war. Some of them were barely into their mid-forties. That was a shock. The Great War where they had sacrificed parts of their bodies was only twenty-five years earlier, when they had been no more than boys of eighteen or nineteen.

A man of about thirty, tall, thin, saturnine, wearing a dark green tweed jacket, dark glasses, a smoking Gauloise on his lip, leaned against an ornate cast-iron pillar. He carried our prearranged signal, a copy of *Figaro*. He didn't need it. He was a younger, darker Charles Boyer. He was everybody's idea of a submarine captain.

I found Julien intimidating. He was the first Frenchman I had ever met and I didn't understand his sardonic sense of humour. As a young boy, I suppose I was just unable to evaluate it. I concluded that he didn't like the British much even though he had married an English wife. Later I would understand a little more. I think he found it near-impossible to accept that Britain had emerged into the post-war world impoverished but widely admired for her stand against Hitler while France had emerged impoverished and with its World War I reputation in shreds. In 1945 French self-belief was at its lowest ebb. Despite de Gaulle's desperate claims, few of his countrymen in 1945 believed they had liberated themselves. That was a belief possible only when the Allies had passed through and on into Germany. Once the physical evidence of American tanks and marching columns of British troops had disappeared from the streets, the French were slowly able to construct their great guiding myth of the late twentieth century: a France freed substantially by her own efforts.

We took the train to La Frette directly from Saint Lazare. It was crowded, the automatic doors held open by young men who stood in the doorway, sat on the high steps, or even, one hand gripping the mounting post, swung out over the track, smoking with their free hand. Anarchy, I thought smugly. I asked Julien about the customs inspection. He laughed without too much humour.

'Coffee,' he said. 'She was looking for coffee.'

'Why coffee especially?'

'For herself,' he said. 'She confiscates it and makes fifteen hundred francs. Say, two English pounds on the black market. A small tin of Nescafé's worth more than money in France today,' he said bitterly. 'Like a half-kilo of coffee beans during the war.' He paused and added, almost to himself, 'More than a woman's virtue.'

Wow! I thought. Who is he talking about? I knew he had been married before. My father had said there was something about a German officer while Julien was away in England. Who could tell?

We passed the football Stade de Colombes and the train slowed through an industrial suburb called Argenteuil. Julien told me that it was a place where some of the great painters of the last century had worked: Monet had painted a view of that river bank. Of course, you'd have to go to Washington to see it now. They all painted here, Monet, Manet, Renoir, Sisley . . . had I heard of them? No.

Which French artists had I heard of?

A moment's hard thinking. 'Picasso.'

'Spanish.'

He seemed to find all this significant.

'Have you heard of Racine?'

'Racine? No.'

'Molière?'

'Uh . . . no.'

'Victor Hugo?'

I shook my head, hot and embarrassed. 'Perhaps.'

He grinned, but it was to himself. 'Anyway you've heard of Shakespeare, I suppose. That's all that matters then, *n'est-ce pas*?'

★

La Frette itself was a suburb which had been a village only yesterday. The high street was easily differentiated with its church and cafés but, I suppose just before the war, several streets of villas were built to cross it, running down to the Seine. The house Julien lived in, La Maison Blanche, was rented by two other families besides his own. It gave me a deep frisson to be told that it had been Gestapo district headquarters until the Germans pulled out last year.

I got along well with Jane, Julien's English wife. She didn't ask me about French painters. It was a little different with Julien himself. I came to think he both liked and disliked me. I realised later that he struggled with the problem of many Frenchmen, both admiring the English and envying them. Beyond even that he distrusted them. They would, he believed, always put England first. But perhaps, as a Frenchman, this was what he most admired. It was what de Gaulle's politics aimed to teach the French to do for themselves.

Sometimes I found it difficult to take Julien's bitter, sardonic sense of humour. He had left England a hero, and arrived back in France a stranger to the attitudes, slang, and above all occupation experiences of his own people. I think he felt a great need to attribute blame for the invidious position in which he found himself. Using tactics now familiar to us, but which baffled me then, he decided to vent his anger on the Americans. Their wealth, the pure swagger of their lifestyle, he found intolerable. All this was exacerbated by his own miserable situation. The French Navy had found him a job in the Ministry of Marine off Place de l'Etoile. It was a miserable job, far below his expectations, and the salary was pitiful. To eke it out he took home work for an entrepreneur who supplied medal ribbons to the American Army in Paris. Night after night Julien, former Légion d'Honneur submarine commander, would sit at the kitchen table in La Frette, wrapping and sewing coloured ribbon round inch-long pieces of cardboard, campaign medals for American soldiers.

He saw the British differently, but no more affectionately. He thought that I, as an English boy, was inheriting the future of Europe, assuming the mantle of France which for a thousand years had claimed the cultural and (for most of the time) military leadership of the continent. Of course, he was wrong; that was not to be Britain's heritage. But it made his bitterness no less acute.

I was excited, intrigued, bored, fascinated, embarrassed, bewildered, and above all made homesick by my fortnight in France. During my time there I had never suffered or enjoyed such a rush of new experience. On my second morning in La Frette I was sent shopping by Jane Lelong, with the precise instructions necessary to shop in France. 'A dozen large eggs. You ask for them *sans tickets*. And then on to the café for twenty Gauloise, *sans tickets*.'

'What does that mean exactly? Without tickets?'

'Off ration.'

Alarm bells. 'Black market?'

'That's it. An extra ten francs an egg.'

'Illegal?'

'Of course.'

I went out very tentatively into the August sunshine, francs in my hand. Dozen eggs, *sans tickets*. Packet of cigarettes, *sans tickets*. Before I was a couple of hundred yards down the street an old lady stopped me. 'You are the English,' she said. 'With Julien and his English wife.'

'*Oui*,' I said, stretching my French vocabulary to the limit.

'*Sa femme* Olivia, 'is first wife . . .' She gave a short whistle and lifted the back of her skirts a few unappealing inches. 'Germans,' she said. '*Boches*.'

'Yes?' I said.

'And see this old flirt . . .' She pointed to a woman, not young but considerably younger than herself, who was mounting a bicycle a few houses down the street. The old woman with me raised her voice. '*Collabo, vous savez?*'

'What?'

'Collaborator. Used to teach English to German officers during the occupation.' She hurried away, sucking her teeth in disapproval.

The '*collabo*' stopped her bicycle. She had heard or guessed much of what was being said. 'You're the young man staying at Julien's.'

'Yes, Madame.'

'He's a good man. He talks to me in the street. He really did fight the Germans so nobody can call him a *collabo*. Bitter about all that's happened but a good man.' She was about to move on, then stopped. 'I used to teach English, private lessons, before the war,' she said. 'When the Germans came, naturally nobody dared take English lessons except for the Germans themselves.' She paused. 'Should I have starved instead? Life's hard in France today for everybody, but less so for anybody who can claim they are Communist. Today, it's the Red Badge of Courage. Do you know that American novel?'

No. So much I didn't know.

'Not important. They shaved my head last year, you know, the Communists. They claimed to know that I was having relations with one of the German officers I was teaching. You'll notice it always has to be an officer to make it really heinous. But . . . you're too young to know about these things. Where are you going, shopping for Jane?'

I told her it was my first shopping expedition in France.

She looked down the village street. 'How long, I wonder, will it take life to settle down, be normal again? Shopping and drinking a *petit vin blanc* in the café.' It was clear these simple pleasures weren't available to her. 'I have to go out into the country. I know a farm there. They're willing, out of the goodness of their hearts . . .' she smiled bleakly '. . . to sell to me.' She paused. 'There are many good French people. They'll come to the top again soon, I believe. For a few years France lost her way under the occupation.'

She got on to her bicycle. 'Just remember, there are many good German people too.' She smiled. 'Only don't tell anybody I told you that.'

She pushed herself forward and began to pedal slowly up the road. I went on down a cobbled street to the *boulangerie*. A gendarme in kepi and leather gaiters passed by on the other side. '*Bonjour, jeune homme*,' he said, saluting smartly. '*Bonjour, Monsieur. Il fait beau*,' I answered and felt ridiculously proud of my limitless command of the language.

This part of the village was probably not unlike Argenteuil had been when all those painters were working there. I could see the café on the corner. A man with a fishing rod strapped to his old bicycle pedalled laboriously towards the Seine. Women stood in pairs talking and pointing, thank God not at me, on the street corners. Most of the streets seemed to be named after politicians. I wondered which street last year was named for Marshal Pétain.

The bakery window was stacked with long loaves and fruit tarts. The smell of baking bread is one we all quickly come to associate with France. Through the window, its scratched gold paint reading *Boulangerie, Patisserie*, I could see a big bowl of eggs on the counter. Inside there were two women serving and four others buying and talking. This was a problem. I was on an illegal mission, to buy black-market eggs. I was much too sharp simply to stand in line and ask for my eggs *sans tickets* with others in the shop. I wasn't going to compromise the baker's wife and her assistant or risk arrest for myself by the gendarme who could only have been a few yards further down the street.

I hung about inspecting the dozens of posters on every ancient wall surface stencilled '*Défense d'Afficher, Loi du 17 Septembre 1898*'. Most of these appeared to be for de Gaulle. There was a butcher a little further on and, suppressing memories of Jinny Carey's cupboardful of dead rabbits at Windsor, I gave it a quick once over. Meat on hooks. Sausages. Meat pies. Plus sinister bits of animal I wasn't at all sure about. One dish was marked '*Museau*' which I hoped I was wrong in translating as 'muzzle'.

I turned back to the bakery. Empty of customers. I crossed and, with a last look each way down the road, entered. To my horror there was another woman in the shop, feeding a long loaf into her string bag. I loitered.

Bending to examine the cakes, I ignored an attempt by the assistant to ask me if she could help. I shook my head and tried to flick my eyes significantly towards the eggs. Too significantly. The assistant said: 'Ah, *des oeufs?*' The bowl, I saw, carried a hand-written sign reading: *Tickets.*

The woman with the string bag was still there. Worse, the gendarme was mooching past, looking in the window. '*Avec tickets ou sans tickets?*' the assistant said in a voice I was sure could have been heard down the river (and the centuries) to Argenteuil. Couldn't she see the gendarme standing behind me in the doorway? Now, even worse, she was pushing a second bowl of eggs towards me. It had a clip on the edge of the bowl and a prominent hand-written card saying: *Sans tickets.*

In a fluster of confusion over numbers of eggs in a dozen and the additional price *sans tickets* which the woman kept explaining, I bought my eggs and pocketed the change. The gendarme no longer filled the doorway. I peered outside, left and then right, hiding the string bag of eggs behind me. He had disappeared. Weak at the knees, I passed on down to the café to buy my black-market cigarettes.

At the bar, kepi on the back of his head, the gendarme was enjoying a mid-morning brandy with the *patron*.

The *patron* saw me as I tried to shuffle past. '*Ah, Monsieur L'Anglais. Tu viens acheter des cigarettes pour Julien?*'

'*Oui,*' I croaked.

'*Pour des cigarettes sans tickets il faut un supplement, tu comprends?*'

A supplement. Of course. Anything you ask.

We exchanged cigarettes and money.

The gendarme yawned, reminded that he'd run out himself. He counted off the black-market sum on the counter. 'I smock too many,' he said to me in explanation. 'I 'ave no longer *tickets*.' He raised his glass. '*Vive le marché noir.*'

FOURTEEN

A Shot in the Woods

I was too young to understand much of the turbulence swirling around me in France. Mid-August 1945 was still a few days short of the first anniversary of the liberation of Paris; a few months only since the last Germans had been driven from eastern France. People were still being murdered in the savage purges which Communist and Gaullist *Résistants* were carrying out that summer. Everybody had a story of courage or treachery. From the highest to the lowest, men claimed they had been secret *Résistants* when, in fact, they had worked for Marshal Pétain's Vichy government. During the war so many people were involved in denunciations of Jews or of members of the Resistance that it was necessary for the Préfecture in each *département* to lock away parts of its archives after the war to prevent the widespread revenge-taking of 1945 from becoming a national blood-letting. Many of these denunciations had been motivated by simple commercial greed, to put the garage, business or shop of a competitor out of business. Many were politically or racially motivated. There were, of course, very many examples of French courage in concealing Jewish families, but sadly many more examples of denunciation. In Marshal Pétain's France 75,000 Jews were transported via Paris by cattle-train for Auschwitz with the consent or connivance of the Vichy government.

For many months after the war ended scores were still being settled by any means from petty village feuding to murder. A shot in the woods at night announced the disappearance for ever of many a collaborator. For some Pétainists survival meant going into hiding, sometimes for years. For others it meant buying documents to disguise their activities during the war. Classically it meant acquiring one of the crudely made little red booklets, internal passports of the time, signed preferably by a well-known local Communist leader. Of course some red books were perfectly genuine and the holder *was* indeed a former Resistance member. Inside, the red book said simply: '*The under-mentioned is a man of honour*'. It would be stamped by the local Communist Party headquarters. It was a crudely produced booklet but in the terrible days of the Purges immediately after the war, it was a passport to survival.

Later in life I married a Frenchwoman. Sometime in the 1980s, dealing with her recently deceased father's papers, as the family had asked me to, I came across one of these little red books in his name. He had been decorated with the Croix de Guerre and the Légion d'Honneur for his courage when the Germans invaded in 1940 and he was taken prisoner. He never talked about the war after his return from Germany in 1941 beyond shrugging and saying that he had been in the Resistance.

Today I have inherited part of his library. Taking down a book on old Paris recently, a photograph fell out. It showed the glossy interior of an opulent office. Marshal Pétain's. Two men, at ease with one another, are casually discussing some issue. The white-haired marshal makes a point. My father-in-law smiles in agreement.

The period immediately after the war revealed the deep divisions within French society. Both Gaullists and Communists struggled to convince the people of France that they, virtually alone, had defeated the Germans. Both sides tried to ignore the Anglo-American contribution, although the Communists were prepared to give full credit to the Soviet Army's victory in the East. The enmity between the two sides was held just short of armed conflict by de Gaulle in the months after the liberation of Paris, but by the war's end both sides were convinced Civil War was just around the corner. Julien Lelong, a passionate Gaullist, certainly thought so. One night he gave me good reason to believe him.

He had been trying to tell me something about the crisis boiling up in France and was astounded when I said that I didn't think people in England thought there was going to be a Civil War.

'That's because England is not really interested in France.'

'We fought on when everybody else was occupied,' I retorted. 'You were there, too.'

'You think England fought for France?'

'Among other things, yes.'

'England fought for England. As she always has.'

I was embarrassed. 'You were telling me about Civil War?'

'Come with me.'

We went up on to the sleeping gallery of the house where he kept a steel cupboard about six foot high. Taking keys from his pocket, he unlocked it and threw open the double doors. Inside, it was racked with rifles. In separate pockets to the side were a whole series of German Mauser pistols. Two boxes of grenades sat on the cupboard floor.

He pulled out one of the rifles, worked the bolt and clicked the trigger. 'Know how to clean a rifle?' he said.

I shook my head.

'I'll teach you. Rifle rods in the corner there . . .' He pointed. I handed them to him.

'Are these all yours?' I asked him.

He laughed. 'I'm the quartermaster of my cell.'

I didn't understand.

'I look after the weapons for the Gaullist group in this village. The village up the road, La Frette Montigny, is eighty per cent Communist. They're well armed, ready for the coup against de Gaulle the moment Stalin gives the word. In villages all over France it's the same. Weapons buried in barns, hidden in lofts. Communists hating Gaullists and vice versa.' He handed me a rifle to clean. 'Do you still believe we're not headed for a Civil War in France?'

Many years later when I was restoring a house I had bought in the Department of the Lot, I employed a none-too-competent electrician named Jean Paysin. His passion was the history of the Lot during the German occupation. The British and Americans, he conceded, had helped keep the Resistance in the area alive by arms drops. But in that area, he claimed, practically everyone was Communist (not by any means true) and when the war was over his father, as a senior Communist *Franc Tireur et Partisan* fighter, had ordered all Sten and machine guns to be wrapped in cloth soaked in walnut oil (olives don't grow in the Lot) and buried under barn floors.

'What for?' I asked him, *faux-naïf*.

'For the revolution,' he answered. 'We dig them up every year and clean and re-oil them. In France, you have to be ready for events.'

And this half of the Civil War conversation took place in 1989!

The savagery of the *épuration* in 1945 and the torrent of abuse against Vichy in the press, some of it purely vengeful, some self-serving, rose to flood level as the *déportés* and *transportés*, the men, women and sometimes children who had somehow survived the death camps or the murderous working conditions in Germany and Poland, began to arrive in trainloads at the main Paris stations. Parisians were deeply shocked by their physical condition, so emaciated and weak that it was not unusual for very old ladies to surrender their seat to them on the Métro. I was never present at the Gare de l'Est when one of these reverse transports arrived from Germany, but I have since heard from my French brother-in-law how shocked he was when a mass of people who might have been from another century arrived as he was buying a ticket there. A sort of babushka wrapped round shaven heads, faces covered with sores, teeth blackened with rot, they were often too weak to lift their bundles, too confused to scan the faces of the waiting crowd for family members. Too cowed to do more than to drop their heads when their name was called.

I never witnessed the return of the *déportés*, but I was present at an equally poignant event of these times. In 1940 the winds of war had carried Julien Lelong, the man I was staying with, to continue the struggle from across the Channel. I was about to discover that behind him, in La Frette sur Seine, he had left, with his former wife Olivia, two very young children, Yves and Pierre, known as Pierrot. I would think his wife, in 1940, was in her late twenties, Yves was probably four, Pierrot two or three years old.

I knew nothing of this until Julien came home from his job at the Ministry of the Marine one day and invited me down to the café for a glass of *jus de fruit* before dinner. He had things to do in the village. He would meet me down there, he said.

Before I left, Jane called me into the kitchen. She continued preparing dinner as she talked so that most of the time she had her back towards me. Did I know that, before the war, Julien had had another wife?

I said no, I didn't. I must have sounded slightly wary, embarrassed perhaps. Jane glanced over her shoulder. 'It's necessary you know. Julien has something to ask you, but first he wants me to tell you about what happened. Julien and Olivia were divorced just as the war began. They had two children . . . boys.'

She turned back to chopping carrots. As soon as Paris was liberated, she said, Julien got leave to come to La Frette to see what had happened to his children. He'd imagined his ex-wife and the boys had all stayed with his parents who lived nearby. He had had, of course, no contact with his parents or anybody else in La Frette since he had left for England four years earlier. But when he returned to the village there was no sign of his ex-wife or his sons. His parents had seen none of them since Olivia had left the village with the children some time in 1941.

'There were of course stories, you know what I mean?'

'I think so.' I was fearing this.

'The local gossips talked, but they would. The usual stories were spread about.' She leaned against the kitchen table. 'She had taken the children with her. But then there was the inevitable someone who had heard of her in Paris a year or so later. This someone reported that the two boys had been placed in an orphanage for children whose parents had died or disappeared during the war.'

'Did she do it?'

'Perhaps. Perhaps not. Nobody knows.'

She finished preparing the vegetables and turned round, hands braced on the kitchen table behind her. 'Go down and have a *jus de fruit* with Julien. The rest of it is his to tell.'

Mystified most of all by the way I, a teenage English boy, was being drawn into this, I walked down to the café. I think I was quite shaken by the idea of any mother putting her children in an orphanage, if that's what Olivia had done. I'd heard of it in England in Victorian times when a woman could no longer support them. Perhaps it had been the same in Paris during the Occupation.

I got to the café and the *patron* waved to me. Julien immediately left the bar and came to sit at one of the tables beside the double doorway. He smiled at me, not the slightly twisted sardonic smile I was by now accustomed to but a quieter smile, more friendly. '*Un jus de fruit? Ou un petit vin blanc?*'

'Wine?'

'Why not? In France girls of your age have been drinking wine since they were seven or eight.' That put-down he always seemed to find necessary. 'Go on, have a glass of wine. Buy you a *jus de fruit* afterwards if you don't like it.'

He ordered and the *patron* brought two wine glasses and left us the bottle.

'Jane told you about my children?'

'She said you'd finish off telling me.' I sipped the wine. It was bitter, not at all like *jus de fruit*.

'I remember Yves well. Pierrot was just a baby. Today I wouldn't be able to pick either of them out of a crowd.'

'Why did your wife put them in an orphanage?' The question that had really been on my mind.

'I suppose she found they were getting in the way. She was looking for a good time, perhaps. Easier without kids. Who knows what happened to people here during the war? Maybe she felt it was better for them.'

I could see he didn't believe that. I drank again, a big gulp this time. I wasn't enjoying any of this, the wine, the way Julien's eyes were glistening.

'Do you know where they are now, your boys?'

'My boys?' He paused over words that seemed so natural to me. My father always referred to Kit and me as 'my boys'. 'I came back to France to look for them as soon as I could. But they were in a *département* still in German hands. Even after the Germans surrendered it took me nearly three months to get the paperwork sorted out.' He poured us both more wine. This glass tasted better. Not so acid. He drank. 'Yes, I found out where they were.'

He lit a Gauloise and blew smoke in a feathery plume across the table top. 'Help yourself to another glass. Don't get drunk or I'll never hear the end of it from Jane. Then we'd better go back.'

I wondered why he'd told me all this. 'When will the boys be coming back?' I asked him.

'Saturday,' he said in a rush of words. 'Gare de l'Est in the afternoon. A special children's train.' He paused, twisting his head to look down the street. 'I want you to come with me to meet them.'

The *patron* passed on his way to serve another customer. '*Il aime bien le vin, ce jeune anglais.*'

Julien twisted his mouth in acknowledgement. I pushed my wine glass away. I was feeling slightly sick. I no longer wondered why he had told me all this.

'They won't remember me,' he said. 'I'm a stranger. Just an old stranger to them. It'll help to have someone young there. You're just a few years older than Yves . . .'

He moved to pour me another glass. I shook my head.

'What?' He looked anxious. 'You'll come with me, won't you?'

'If it'll help,' I said. 'I'm just feeling a bit sick.'

Even, or perhaps especially, in wartime England the myths of Gay Paree, of beautiful, chic and available Frenchwomen, were constantly repeated in the press, magazines and films. Among the boys of the newly constituted Sloane School there was also a good deal of talk about the prevalence of high-class courtesans who, it was imagined, crowded the boulevards in the evening, distinguishable from their more respectable sisters by the poodle dog that accompanied them and the thin gold chain round their left ankle. As the school's first visitor to the capital of vice (I left a week or two before Harry Little's Commando set sail) I was expected to bring back all the details.

In fact it was proving difficult to find an opportunity to get to the home of vice on my own. Julien's father, a First War veteran, had volunteered to show me the city. A few minutes with him were enough to show me this was not entirely the Paris I wanted to see.

Our first visit together confirmed my worst fears. Monsieur Lelong had planned for us less a tour of Paris itself than a pilgrimage to every known Parisian statue of Joan of Arc. We would trudge up to each statue and stand reverently before it. '*Brûlée par les anglais.* Burnt by the Englishmen,' he would say with morose satisfaction. I would nod sadly and he would purse his heavy lips at my acknowledgement of guilt before we moved on to the next monument.

When we returned Julien laughed at my ordeal. 'Serves you right,' he said. 'The English have never suffered enough for their history.'

I let that pass. 'Why does she have so many statues?' I asked him.

He was in a jocular mood. 'You burnt her . . . doesn't she deserve her statues? Anyway my father is a Monarchist,' he said. 'Joan of Arc's famous for crowning Charles V at Rheims and upsetting the English.'

'So it was a sort of anti-English tour?' I said boldly.

'Perhaps,' he said. 'Perhaps it was more a tour to remind you that we are, despite present circumstances, a great nation. As great as the English. You agree?'

I puffed out my cheeks, hesitating. I didn't want to say yes. I didn't believe a word of that.

'There.' He nodded in confirmation. 'As I said, the English have never suffered enough for their history.' Suddenly he was bitter again. 'It takes us French to do that.'

The following day I escaped to Paris alone. I took the train from La Frette as excited as I could ever remember being. At mid-morning it was almost empty. Nobody blocking the sliding doors with a foot jammed against them. No young men swinging out crazily from the central bar over the rails, one hand stretched out to touch (almost) the train passing in the other direction. In my fractured French I talked to two old women who were going to a market in Paris. Or perhaps they said they were going to a black market in Paris. By now I was as morally easy about such activities as Julien. After all I had smuggled money, I had bought black-market eggs and cigarettes several times, as often as not with the gendarme in the café looking on.

But I could not go back to school without an adventure to recount or some shocking piece of knowledge to reveal. Black-market stories would not have cut much ice with most of my third-form friends. The money smuggling was quite good but I had promised my father not to talk about that. Instead I'd set myself a task which would certainly appeal to the other boys. I planned to track down a real, functioning brothel of the sort we thought we knew existed. The sort Harry Little had *told* us existed.

At St Lazare I left the train and headed for Notre Dame. I walked miles. I got hopelessly lost searching backstreets and alleys that seemed to me suitable locations for a brothel. But nowhere did I find anything suggestive. I realised that my deep ignorance of the city meant I might have been searching in the Paris equivalent of Cricklewood, not the accepted red-light centre of London. But I could not give up. After buying a vastly overpriced split baguette with a slice or two of fatty ham inside, I continued my sleazy researches into the afternoon.

As the travelling world now knows, the sign for a tobacconist in France is two red cones joined at the base and, by law, suspended over the entrance to any café or bar licensed to sell cigarettes. Among the advertisements, the flyposting, the street furniture of Paris, I had not noticed them until I found myself walking down the Boulevard St Michel towards the Seine, by this time dragging my feet, almost prepared to give up my search. The Boulevard St Michel struck some sort of bell. Perhaps Harry Little had mentioned it as one of his stamping grounds? Promising.

I looked up, over the heads bobbing along the busy sidewalk. And with a jolt in my stomach I saw it. Over the Café de la Paix, corner of the Rue St Sévérin, what was obviously a *red light*. I stared at the *tabac* cone. At night that would no doubt be lit up to lure clients in. Yes!

But there was more to come. The hanging fringe of the blind was inscribed with the café's name, of course, but it was flanked on either side by the words *Blondes* and *Brunes*. A choice of blondes or brunettes on offer! I was transfixed. Stunned. These Parisians were obviously totally unabashed. Of course, this was what Gay Paree was all about, a totally uninhibited attitude to these matters. I looked down the boulevard. There were red-light signs over almost every café bar. Hotels too. I looked across the street. Yes, more advertisements for blondes and brunettes. Unbelievable, these French! I must be bang in the centre of the red-light district. There was hardly a building the length of the street that wasn't blatantly advertising!

I had one more thing to do. I sat down boldly under the canopy of the Café de la Paix, directly under the word *Blondes*, and ordered a *vin blanc*. If only someone had been there with a camera. I sipped my white wine nonchalantly, while craning my neck to see if I could see any sign of the blondes and brunettes inside. It must have been a quiet afternoon. No matter. Would I have something to tell the boys about when school started next month!

Unfortunately I took another step forward in my understanding of France and the French before I had time to recount my story. At the local café in La Frette next day where, mystifyingly, I'd noticed for the first time a red cone hanging over the door, Julien ordered a beer, a *demi*. '*Blonde*,' he had added. A half-blonde? Couldn't be.

My confidence in my own translation oozing away, I asked him. A *demi* was a half-litre, he explained.

And why blonde?

'Bad luck, Dee,' he said as if he knew. 'Nothing to do with blondes. It's the beer, *blonde* for light beer, *brune* for dark.'

'I see,' I said, totally deflated. 'Yes, I see.' There went my status as a devilishly knowledgeable traveller in Paris.

Saturday came. I was not looking forward to this at all. I had taken the train from La Frette by myself. I didn't feel I could ask why Jane was not coming with me. Going into Paris, the train was more or less empty during the day. I stared at the new-looking football stadium at Colombes, bright in the August sunshine, thinking with more than a touch of homesickness how much Kit would like to play there. We passed through Argenteuil and I tried to pick out the spots where the Impressionists had painted the pictures Jane had shown me in a book the night before. But mostly I thought of those two small boys coming all the way from Eastern France to live with a man they didn't know. Had they been well treated in the orphanage? Of course in those days, even had I been an adult, I would never have thought of sexual abuse. But had they been bullied, shouted at, made miserable?

Julien met me at St Lazare and hardly said a word. Now that I was not engaged in a brothel hunt, there was plenty for me to look at as we travelled by bus across Paris, plenty of questions I wanted to put to him, but a glance at Julien's face told me this was no time to ask. I could feel his tension in the clenching of his hands, the number of cigarettes he smoked, in the way he kept jerking and stretching his neck as if his loosened tie was still too tight for him.

I wanted to ask how would we know them, did he have photographs? But his anxiety was just too intimidating.

It was the usual shabby scene common to any Paris railway station in those days, a sense of stress and bad temper in every encounter. Hissing steam, people lugging roughly tied parcels of food back from the country, irritable nuns shepherding groups of girls across to trains as if expecting their charges to be pounced on at any moment by white slavers. Gendarmes leant against the wall of the ticket office, one gaitered leg crossed at the ankle, a cigarette pinched between thumb and finger in the hand below the cape, their whole manner proclaiming that anything that happened on the station forecourt was nothing to do with them, certainly not requiring their inter-vention. Soldiers were everywhere. American and French were difficult to distinguish when America had supplied the French Army's uniforms. A few French sailors with red pom-poms on their hats did something to brighten the atmosphere.

We were early and went to a café inside the station. Julien drank coffee, a small black, and a cognac. I stuck firmly to *jus de fruit*, pineapple juice. After a few moments it seemed to me the forecourt was getting more crowded, at least on one side. People were coming in by the various entrances but all drifting towards this side of the station. Many of them were quite old; some of them young couples clutching each other . . . or quite often a man alone, standing apparently unmoved except that he kept glancing at the big chalked blackboard declaring: '*Train des enfants, 16.40 heures.*' Julien would have been one of them if he had not asked me to come with him.

The train was near enough on time. By now a number of railway officials had appeared and were corralling the waiting adults into one corner of the concourse. I noticed one or two of the single men drifted off during this process and sat at a café table. Like Julien, I suppose, they were too proud to be controlled, directed, ashamed to be thought somehow responsible for the abandonment of their children.

At just a few minutes after 4.40 as the train pulled slowly into the station Julien got to his feet and dropped some money for the waiter. The officials had linked arms by now and were trying to contain the waiting crowd in the corner assigned to them. Julien lit a cigarette, cool as a cowboy.

Who knew what to expect? Some people among the waiting crowd perhaps. Not me. And, I think, not Julien. The train came into the station and stopped. No doors opened. For several minutes the people behind the barrier of officials, the parents, grandparents, uncles, aunts, stood staring, lips pursed, at the silent train. Then the doors of the front carriage opened and officials stepped down on to the pavement. I think the wheelchairs came from the cattle-trucks hooked on to the rear compartments. I won't forget that fearful gasp from the waiting crowd as the chairs were wheeled up to the front carriage. Children were lifted or helped from the train into them. Parents or grandparents who still knew no more than Julien about the condition of the children they hoped to meet craned their necks to see if any of the wheelchair children were their own. By now the whole station seemed to have stopped to watch. In the silence I could hear the sobbing all around me.

Officials with armbands ordered the other children down from the train. Struggling lopsidedly with heavy suitcases and French school-bags, they marched in pairs down the platform. They were most of them very young, some could have been no more than babies at the beginning of the occupation. I couldn't help being reminded of our evacuation from London's Clapham Junction two days before war began on 1 September 1939. But it was just about to become very different.

Suddenly the whole forecourt dissolved into chaos. The orderly line of children scattered under the adults' charge. Women were running forward and throwing their arms round children; others, unable to recognise a child, were pushing them forward, snatching at the card pinned to their jacket, bending to read then pushing them on again. Names were screeched or shouted. In total confusion children looked over their shoulders towards the familiar officials as strange adults hugged them and sobbed over them. The two gendarmes leaned against the wall of the ticket office in the same attitude as when we had arrived, one leg bent across the other, cigarette held between thumb and index finger, and watched.

I stayed close to Julien who had climbed on to a luggage cart and was glaring down on the swirling crowd, glancing every few seconds at the two photographs he held in his hand like playing cards. I could see very little from where I was. Sometimes the crowd parted and I saw officials had imposed some local order, gathering children in a half-circle to be examined. Men and women circled around them, staring at a child's face, twisting the card pinned to them to read more easily, suspicious it seemed that they might be palmed off with some other child, stopping just short of pinching them for quality. Like a slave market almost.

Suddenly Julien jumped down beside me. He grasped my arm

hard. 'Stay put,' he said. 'Don't move from here.' And he was gone, angrily barging his way through the crowd.

Two boys stood before me, Julien between them. The elder, Yves, was dark-skinned, very small for his age, thin, with darting eyes and uneven teeth, already smiling ingratiatingly. Pierrot was snuffling after tears, his round face streaked with dirt. Beside Yves he looked well enough fed, shy, blue-eyed, a charmer in his over-long shorts and name placard that was too wide for him to get his arms around.

'*Eh bien, mes enfants*,' Julien began but couldn't continue. He pulled a packet of cigarettes from his pocket and fumbled with them.

'I'm English,' I volunteered to the boys to fill the gap. '*Je suis anglais.*'

'Like the bombers?' Yves said with a smirk and an upward glance to what might have been the sky.

FIFTEEN
Stamford Bridge

I returned to London just after my fourteenth birthday. The last few days in France had not been good. The boys were clearly not accustomed to family life. Both were, not unnaturally, disturbed by their experiences, Yves more so than his brother. I never learnt much about these experiences, probably because a degree of family and even national shame attached to the history of so many children caught up in the tragedy of the last six years. I believe Julien's English wife found the boys, Yves particularly, surly and rowdy by turns, difficult to deal with. The house was not big enough for us all and I think everybody was now looking forward to my return to England in a few days which would obviously ease the shortage of bedspace.

La Frette was a small enough place for most people to have known me by sight, and indeed as an English boy I was something of a curiosity, my school blazer coming in for frequent inspections. It was therefore no great surprise, shortly before I was due to return to England, to be told that a family living on the other side of the village, the Linquiers, wanted to meet me. Monsieur Linquier was a water standards inspector, short, lively, gesticulating. Madame Linquier, originally from the Italian–French border, was dark-eyed and laughing. They had a small daughter born in the first year of the war and given the popular patriotic name, Marie-France – and, the reason for wanting to meet me, a boy of almost exactly the same age as myself, Daniel, a tall, good-looking boy who looked on me with that very French combination of wariness and disdain.

The Linquiers knew Julien and his wife's house and knew that there was no longer room for me to go back there. Perhaps they had already discussed the matter with the Lelongs. As far as I could understand, Monsieur Linquier and his wife, both of whom I immediately liked, were proposing I should come back next Easter to stay with them. Daniel and I were the same age, we could make an exchange. Be friends.

Friends? I wasn't too sure about that. And nor, I think, was Daniel. Parentally encouraged friendships are not always notable successes. I said I would have to speak to my parents first. '*Bien sûr*,' said the amiable Monsieur Linquier. '*Bien sûr*.'

Life back in Primula Street was comfortable even in those bleak post-war years, my father obtaining some of the good things of that life (PX rations, even a second hand refrigerator) from the American officers and diplomats who were still stationed in London. But most importantly we retained a strong link with our roots in the World's End, through school, through my father's work at Whitelands and his Saturday evening job at Stamford Bridge. From Shepherd's Bush my mother would take the 11 bus down to see my Aunt May and the rest of the Easts who were back, rehoused in the repaired block of Guinness Trust, and in the process would meet and report back on the fate of a dozen old neighbours. On my father's side we still had family living there, most closely his elder brother Fred, our favourite among his brothers and sisters. And Kit and I were getting off the bus at the World's End every day in term time, of course.

Why this connection was so important to us, and to many others who left the World's End after the bombing to live in places like upper Chelsea, Victoria or Battersea, is not easy to understand.

Chelsea Borough Council had an extensive requisition programme for the bombed out. Most people were now more sumptuously housed than they had been before. All requisitioned properties would have had a bathroom. There would have been less or none of the overcrowding that we had almost all grown up with. But there was no replacing that special warmth that comes from growing up with the same people, knowing so much about them. A life lived almost entirely without strangers.

White City may well have been dull in comparison but I think it no exaggeration to say that our home-life in Primula Street was different from almost any other in Britain. We had a telephone. That alone was rare among people like us, but what made life really different for us was the way it was used. My father's street bookmaking business had flourished since the wartime nights when Fatty the Yid and Darkie Evans collected for him in the streets of World's End. Fatty and Darkie no longer worked for him, presumably having only been on loan, but had rejoined their old boss Alf Gordon when he emerged from Wormwood Scrubs or wherever he'd done his time. That meant my father, though still working as a clerk for Alf, was now without a territory of his own. And even if he had found one it would have meant recruiting new runners.

His solution was not to have any set territory where he might clash with the established street bookmaker. Instead he abandoned the idea of having his own pitch altogether and took bets from anywhere in West London where he happened to have a friend or contact from his early life as a plumber, people he'd met during his wartime spell in the Home Guard, or even through the agency of the travelling Mayfair Laundry van driver who was already closely connected with a number of my father's 'arrangements'. There was a contact in the Fulham gas works; another at Lyons big packing plant at Olympia, others from Chiswick and the Acton Underground train repair works. All bets would be transmitted by phone. In this way he avoided any physical presence in any district that was already 'spoken for'.

It was a daring innovation. But it meant that the phone had to be manned day and evening (by my mother during the day, Kit and I several evenings a week) taking down careful details of a long list of shilling accumulators and sixpenny each-way cross doubles from hoarse-voiced and weirdly pseudonymous runners, Jack the Lad, Joe Lyons and Harry Gas Board, or individual punters like Bald Albert, Ethel Rose and Crown, Green for Danger, Desperate Dan and Fred Fireman.

This was all illegal, of course, and certainly enough to lose us the house if my father had been prosecuted. And the memory of Alf's difficulties with the law was still fresh. The result was that we lived, if not in terror, at least in fear of any passing policeman. It meant that our telephone shiftwork at home had to be concealed from friends at school and could never be given as an excuse for late delivery of homework. I think the need for secrecy, the sense of shared responsibility in a matter so important to the four of us, deeply influenced both Kit and myself. Some evenings the phone could ring ten or a dozen times; calls could be a brisk two or three minutes long or a mind-numbing half an hour. During the day, when my mother manned the phone, it was worse. It was not easy work.

The illegality of it didn't worry us because we believed the betting system to be unjust. But it was difficult work maintaining the secrecy when a friend or neighbour came to the house and you had to disappear for twenty minutes, taking and reading back whispered bets in the front bedroom.

I thought a lot about my future at this time, doctor, lawyer, pilot, millionaire businessman, and had been attracted to one or other of the professions in turn – but it was writing that attracted me most. I had after all been brought up on the tall stories of my grandmother, Eliza Toop, story-teller, fortune-teller, one time barmaid at Dirty Dick's during Jack the Ripper's day, who claimed to have driven him off by brandishing her stiletto-like hat pin. Many of her tales, some even true, have appeared in my earlier book, *World's End*. My grandmother telling stories, acting them or singing them out, formed the background to my life and Kit's as we grew up. I never acquired any of her terpsichorean skills but under her influence or less directly via her genes, I had begun writing my own stories just after the war ended.

Of course, my problem was that I had never read any books except *La Mission de Slim Kerrigan*, a tattered French-Canadian tale I had struggled through in France. The result was that my writings were heavily based on the comics *Wizard*, *Adventure*, *Champion*, or on the one Agatha Christie I'd started and maybe even finished. Titles were pretty derivative too: *Murder on the Amazon* or *The House on Chaos Street* . . .

My father had begun taking me with him to Stamford Bridge dog track on Saturday nights. I knew there was something going on, some plan in mind, but in answer to any question he'd say 'Nothing special. I'll tell you when it is.' He was still working as Alf Gordon's bookmaker's clerk as well as running his own phone business. My dog-track friends, Darkie Evans and Fatty the Yid, liked to keep up with what I was doing. When I told them I was writing a story they looked at each other, puzzled. 'Homework?' Darkie said. 'Is that what they give you? Stories to write? I thought they was teaching you Latin?' Darkie was very keen on the idea of me learning Latin.

'I'm learning Latin at school but I'm writing stories because that's what I like doing in my spare time,' I explained. 'I think maybe I want to be a writer.'

'A writer? That's weird, Dee, no two ways,' Fatty said.

'I thought you was genna be a doctor.' Darkie was clearly concerned. 'All that Latin gone to waste, then?'

Fatty laughed. 'He only wanted to be a doctor because he knows the gels go for doctors. That right, Dee?'

Do they? I thought. Interesting. Maybe I should give up writing and become a doctor after all.

'Yeah . . . *"All the nice girls love a . . . doctor"*,' Fatty half-sang, smiling broadly. 'The 'ealing 'ands,' he said, making a big show of dropping both aitches and holding his huge hands up before me.

Darkie nudged me. 'Stay with the Latin, Dee. That'll take you places. Doctor, that's something.' He shook his head. 'Wish I'd done a bit a' Latin. Yeah, doctor, that's quite something.'

My father bustled up. 'Stiffen the Prussian Guards!' he said. 'Haven't you got that stand up yet?'

Darkie feinted and whipped a quick hook to my ribs. It would have floored me if he hadn't held it back. 'Stay with the Latin,' he said. 'That way you can make something of yourself.'

SIXTEEN

The Red Light

Perhaps it happens to all young men and they never express it to each other but the discomfort of my burgeoning sexuality was now becoming intense. Furthermore, during my early teenage years, my sights were set hopelessly on young women of perhaps eighteen to twenty. I was neither inspired to love, nor excited to lust, by girls of my own age. Not that it would have been very easy to meet them. We had a girls' school, Carlyle, next to Sloane but the authorities had clearly plotted deep into the night to keep the two sexes apart. Times for morning arrival and afternoon departure were staggered. I can barely remember seeing a Carlyle girl out on Hortensia Road despite the fact that the main gates of both schools were no more than forty yards apart. In addition the two schools shared a playing field up at Roehampton but our apartheid was too well organised for any useful contact to be made. Would it have made any difference to me if we had been a mixed secondary school? Today I have no real idea, but I think it probably would. Several friends and indeed my brother Kit married girls from Carlyle but this was as a result of meeting them later. At the age of fifteen separate development was the order of the day.

The problem is that such separation does not march in step with the hormonal development of young boys. And these years before any sexual expression with the opposite sex was possible could be years of real isolation. You still have your family, your friends, but other things are preoccupying you. There's a sense of shame about the direction your instincts are taking you. There's also determination to gain some sexual experience, no matter what or how. There's fear, too, played on outrageously by well-meaning commentators like the reverend author of *The Red Light*, a tract we had all read by the age of fourteen, a tract that warned in the most sensational terms of the dangers of Venereal Disease if you should so much as kiss even a perfectly virginal Carlyle fourth-former. A kiss could lead anywhere – and usually did, warned the Reverend. Somehow he knew. Strangely, the other, and more acute, danger of unwanted pregnancy was not emphasised. Perhaps this was given full and lurid treatment in a similar booklet for girls.

I can see the cover of *The Red Light* to this day, an empty street scene late at night with foreground traffic lights stalled at red, and do I imagine the split skirt and fishnet-stockinged leg of the woman in the shadowed doorway?

Where did we get these cheap pamphlets? In my case it was a shady shop selling trusses, Durex condoms and second-hand paperbacks, just off Hammersmith Broadway. One or two thumbed copies of *The Red Light* were shelved under Medical along with books on anatomy and women's health. My initial reason for using the shop was an untutored interest in Shakespeare. For a few months I had become an ardent Baconian, a believer in the theory, first put forward a century after Shakespeare's death, that none but Francis Bacon could have written the 'Shakespeare' plays. The shop was the only place I knew selling the fiendishly clever, though slim and ill-printed, volumes of Bacon theory. The argument would frequently take the form of a covert message deciphered from a line of Shakespeare:

'*To be or not to be, that is the question . . .*'

Now simply take letters number 12, 16, 23, 29, 30. Don't ask why those numbers, all will become clear. Apply them to the text, extract the relevant letters and you have Baqon! Convinced? If not there are thousands of similar clues for those with sharp eyes and nimble brains scattered throughout the plays. In addition you'll note that whenever the name Will or William appears in the text of the plays, he is a rustic duffer incapable of writing the Queen's English. (Not in fact true but this never bothered Baconians.)

Fellow conspiracy theorists in old fawn raincoats were to be found in the shop on wet afternoons, rolled cigarettes in the mouth, hands free, as they studied various texts. I quite soon noticed that it wasn't just Bacon that attracted them there. The Medical shelf was well frequented. As was the History shelf. There, the searcher after historical enlightenment could find a whole range of paperback volumes on the Turkish 1917 atrocities in Armenia. Most of these discussed the rape of Armenian women in generous detail. There were other tomes of Hitler material. *The Diary of Hitler's Maid* and *Hitler's SS Procurer-General* were favourites, both probably illustrated by the same artist, I guessed, since both showed half-dressed young women being carried kicking helplessly into the Führer's opulent bedroom. Come to think of it, the Turkish Janissaries in Armenia were always carrying high-kicking Christian girls into opulent boudoirs on the front cover of the 1917 atrocity books. Ancient history was not ignored and the sufferings of the Sabine women figured on several covers (their shapely legs, too, were inclined to Betty Grable high-kicks as they were carried away). Certain Greek and Norse myths also excited interest. I don't know who published these pamphlets or whether there were a dozen different publishers, but they were clearly offering a very similar view of the world.

With the exception of the Bacon Society volumes most of these booklets were dog-eared and dusty. Some of them had probably been in the shop since before the war. As a recognised Bacon enthusiast I was allowed to browse through the upper shelves. It's not that I wouldn't have preferred my reading to have been more devoted to *consensual* sex but I think the shop owner knew that this would have less appeal to the scholars in fawn raincoats.

Among what would now be considered this low-grade but fairly harmless material there were some nastier pieces of anti-semitic porn from an earlier time. Those I looked at certainly antedated the Holocaust and the liberation of camps like Belsen. It was material that shocked me. When I showed the owner one of these pamphlets he glanced at it, grunted, and tossed it into the waste-bin without another word. I couldn't tell whether he had known it was there before – and would retrieve it the moment I'd gone.

I didn't realise at the time that this was the field of interest of a young man whom I met in the bookshop. In his mid-twenties, with dark hair brushed back and bright blue eyes which emphasised the intensity of his manner, he claimed he had seen me in the shop before but had felt shy of starting a conversation. I was too easily flattered. He was, he told me, a convinced Baconian and was at this time writing a treatise on the real events behind the theft of the Shakespeare titles from their obvious author. He seemed to me to have read a lot about the Bacon controversy and spoke fluently of its origins in the English eighteenth century before it was picked up and amplified in the next century by American writers. His name, he said, was Freddie.

Over a cup of coffee in the Black & White milk bar in Hammersmith Broadway we talked about Francis Bacon, the state of the world (of which of course I was profoundly ignorant) and discreetly of sex. Freddie asked if I'd ever been betrayed by a girl. I was fourteen. I told him chance would be a fine thing, but Freddie didn't see the joke. Later, I realised he didn't see the joke in anything. Passionately he began to outline the dangers of having anything to do with women. Disloyalty was only the most obvious threat although that could damage your manhood as much, at least as much, as the other ever-present menace in consorting with women: disease. He was beginning to sound like the reverend author of *The Red Light*.

'In my opinion, Dee,' he said, 'a woman does not have what we call a heart. Of course she has an organ which pumps blood round the system as Harvey discovered in 1610. But if you look at Francis Bacon's portrayal of women, you'll see time and time again the true depths of their cold-heartedness. Look at Regan and Goneril in *King Lear*. Look at the Queen in *Hamlet*. Look at Lady Macbeth. Bacon knew what he was talking about.'

'Mmm,' I said.

'And I don't have to tell you anything more about disease, do I?'

'No,' I said. Please.

'Women . . . girls . . .' He lifted his hands wide. 'Stay away, Dee. That's the advice of a friend.'

I pursed my lips and shrugged.

He looked at me grumpily over his raised coffee cup. 'But you probably like girls?' It was a question.

I tried another non-committal shrug.

'You had many girlfriends?'

'One or two,' I lied. I couldn't tell him twelve-year-old Kathy Davis was the last, and she probably didn't even realise she was my girlfriend.

'What do you do with them when you take them out?'

'How do you mean?'

'You know. You take them to the pictures. Take them to the back row. Then what?' His knee jerked up. He clasped it with locked fingers and lowered it to the ground. Giving me a nervous half-smile, he said: 'What d'you like doing to them?'

I think he saw his questions were making me very uneasy and quickly changed the subject back to Francis Bacon. The son of the Belgian Ambassador, he told me, was a very keen Baconian. Freddie was sure he would like to meet me. He thought all three of us should meet for tea at the embassy where the ambassador's son had a collection of books on the subject. He stopped for a moment, humming thoughtfully to himself. The ambassador's son, he said slowly, was very keen to improve his English. I could be just the one to help. Again I was flattered. My unease dissolved. I'd never been to an embassy. I agreed to meet Freddie in Trafalgar Square the following Saturday from where we'd go on to the embassy together.

The next Saturday was a damp, blustery day. In the early afternoon I caught the 11 bus down to World's End and along King's Road. At Sloane Square the conductor warned us all it could be slow going from the Houses of Parliament because there was some sort of demonstration being held in Trafalgar Square. I got off the bus at Westminster Abbey and began to walk up Whitehall towards Nelson's Column. I was never going to find Freddie if there were thousands of people milling about in the square as I'd seen plenty of times on newsreels. But as I got closer it occurred to me that if there were thousands there they weren't all approaching from this direction. There were a few dozen people on the pavements, some of them carrying rolled up Union Jacks, but probably no more than there might have been visitors come to see Downing Street and Horse Guards' Parade.

'If you want to know the time, ask a policeman,' Eliza used to say. So I asked a pair of uniformed officers standing opposite Horse Guards if there was a demonstration on this afternoon.

'Of some sort,' one of them said, nodding.

'The sort you want to stay away from,' the second one said.

'I'm meeting someone at Nelson's Column.'

'Just don't hang about for the speeches is my advice, lad.'

'Why not?'

''Cause we fought the war to get rid of these types.'

'Who are they?'

He shrugged.

'Fascists?'

'They don't call themselves that. League of Empire Loyalists most of 'em.' His colleague had started to walk away.

'You just meet your girlfriend and pop off to wherever you're going.' He bustled off to catch up with the other officer.

How was I going to find Freddie if the square was crowded with these people? I walked on. Past the Banqueting Hall on the balcony of which King Charles I had lost his head, past his equestrian statue which had been found dumped by Cromwell's militant wing in somebody's back garden, then into Trafalgar Square itself.

Opposite the National Gallery the base of the column which formed the speaking platform was decked with Union Jacks and placards for the League of Empire Loyalists. There weren't more than fifty or sixty people standing listlessly at the platform base listening to the speaker. But I was immediately riveted. The speaker was the man I was here to meet. The speaker was Freddie!

He wore a trenchcoat, a black beret and black leather gloves. The speech was horrible stuff. Ostensibly about immigration, it was in fact a plea to keep the Empire (India in particular) and pass new laws to keep the inhabitants of the imperial lands out of Britain. Even as a fourteen year old I could see that it was an outrageous demand to have your cake and eat it. But there was more. Somehow the Jews were brought into the act. On what grounds I can no longer say, so smoothly did Freddie slither from anti-immigration to anti-semitism.

There were at this time, of course, huge numbers of Jewish displaced persons in Europe. Their goal was America, Britain or Palestine. Britain and Palestine (a British mandated territory) must refuse them, Freddie told his audience. He was cautious in his choice of words but the thick, twisted vein of anti-semitism was unmistakably there. One of the legacies of war for all my schoolfriends was that we felt passionately about these things. It was not so long ago that we had all watched the film of Belsen. Since then we had heard other names that inspired even greater dread: Treblinka, Sobibor and Auschwitz. I couldn't believe someone I had talked to, had a coffee with in the Black & White milk bar, could harbour such ideas. He might have been reading direct from the Protocols of the Elders of Zion.

About then he saw me, paused in his speech, grinned and waved before continuing. I didn't care about the snob value of going to tea at an embassy any more. Indeed I very much doubted he knew the Belgian Ambassador or any other ambassador's son. I turned round and hurried back down Whitehall.

It was a time when I wandered about London a lot on Saturday afternoons. I enjoyed the seedier parts of the city, the backstreets of Victoria, Charing Cross Road, Hammersmith Broadway . . . I enjoyed watching the passers-by, listening to the arguments outside the pubs, taking in the life on the streets. Most of all I enjoyed being alone.

Because of our close family background, isolation never turned to alienation, I never became a surly teenager. At home, life for me continued as though the sex drive did not exist. I did my usual shifts at the telephone taking bets, Kit and I dug out the concrete shelter in the back garden and sledge-hammered it to pieces small enough to have the council carry it away. I went with my father to the dogs and joked with Fatty and Darkie. But I was always anxious to get away on my own.

Perhaps my grandmother, had she still been alive, might have helped. I might have been able to drop a few hints to her. She might have assured me that there was nothing freakish about what I was feeling and reassured me that there were hundreds of thousands of young people wandering around London in the same dazed, hypertensive state.

But she had died in the autumn of 1943, a few months before we were bombed in early 1944. Much as we missed her, I think we all felt her death had come at the right time. She had suffered acutely from angina when the earlier blitz was at its height. There were no palliative drugs available and her failing heart would certainly not have survived the bombing of the World's End.

I was finding that I needed to live some part of my life independent from my family. Independent not from prying eyes, because I never had a sense of being disapproved of, but quite simply to live some of the time free from the presence of anybody who might know me. I had felt this sense of personal liberation most strongly in France. Mildly homesick as I was, I'd relished being on my own. Relished perhaps being or trying to be an adult. I was happy with my schoolboy life, but it was a path already laid out for me, and it wasn't enough. I needed to move outside the circle. I needed a measure of anonymity.

It was the dog track that gave me the opportunity. Stamford Bridge Greyhound Racing was also to give me the chance to earn money. In the 1940s it was not easy for children to earn. Regular jobs were a paper or milk round, both of which Kit and I had done in our World's End days. We'd also earned money carting coke from the Gas Light & Coke Company across Chelsea Creek back to our neighbours at Guinness Trust during the war, but profits were measured in pennies. At the dogs, however, I had a skill to sell.

My father's plans had come to fruition. The new developments he had hinted at had come to pass. My mother, of course, had known all along, but he announced the news to Kit and me at dinner one Sunday. He had made a bid for a bookmaking stand at Stamford Bridge and had just heard that the bid had been accepted and the licence granted. He was now a fully fledged legal bookmaker working under the pseudonym 'Mick Burns'. At the same time he maintained his illicit phone bookmaking business. As always he involved Kit and myself immediately. He regarded all his extramural work as a family activity, carried out for the benefit of all four of us, and thus requiring the commitment of all four of us.

'Mick Burns' was an enterprise that had to be kept secret not only from Whitelands House but from our neighbours in White City too. If it had been known by the London Underground Housing Department that my father was a licensed bookmaker we would undoubtedly have lost the house. This meant the postman had to be given a story to cover some of the official-looking envelopes he had to deliver to Mick Burns. It meant keeping the bookmaking stand and money bag, with 'Mick Burns – Turf Accountant' painted in bold red and white on the side, at my uncle's house in the World's End. On Saturdays, while my mother and Kit manned the phone at home for street bets, my father and I would go to Stamford Bridge where I would earn ten shillings and sometimes a half-crown more as a white-gloved tick-tack man at our stand a few books along from Darkie Evans and Fatty the Yid.

By my fifteenth birthday, if the book had had a good day, I sometimes made as much as fifteen shillings in a week.

I spent most of this on Friday nights. My brush with the Bacon Society had led to a genuine interest in Shakespeare. Perhaps I had gone to one or two plays with the school as an introduction, but as my fifteenth year came round and we began to study *Macbeth* for Matriculation, perhaps once a month that autumn and winter I would go off by myself to the West End to see a Shakespeare or perhaps a Shaw play, or more boldly, and much more rarely, something by Christopher Fry or Sartre.

I soon discovered the West End was Soho. Off Piccadilly was Soho. Off Shaftesbury Avenue was Soho. Turn out of Oxford Circus or Leicester Square Station and it's Soho. Narrow gaslit streets and courtyards where the lights shone from foreign restaurants. Deep cream-painted doorways where a shaded red bulb lit a single bell inscribed 'Model' and an arrow pointing to a narrow carpetless stairway. Up and down the streets foreign languages were spoken: Italian, Arabic, lots of French. Painters carried their canvases wrapped in newspaper, shady figures tried to lure you down into basement clip-joints, and of course street walkers, seldom less than middle-aged, whispered invitations from cavernous doorways. Drunks who might have been Francis Bacon (the painter) and his friends came staggering out of one pub and headed for another. Heavily made-up 'girls' clicked busily along the street on their high heels. I loved the sheer raffishness of the place.

I timidly pushed open the door of a few pubs for a quick glimpse inside. The air was always thick with cigarette smoke; men in suits and ties leaned on the bars, deep in talk. There seemed to be no working men's pubs here. No Friday night fights. The women's voices carrying into the street as the doors swung open were all upper class, though more often than not slightly tipsy. Newspaper and magazine articles said writers gathered here, painters, crooks, black-marketeers, alcoholics . . . And every week the *News of the World* carried an exposé of some sex scandal involving the Square Mile.

After a few visits the excitement I felt wandering about Soho at night had far from worn off but it began to be tinged with a sense of exclusion. Everybody else seemed to know where they were going. There were membership-only clubs like the Gargoyle on St Anne's Passage, busy pubs like the French pub as I later learned to call it, restaurants like the Gay Hussar or Leoni's.

I had never been in a restaurant and was very curious to know what happened there but I guessed I didn't have the money just to walk into the Gay Hussar and sit down, especially when I saw Aneurin Bevan and another Labour Minister going in. A pub was more of a possibility. I was well below the legal limit but knew I was quite tall for my age and, desperate as I was to shoulder my way into this raffish Soho life, I thought it was worth the risk.

On my third or fourth visit, on a misty Friday night after a Donald Wolfit performance of *Julius Caesar* in Nazi uniform, I walked past several possible places, narrowly rejected the Fox and Grapes as not looking quite literary enough and finally plucked up courage to push open the door of The Wheatsheaf on Wardour Street. I had decided it was time to experience a post-theatre drink in a literary pub, possibly exchange opinions with a few *litterateurs* about the value of an SS setting for *Julius Caesar*.

There were about a dozen men at the bar and three or four women. Everybody there seemed a lot older than my parents (who were about thirty-five and thirty-six at the time) and there was a generally shabby or tattered air to the clientele. As I walked across to the bar I was terrified, certain that my own underage appearance would show up particularly strongly against this greasy bunch of old codgers. At the bar I stood as tall as I could, which, I was pleased to see, was taller than the man I was standing next to. He gave me a quick glance. 'Get you,' he said.

That didn't seem entirely friendly. The barman stood in front of me, raised an eyebrow as if he'd come to a decision and said, 'OK then, what's it to be?'

I had the answer already worked out. I'd drunk enough wine in France in my short stay. 'I'll have a *petit vin blanc*,' I said.

'A what!'

A moment's panic. 'Wine,' I said. 'A glass of white wine.'

He screwed up his face. 'White wine? The only wine we sell here is port wine,' he said. 'And that's red.'

'I'll have a glass then,' I said hurriedly.

'On me, Tyrone.' The man next to me pushed a half crown across the wet counter with his finger tip. I saw that he was wearing pale pink nail varnish.

'No,' I said. 'Thank you but no, I'll get it myself.'

'Independent,' he said.

I took the glass of port and paid for it. Moving away from the bar I lifted the glass to my mouth, intending to take a small sip. At that moment I caught the eye of a woman in her forties who was sketching rapidly on a pad propped on her arm. She wore a black roll-neck sweater and a man's jacket with coloured pencils sticking from the top pocket. She turned the pad so that I could see her sketch. It was of me. Or rather, a grotesque, distorted, lipsticked version of me.

She winked. I gulped. The strength of the port caught in the back of my throat, burning as it went down. I loosed a rasping cough, spluttering port wine. The man who had offered to buy my drink was at my elbow, grasping my arm.

'You all right, Tyrone?'

I nodded and pulled my arm away. 'I'm fine.' I put the glass down. 'My name's not Tyrone.' I turned for the door.

'Suits you,' he whispered as I pushed at the door and stepped hurriedly past him into the enveloping comfort of the mist.

SEVENTEEN

The Schoolboy Republic

Things were now dramatically different at Sloane. The masters who had returned from evacuation had begun to introduce us to the idea of work. Developing in us an interest in their subjects that, for the first time, went beyond acquiring enough termly marks to stay in the 'A' form with our friends, did not happen overnight. With some masters and some pupils it didn't happen at all. But I think that, before too much time had elapsed, something was stirring in our heads.

Young teachers were returning from the war, in one case from a German prison camp having spent four years reading German and French literature. And an Australian master brought his own refreshing attitudes to teaching, questioning our views on the shape of the post-war world. Our intellectual somnolence of the last six years came heavily under attack by teachers who now enthusiastically accepted the challenge that such woefully uneducated pupils presented them. Our ancient English master, possibly younger than he looked, rocked his slight body in his chair, passed a hand over his veined bald head and smiled spectrally round the class. 'What I enjoy about teaching you boys,' he said, 'is that wonderful sense of making the first faint scratches on a *tabula rasa*.' We didn't know what he meant. Somehow we didn't think it was entirely a compliment. But we began to enjoy *Macbeth*.

Our new History master, Leslie Berkeley, was to remain a friend of mine until the end of his life. His teaching was flawed only by an excessive modesty, a sense that some of his pupils deserved something better than a Third class degree from Oxford to instruct them. 'Mr Gorman,' he would say with something approaching reverence, 'has a double First from Cambridge.'

Latin, Darkie Evans' favourite subject, had once been a matter of learning a few meaningless declensions under threat of a flick under the nose from Mr Colon's fat finger. It now became a life or death struggle against the determination of Isaac Gorman to reveal to us its subtleties and pleasures.

We had a long way to go. The need to catch up the largely lost years of the war was rapidly sinking in. When every returned or newly arrived master in every subject told us that we lagged far behind the standards of 1939 we at first believed this was no more than an extended pep-talk. But when the standards we were going to have to reach for Matriculation, the O-level of its day, were laid out for us, we were convinced. In those days the core subjects, in my case English, English Literature, History, Geography, Maths and French, all had to be passed at one sitting. One failure meant total failure.

But other things were happening to us, too. You can't activate young people's thinking processes on one level only. As we came to appreciate a little Virgil, get a thrill from the poetry of *Macbeth* or find ourselves intrigued by the causes of the French Revolution, we also began to move towards breaking out of the mind-set of most of us which was still, a year after the German surrender, waiting for the war to end.

One or two of us, though not notably myself, had consciously begun to think about our post-war political direction. These were mostly Jewish boys or those whose parents were members of the Communist Party. My friend Ted Simon was very definitely ahead of the pack here, a signed up member (as we used to say) of the Young Communist League. When one of the masters, the one who had recently returned from a prison camp, set up a mock election, Ted put himself forward as the Communist candidate. There were Conservative and Labour candidates and each was allowed a week to canvass the fifth form (we didn't at this stage have a real sixth). I had a strong feeling that the headmaster, Guy Boas, disapproved.

I suppose the Conservative Party candidate never really had a chance although most of us continued to admire Winston Churchill. I no longer remember the name of the Labour candidate. He had the predictable uphill struggle of any champion of a party that had already spent two grey years in office. And they were grey, austere years. When people today think of rationing they tend to think only of food rationing. In fact post-war rationing entered every corner of the national life. It applied to clothes, shoes, coal, building materials like wood and glass . . . even, unknown during the war itself, to bread. To a large extent rationing set the scene in post-war Britain: shabby, ill-shod, poorly heated, no more than adequately fed. After six years of war the country lacked the sort of sparkle that was already apparent in Paris. And the National Health Service had yet to appear as the great justification of Labour's post-war period in office.

Later in life, in the late fifties, I myself taught for a short, disastrous spell at a prep school near Great Missenden. At a party given by one of our neighbours, I met Clement Attlee, Prime Minister of the first post-war Labour government. He was small, rather pleasantly cocky, a man with a no-nonsense attitude to politics and to his own place in history. Rather brashly I asked him if he had ever thought that his Labour government had imposed an unnecessary degree of austerity on the country. He thrust his thumbs deep into his waistcoat pocket. 'Hmm,' he said, and I thought he was going to rip into me as he was clearly quite capable of doing. Instead he nodded thoughtfully.

'Wondered about that myself, a dozen times,' he said. 'But I think when we saw the real state the country was in at the end of the war, the finances, the economy, the railways, the housing stock, we all went into a blue funk. Scared the pants of us, as the Americans would say. Austerity and more austerity seemed the only way out. You're asking were we too heavy on the brake? Yes, I think we got it wrong there.' It was a candour that would have been extremely rare among Western leaders at that time: today I can think of none who would risk such an admission to a young school teacher from down the road. But then today that school teacher would have been on the phone to the red-top press within minutes of the party ending.

Ted was much more politically aware than I and he had begun to urge me to join the Young Communist League. Not as a Communist, he cleverly argued, simply as a sympathetic searcher after truth. I hesitated.

We were still some days off the election when Ted asked me to go with him to a meeting of the Young Communist League. I think we went to King Street, Covent Garden, Communist Party head-quarters. We were wearing our school uniforms but I remember being impressed by the way adult members of the party treated Ted, calling him Comrade, looking out posters from the files for his election speech or explaining carefully the party line on Soviet policies or events in Germany and Eastern Europe. An admissions secretary asked me if I would like to join the Young Communist League. Again I hesitated.

On the day of the school election the three candidates delivered their speeches. The Conservative spoke fluently enough but had nothing to offer that might dent the Labour candidate's recitation of the step-by-step process by which the Welfare State was being created. My Stamford Bridge friends Darkie and Fatty the Yid would already have had their money on the Labour candidate. But there was one more speech to come.

Ted's speech was remarkable. It was by far the best prepared of the three. He stood at the lectern in the school hall, dark-eyed and intense, his great mop of black hair untamed. He was offering an entire world view: at its heart, revolutionary policies of immediate nationalisation at home, the abolition of the monarchy and the public schools, and abroad, realignment with the Soviet Union rather than the United States. I seem to remember that few of us had until then seen the necessity of a choice between America and Russia. 'Good old Joe' slogans still daubed the walls of most working-class districts of London. Stalin was avuncular and popular, Harry Truman unknown.

For Ted it was a landslide victory. He was duly elected Communist Member of Parliament for Sloane School, World's End, Chelsea.

Guy Boas was furious. His school had voted for a Communist candidate, one proposing, as a key element in his programme, the abolition of the monarchy and the formation of the People's Republic of Great Britain. What was he to tell Pussy and our august Chairman of School Governors, a member of the Bowes-Lyon family and uncle of the Queen!

On our way to the dogs that night I reported the result to my father with some glee. But I saw the look on his face when I told him I had voted for Ted. 'And were you just voting for a friend?'

'I don't know. I've been thinking about it. Ted wants me to join the Young Communist League.'

'Is that what you want to do?'

'I like a lot of the things they say they're going to do. And I think they mean what they say.'

'They probably do.' We turned into Stamford Bridge and headed for the turnstiles. 'But just watch your step, Dee. I'm not saying you're too young to make up your mind. I'm saying none of us knows enough yet about how it's all going to turn out. The world's splitting in two. Joining the Communists now could leave you stranded on the wrong side of the fence. You're certainly too young to let that happen.'

It was, of course, just what the Communist Party was saying, though from an entirely different set of motives – the world was dividing into two camps. One day I knew I was going to have to decide which camp I was in. Like the decision we all made as World's End kids about whether we were Oxford or Cambridge, it was an allegiance that would stay with most of us for the rest of our lives.

EIGHTEEN

On the road

We were not, for obvious financial reasons and the demands of life in wartime, in the habit of taking family holidays, although we had once had a long weekend at Margate. During our late-fourth and fifth-form year, however, a group of us, friends from the same form, began to spent part of our school holidays hitch-hiking around the country of which we had so far seen so little. Our Geography lessons spoke of steel-making in Wales, the Yorkshire coalfields, shipbuilding in Glasgow and on the Tyne, the splendours of Durham Cathedral or Georgian Edinburgh. It was time we took a look for ourselves.

I was unaware of it then but these journeys round the country, sometimes by Rolls Royce, sometimes on the back of a coal lorry, were another element in forming my view of the world, or at least of this country.

We soon found, after the first few times, that putting up tents, laying down groundsheets and the whole process of conventional camping, was not what we wanted. It was too comfortable; the only adventure you were likely to come across camped in a field would have involved an inquisitive cow. So we abandoned our tents and camp-fires made from a wigwam of damp twigs. We chose instead to rough it at night on the streets and in the doorways of Birmingham,

Salford, Newcastle and Glasgow. At the time this seemed to us just an opportunity to see how well we could fend for ourselves, an opportunity to talk to a whole new range of people, to seek new experiences, adventures. We mixed with miners coming off shift, we talked to a hundred lorry drivers from all over the country in their cabs or in all-night transport cafés up and down the A-roads. Some nights we froze; some nights we sat under the shelter of a covered market and drank tea with the local police; some nights we slept on the back of a lorry as the driver pushed on to Cornwall or Manchester or Dundee; one night we burnt paraffin rags in soup cans to keep ourselves warm by a monks' frozen fishpond in the grounds of the Abbey of St Albans.

In one Lancashire mill town on a freezing February night we were dropped off a lorry at about 4.30 in the morning. It had been a long lift but most of us had slept no more than a fitful hour or two through the night. As we waved goodbye to the driver I could barely speak for the chattering of my teeth. The main street was bleak, a few low-level gas lights were all the fuel crisis allowed, no illuminated shops, no cars or vans offering the hope of another lift, not a soul in sight. The wind cut down from the hills, its bitterness almost personal.

We huddled in a shop doorway but there was no sleep to be had and no escape from the Siberian wind. At that moment I had a serendipitous thought. I had recently read a Russian novel, *The Road to Calvary* by Alexei Tolstoy. In it freezing soldiers in the Russian Civil War had stripped off their clothes and rolled in the snow. When they put their clothes back on again they found the cold more tolerable. I suggested this procedure to my friends. Unsurprisingly (quite apart from the lack of snow to roll in along the cobbled main street), they thought I was mad.

'The wind's gone to his head,' one of them said through chattering teeth.

I was going to have to demonstrate.

I stepped out of the doorway and was nearly struck down by the lash of sleeting wind. I took a deep breath, peeled off my ex-Army jacket, dragged sweater and shirt over my head and took off my trousers. The cold nearly took my breath away.

I jumped up and down, ululating to an indifferent high street, rubbing my chest, running on the spot. I was blue with cold, wet with sleet – but suddenly it started coming right. I wasn't warm, but I certainly wasn't freezing.

One of my friends came to the edge of the doorway. 'It doesn't really work, does it?' he said doubtfully.

'Old Russian remedy,' I puffed out frozen breath. 'If we had some real snow and a few birch rods we could do the job properly.'

He unbuttoned his jacket. One of the others followed him out, crouching against the wind. Within minutes there were four naked youths doing callisthenics in the High Street at not long after 4.30 on a freezing February morning.

I had heard the distant sound a moment or so earlier, although I couldn't quite place it. It was familiar, even evocative. Something from when I was a boy, I was fairly sure. We were all on the *qui vive* for a truck which might have given us a lift, but this was definitely not a truck. I was not even sure whether the strange metallic susurration was moving towards us or away.

I stood apart from the gymnasts to listen. And remembered! The girls in the World's End Watney's Bottling Plant opposite Guinness Trust Buildings had worn clogs. Ten or twenty of them walking together could create this strange metallic shuffling sound. This empty Lancashire street was about to come alive.

Staring up the street, I yelled to the boys to get their clothes on. It didn't take a lot of imagination to guess how 'jokey' a couple of dozen mill girls could be with a lucky find of five naked seventeen-year-old boys. My eyes were fixed on the corner just fifty yards away. When a mass of young women appeared they seemed not to notice us at first and were about to move on up the hill when one of them turned and stared unbelievingly. 'Lads!' she screamed, and pointed.

'Bollock naked the lot of them,' another exulted at the top of her voice.

Twenty or thirty women, not all young, detached themselves from the group and began to run clacking down the cobbled street towards us. We snatched at abandoned clothes, grabbed up our rucksacks and stumbled downhill, but it was hopeless. What passed for obscenities in those innocent days filled the air. They were upon us, prodding us back against the wall, sizing us up, screaming with laughter.

We were saved by the bell. Or rather the hooter. From not far up the street a factory klaxon sounded twice, then twice again. The women went quiet, still staring but not laughing so much. As the klaxon sounded one long blast they all looked towards it.

'Lucky boogers,' one of the older women said, with a gap-toothed grin at me. 'Here tomorrow morning and it'll be a different story, lad.'

But what struck us most on our travels was the simple goodwill of so many people we met along the way – in Darlington a woman coming out of her house to invite us in for tea and jam butties when we sat disconsolately on the kerbside, having run out of food and money; two Glasgow police sergeants debating which doorway beside the Clyde would be likely to be more out of the way of driving snow and scuttling rats as we settled down for the night in the Gorbals; middle-class people driving miles out of their way simply to get us to the most favourable road for a lift; one of the Wingfield Digbys, who had been there since at least Charles I's time, spending a morning showing Ted and myself round the ruins of Sherborne Castle. Such a lack of friction, of suspicion in casual contact. Was this one of the things that had come out of the war? Certainly, I thought, this was not a country ripe for revolution.

And there were unforgettable sights. A lift on a January night north from Sunderland on the open back of a lorry carrying heated oil drums (heated to stop the oil congealing in the extreme cold). We lay wrapped in our sleeping bags, on the warm drums, as we drove through the freezing starlit night along the Northumberland coast road and watched the dawn break over the North Sea. Or a camp pitched high above a Welsh valley as a steelworks bellowed flame and sparks into the night air. I think I have never lost that sense I had then of a country of great variety of landscape, accent and class but a country united by the same essential values, the same essential myths to back them up.

Britain was struggling. But the countries of Western Europe were drowning. France and Italy were wracked with strikes. Germany was a land ravaged by warfare. Throughout Europe, East and West, there was a desperate need for American Aid. The year 1947 was the watershed. It was the year of Marshall Aid, the American offer of $17 billion to restore Europe, East and West. It seemed an act not only of unparalleled generosity but of world statesmanship.

But Russia refused the offer. Communist Parties in the West denounced it as American Imperialism. The near-left spoke knowledgeably: the United States was in crisis, desperately needing to give away seventeen billion dollars to keep its own economy afloat. The object of the whole exercise was to increase American markets in Europe. And when that happened the standard of living of European working men everywhere would be lowered.

I was baffled. If that were the case, why was the British Labour government in favour of Marshall Aid? Why were French Socialists equally enthusiastic?

Events in the wider world seemed to provide pointers. The actions of the Soviet Union itself were throwing into doubt the views of my friend Ted and the kindly men in King Street. Soviet Armies had occupied a huge area of Central Europe with as yet no sign that they were planning to pull back. Ted fought to put to his friends the party line on all this. At this time he was the only Communist in our group. But his certainties looked less certain now.

I went with a friend to a meeting called to discuss the Marshall Plan at Chelsea Town Hall. The big dance room had been booked by the Marshall Aid Group. I sat down with Tony Bracking, who had been the Conservative candidate in the Sloane 'election', and we looked around wondering where the audience had got to. There were ourselves, a middle-aged couple or two, and eight or nine men who obviously knew each other and were talking among themselves and casting concerned looks towards the door.

Twenty minutes late the meeting began. There was no discussion. The evening consisted of a straight diatribe against the Plan, against America, against capitalism. Tony Bracking felt he ought to speak up for the plan. His use of the word 'generosity' caused gales of unamused laughter. The group in front of us turned in their seats and openly sneered. This was another face of the men from King Street.

Everybody present knew the meeting had been a total failure. The speakers were preaching to the converted plus two unpromising prospects in Sloane blazers. Not a good showing to report in the *Daily Worker* next morning.

When the meeting was wound up we all left the hall and moved down the passage towards one of the wide main Town Hall doors. A small man carrying professional-looking camera equipment bundled past us. He was standing at the bottom of the steps as we reached the wide doorway.

'Allow me to stop you there,' he said in a Middle European accent. 'I am from the *Daily Worker*. Please all bunch together in the doorway to give the illusion of more people attending the meeting.'

'To give the illusion . . .' Tony and I looked at each other. I had not yet decided what I thought about the Marshall Plan but I wasn't ready to support an illusion. 'No, thanks,' we called down to the photographer, and to his evident surprise ran down the steps and out of shot. Everybody else who had been in the hall bunched together as asked. One or two raised a clenched fist in the Party salute.

We stood behind the photographer, watching them. It was one of those moments. I wasn't weighing the scales but I was feeling that the dour sincerity of the meeting clashed tellingly with the casual request to fake the number of enthusiasts present.

The faded *Good old Joe* and Hammer and Sickle slogans painted on brick walls began to disappear, sometimes weathered, often rubbed out. The struggle for the hearts and minds of Western Europe hung in the balance. Then the Victor Kravchenko book, *I Chose Freedom*, struck the Western world with cyclonic force.

Kravchenko was a Soviet defector. His book was a record of the murderous path of Stalin's collectivisation programme in the Ukraine. It was a total challenge to the soupy sentimentality in which Stalin was enveloped. It was the first book to bring the point home that the heroism of the Russian people was divisible from the leader and the Bolshevik system. That point was crucial. To read Kravchenko was a searing experience. Nobody could ignore the book. Years before Solzhenitsyn, it proclaimed the existence of a savage Gulag system, the last stop for millions of innocents. It denounced the racism of Stalin's deportations, his hypocritical anti-semitism, terror as an instrument of Soviet government.

I bought a copy.

I found myself struggling with astounding facts, or what were presented as facts. At least as many murders as Hitler, even more betrayal, mendacity and deceit! Could it possibly be true? The *Daily Worker* which I read regularly in the White City public library gave a compelling refutation on its inside pages. Millions murdered? Stalin's friends and colleagues silently imprisoned in the wastes of Siberia? Secret protocols in the Russo-German Pact to carve up Poland – and the murder in the Katyn Forest of 10,000 Polish officers? Pure Hollywood, the *Daily Worker* maintained. Concocted by American Intelligence, the Party alleged. Kravchenko's book deserved burning.

And on my own doorstep there was further condemnation. My uncle Bill was a Communist. Very tall, Scottish, the *owner* of a house in Streatham and thus convinced his view should command respect. 'Marshall Aid? It's for their good, not ours.'

'How do you know that, Uncle Bill?'

'Marx predicted it all, word for word. They don't teach you that at school, do they?'

And there were others, decent people like Ted. And at least two of the masters at school were Communists. They all knew a great deal more about Communism than I did (although privately I always doubted the depth of Uncle Bill's knowledge). He would insist that Russia was the only major combatant who had never bombed civilians, refusing to accept my argument that it was only because they'd had no four-engined heavy bomber – and that when close enough they'd had no qualms about *shelling* civilians.

Perhaps it's easy now to say that some were simply blind to the overwhelming truth about the Soviet Union. But we came from a world that at least *thought* the facts were accessible to us in peacetime. No nation at peace had hitherto misled the world on the scale Kravchenko was asking us to believe the Soviet Union had done, and was continuing to do. Easier to believe that the clearly sinister Senator McCarthy lay behind this somewhere. Easier to believe that rabid American anti-Communists had concocted *I Chose Freedom*.

I was fifteen years old, sixteen in two or three months' time. At home I carried *I Chose Freedom* around. I think my mother was concerned about how involved I was getting with it. My father thought it good that I was trying to decide whether or not it was true and would sometimes even play the devil's advocate. He would remind me of the social injustices in Britain, of class differences, inherited wealth, restricted opportunity. He would remind me that all these things were not abstract. For many people in Britain, and far more throughout the world, they meant living conditions like Joe and Jinny's, small children playing in sewage, the lack of proper health care that my own grandmother had suffered all her life. It was an effective counterweight to my adolescent black-and-white-ism.

About this time Ted asked me again to go with him to the Young Communist League. This time I didn't hesitate. I told him I wouldn't be going. I hadn't yet made my mind up about Victor Kravchenko but I had made up my mind not to commit myself to the Communist Party until I did. The truth was that I was beginning to be haunted by the idea of signing up to a system as foul as that depicted in *I Chose Freedom*. What if Kravchenko were telling the truth?

NINETEEN

A Dream of Fair Women

One Christmas in, I think, my fifteenth year we had a surprise visitor. She was a young airforcewoman, a WAAF, the daughter of the man who had secured the house for us in White City. Bunny, as she was known, was a tall, slim, fair-haired girl of perhaps twenty, notably attractive in her blue uniform. I can no longer clearly remember the circumstances of her coming to spend Christmas with us. I very vaguely recall hearing of a broken love affair with a young officer on the RAF base where she had been posted. Whether he or she broke it off, I can't remember.

For me these were the years of high adolescence, fourteen, fifteen, in all probability the most difficult years of my life so far. My problem centred on the gulf between my sensual needs and the possibility of fulfilling them when my interest remained stubbornly fixed on young women rather than teenage girls. The few girls of my own age I met seemed interested enough but, candidly, they did nothing for my fantasies. These all revolved impossibly around an older woman, by which I probably meant up to mid-twenties, and the imagery was certainly not limited to damp teenage cuddling on a park bench.

The arrival of a young WAAF to spend Christmas was therefore electrifying. Bunny was uninhibited in her talk, candid in her description of life as an attractive young woman on an airbase mostly staffed by men, and a totally exciting guest to have in the house. She seemed happily incapable of listening to any music on the wireless without swinging her hips, fingers clicking as she kicked out her unusually long legs. 'Jive,' she said. 'It's all the rage.' This, I thought, was going to be a Christmas to remember.

One afternoon when she and I were the only ones in the house, she began to tell me about her belief in Yoga. I would have been happy enough to have sat and listened to her expound on her recipe for mixing cement, so I nodded appreciatively and asked what I hoped were the right questions.

I suppose I had got to a broad understanding that the practice of Yoga involved invoking the power of mind over body when my fifteen-year-old scepticism prompted me to ask her what it was good for. I'd heard of the Indian Rope Trick as an illusion perpetrated on the unwary and didn't want Bunny to see me as just a gullible schoolboy.

'What's it good for?' she said. 'Well, pain control, for instance.' She jumped up. 'Just wait a minute and I'll show you.'

She left the room and a moment or two later came back with a pin at least an inch long and a box of matches.

'You're not going to burn yourself?'

'No.' She sat on an upright chair, crossed her legs and, to my gasping astonishment, pulled up her skirt. 'Watch this,' she said. I was. A white suspender held her WAAF pale blue stocking in place.

She lit a match. For a moment or two she held the pin carefully in the blue part of the flame before dropping the match into an ash tray. With a practised hand she undid the exposed suspender and pushed down the stocking.

'Put your finger on my leg,' she said.

'Where?' I said.

'Doesn't matter where.'

I extended my index finger and brought it to a point over her thigh. My hand was shaking slightly.

She looked up. 'You're not shy, are you?'

'No.' I really was shaking now.

'Well . . . press down.'

I did.

'Hard.'

I dropped my other fingers on to her thigh and pressed.

'That's enough.' With her free hand she took my wrist and removed my fingers from her leg. 'Now watch this.' In one of the pink, cupped indentations I had made on her thigh she brought the point of the pin down and broke the skin.

I stood back.

'No pain,' she said. She pressed harder on the pin-head, lips pursed, eyes closed. 'No pain.'

I leaned forward and stared.

With one hand she held the pin upright. With the other, fist clenched, she tapped the pin deep into her thigh. 'There,' she said with an exhalation of satisfaction. 'No pain. No blood.'

I was both inflamed by the sight of her long, stockinged leg and fiercely interested in her demonstration.

'You want to try?'

'In my arm?'

'In your leg.'

That meant taking off my trousers. 'No,' I said. 'I can see it works.'

She laughed, pulled out the pin, put it aside and, two-handed this time, did up her suspender. 'Believe me now, do you?' she said, flicking down her skirt.

'Of course,' I said. 'I always did.'

I had four more days of her presence. Had she fallen in love with me, despite the huge age gap? Had the Yoga trick been her way of saying the unsayable?

I behaved as though nothing had happened between us. As maybe it hadn't. But I didn't believe that. She left on Boxing Day for an unknown destination. I looked for some sign that parting from me was painful to her beyond the relief of Yoga. With the most urgent will in the world, I saw nothing to convince me.

'Wow!' Kit said as the door closed behind her. 'Did she show you that trick with the pin in her knee?'

In the next year I was not completely without 'conquests' of my own but they seemed always to be attended by very dubious circumstances. As part of my attempts to extend my knowledge of France and French life beyond Boileau and Baudelaire, I used to go every so often to the Classic Cinema on King's Road where foreign films, mostly French, were shown. Not furthest from my mind was the possibility of meeting a slightly older French girl, in London to study English.

The Classic was one of those small, extremely comfortable cinemas and, like many other small London cinemas at that time, ran an uncomplicated programme of just one film with a five-minute break before the lights darkened and it was re-run. There were no ice-creams, as I remember, certainly no popcorn, just raw art. I was seeing *Les Enfants du Paradis* for the third or fourth time and we had trundled almost to the end of the film when a movement to my left made me glance up. Coming towards me with that strange sideways movement we all employ in a reasonably full cinema was the shadowy figure of a girl in a pale trench-coat. I half-stood to let her pass, holding my own trench-coat (they were fashionable among the Paris young that year) into my lap. But to my delight she indicated that she was going to sit down next to me.

We settled down, my eyes fixed on the film, my mind fixed not on Arletty but on her fellow-countrywoman in the seat beside me. I was conscious of every movement. So was she. When we bumped elbows she murmured a quite unnecessary '*Pardon*' in her charming French accent. I responded: '*Pardon, Ma'moiselle.*'

We drew closer as the film came to an end. Nothing too obvious but it was nevertheless clear to both of us that we weren't just two strangers sitting next to each other in a cinema.

The end credits rolled and I felt a wave of alarm. I took a quick glance sideways as the lights came up and caught her in profile. Dark-haired, a rather sharp but definitely attractive nose, full lips touched with lipstick, a small chin – and an Hermès scarf casually knotted. Of course. So *chic*.

How to handle this? A few words about the film? Was this the first time she had seen it? For English students, I would tell her, *Les Enfants du Paradis* was compulsory viewing. Not that we were compelled in any way – or rather only by our admiration for the direction and Arletty. No, say nothing about Arletty. The girl might think I'm just here to gawp. Talk about the direction. The lighting cameraman's work. That's what I should be talking about. I took a deep breath – and the house lights went down.

We both felt the tension. We couldn't have got any closer to each other. The merest bump of elbows now would bring a smile and a '*Pardon*' from each of us. Tense but exciting.

Now when to leave? We had passed the point she had come in but were both unwilling to leave in case the other failed to get up too. Tension mounted as the end came round a second time, the credits rolled and the lights came up.

I turned to her, about to pose my question about the number of times she had seen the film, but she beat me to it. 'You're French, aren't you?' she said in the accents of nearby Sloane Square.

I suppose it was surprise. Shock even. To my eternal embarrass-ment I grunted acknowledgement in international tones. 'Aargh,' I gargled. To her it was clearly an affirmative.

She leaned over and grasped my wrist. 'Knew it,' she said triumphantly. 'I absolutely knew it. There's something about you French. It's your *savoir-faire*. I think you inherit it at birth.'

'*Possible*,' I said disarmingly in the accents of La Frette sur Seine.

She stood up. 'Are you coming? Or are you going to see the film round again? You can't be that keen on Arletty.'

'*Nevair.*' I stood up.

We left the cinema and walked towards the river. I was already far too committed. I felt there was no choice but to leap feet first into the accent. 'Tell me,' I said, ''ave you evair been . . . at Paris?'

'No – going next month, though. We'll be living there. Daddy's just been appointed to some Anglo-French committee. He and Mummy have left already. But we're keeping on the flat here in Sloane Square.'

A flat empty of parents. 'Is near 'ere?'

'Walpole Street. Just opposite Whitelands House, d'you know it?'

Whitelands House! Speech failed me. I nodded vigorously.

'Do you live in Paris?'

A deep breath to adjust the accent. 'Vairy close to it. La Frette sur Seine. Like your 'ome counties.'

She pulled a face. 'I just love your accent. But will you speak to me in French? I've just spent three months in Switzerland. Finishing school. More like a prison sentence. Do speak French!'

'Next time we meet,' I said. ''Ere, I am learning the English.'

'How long are you staying in London?'

'Regretfully, I leave tomorrow.'

She grimaced. Then lightened the look. 'But, of course, I'll be in Paris too.'

Yes. 'Of course.'

'Can we meet there? As soon as I get to Paris?'

'*Bien sûr.* Give me your *numéro de téléphone* and I will call you before I leave.'

We stood on Chelsea embankment as the lights flickered in the mist. I put my arm round her shoulders and she put her arm round my waist. I felt terrible. She was a nice girl. Perhaps too upper-class for me. But then that wasn't the only reason that I knew I could never phone her.

★

Another of my 'conquests' dappled with failure was a very different proposition. I met my own Mrs Robinson on an Underground train late in my fifteenth year. I was riding from White City towards Notting Hill Gate in a train that was quite crowded. I had stood up to allow a woman or old man take my seat, a common practice at that time, and was holding on to the bar just inside the sliding doors. At Holland Park a well-dressed woman came into the compartment, stopped just inside the sliding doors and steadied herself by reaching for the same vertical bar. As she gripped it her hand covered my thumb. I gave a half-smile in her direction, but she looked stonily over my shoulder. I moved my hand to try to release my thumb but she turned her head and looked down the carriage as if searching for a seat.

I was baffled. She could not possibly have been unaware that she had trapped my thumb. Her arm was at full stretch holding the pole. There were several people crammed quite close around us and I could not see her face long enough to catch her eye as other passengers swayed back and forth between us with the movement of the train. At Notting Hill the doors opened, the sway of passengers revealed her face and I leaned forward. 'Excuse me,' I said. 'My thumb.' No response. 'This is my stop,' I added.

She raised her eyebrows as if in surprise. As I moved she clamped my whole hand and looked away. The doors slid closed.

We stood, no more than two feet apart, her head turned away, her eyes fixed elsewhere. I could quite easily have prised my hand free but embarrassment had been replaced by that familiar sensual curiosity. An attractive, well-dressed woman, admittedly somewhat strange in her behaviour, had chosen to make deliberate contact with me. She was probably in her mid twenties although women dressed older in the late 1940s, all apparently aiming, like film stars, at the magic young sophisticates bracket. She was certainly by far the most sophisticated woman ever to show any interest in me, even if the extent of her interest seemed so far restricted to my thumb.

As the doors opened at Lancaster Gate she released my hand and stepped out on to the platform. With no more than a quick glance at my old bed-space where I had spent many a dusty night during the war, I left the train and stood beside her.

'You'll come up for a drink?' she said as if we'd known each other since time immemorial.

'Kind of you,' I said. She wasn't the only sophisticate on the platform.

She was not talkative. We got to the top of the station and out into Holland Park Road with just one exchange in which she told me, in answer to my question, that her name was Mrs Buckliss. No first name on offer. And she seemed to have no interest in asking mine.

We walked through a few streets near Holland Park, a rather gloomy unpainted area at that time, the fine houses disguised by lack of any upkeep during the war. By the time we came to a small pale brick block of 1930s flats my heart was thumping. We had entered the hall and Mrs Buckliss pressed the button for the lift when a terrible thought struck me.

'You do realise . . .' I said.

'Realise what?'

'That I . . .' I hesitated, suddenly far less sophisticated. 'That I'm a student.'

'So?'

'If it's a question of money . . .'

'It isn't,' she said coldly and stepped into the lift.

I followed. 'Just saying . . .' I was going to go on to a full apology but she didn't seem to be interested.

The doors closed. We stood huddled in the small lift. I was standing with a well-dressed older woman who had actually picked me up. She clearly wasn't looking for conversation. Within five minutes I might actually be in bed with her. But I didn't feel as I should have, as I would have expected to. The strangeness of her manner was a detumescent.

The lift jolted between floors, stopped a moment and continued upwards. I caught her eye and tried a smile.

The only response was that cold, unsmiling face. The lift buzzed and whined, almost stopped again and moved on past the next floor. 'Do you live on the top floor?' It was the best I could do by way of conversation. She ignored me.

The lift stopped. She turned for the door and paused. 'One thing,' she said. 'It makes no difference to you, I suppose . . .'

A spurt of real apprehension now. 'Difference?'

'My husband.'

'Your husband?' Alarm bells.

'Harmless. But the old goat likes to watch. It's his thing. Especially strapping young lads like you.'

The lift door opened. She stepped on to the threadbare carpet of the landing. *Likes to watch.* I hung back in the lift.

The doors began to close. 'Green button. Press the green button,' she said irritably through the closing grille. I reached for the buttons. No hesitation now. I pressed Ground.

The lift started down, hiccupped to a stop at skirt level, and fell smoothly down to the ground floor.

TWENTY

Fire in the Blood

Speakers' Corner was a Hyde Park institution. On Sundays you might get six or seven speakers addressing their own little crowd of ten or fifteen people. There were some very polished speakers, like the Methodist minister Donald Soper, and some who could only pick their way through a sentence with difficulty. There were serious people like Hammersmith MP D. N. Pritt talking on the British Mandate in Palestine, and left-wingers speaking persuasively against the Marshall Plan. There were performers, people who spoke for fun, and a good sprinkling of crazies warning against visitations from Mars or the dangers of eating walnuts. Heckling and taunting of orators was common practice. I loved the place.

There was no system. You just started talking to someone on any subject on earth. A third person might listen in and add a few comments. Others would drift over to see what was being talked about, and before you knew it you would be addressing your own small knot of listeners. I saw it often; I even nervously hoped that natural selection would make me one of the speakers – but I never made it to more than two or perhaps three people.

We all need rites of passage to mark our journey. Possibly if you're from a more settled background, the rites are marked out for you, at home or at school. For myself, and for most adolescents I knew, there was no given pattern. It was left to you to fashion your own rites, to choose your own hurdles to be cleared or to fall at.

I was drawn to Hyde Park on Sunday afternoons to hear the speakers but soon found that the park, as darkness fell, offered another source of attraction. I'd been to Speakers' Corner two or three times only when, leaving at nightfall, I noticed that a young woman had taken up a spot under the trees that line the carriageway running parallel to the Bayswater Road. Further along I saw that two more women stood talking in the shadows. Whenever a man passed, one of them would step forward and talk to him.

I didn't need telling why. I knew this park. My mother's father had been a ticket collector here in the days when young gentlemen hired a slatted green chair for a penny and watched young women promenading by. And some of the women, of course, especially as dusk approached, were less than 'respectable'. Perhaps my grandmother was one of them. Eliza Toop, as she became after she married my grandfather, had kept her head above water throughout her life by courage, hard work and scant concern for the stifling morality of her day. At the age of fifteen she had run away from service somewhere in the South West and walked back to London. Afraid to go home to World's End Passage, she lay in wait for her brother and asked him to help her. He was a gold leaf tradesman working at that time on the ceilings of the Bank of England. He had taken her up to the City with him and found her a job as a barmaid.

Later, at the end of the 1890s, after she had returned to live in World's End, by now with an illegitimate child, she began to spend time in Hyde Park. I assume her mother, a God-fearing woman with an idle drunk for a husband, looked after my mother's half-sister while Eliza was working in the park. Perhaps I do her an injustice but I don't see how she could have afforded to be sitting there evening after evening without earning. Murky though it undoubtedly is, it all worked out well for Eliza and Jesse James Toop, the ex-butler turned park ticket collector whom she met there. They married a month before my mother was due and spent a happy twenty years together before Jesse James died a month before I myself was born.

I found it difficult to get the women in the park out of my mind. I told nobody at school, of course. For me there was no satisfaction in schoolboy chatter. Perhaps guilt weighed too heavily upon me. Perhaps I already knew what was going to happen.

The following Friday I left at the interval a play whose title I no longer remember and, instead of walking round Soho, took a bus straight down to Hyde Park corner. That evening I walked back and forth across the park, astonished, fascinated, by what I was seeing. There were, by about nine or ten o'clock, at least thirty or forty women walking the carriageways, gathering under the lights, exchanging banter with passing men. Of course I had seen the middle-aged, unattractive streetwalkers of Soho, heard their sharp-tongued exchanges, but these were much younger women, some of them in their mid-twenties or less. They were at the age where my attention was most keenly focused.

Fantasies came thick and fast. The park women resurrected for me the memory of Shirley, the girl who had begun 'going with Americans' when we had stayed with Joe and Jinny at Windsor. She would by now be about eighteen, not far from the age of many of the girls in the park. I began to believe that she could quite easily be one of these young women. She had left her family and I had no doubt that she had headed straight for London. With the return home of so many of the GIs, Rainbow Corner was not the place it had been. As far as I knew there were only two places for her to make a living, Soho and Hyde Park. What was so unlikely about thinking there was a chance of meeting her walking the shadows of the Bayswater carriageway or caught by the winter moonlight on the Serpentine Bridge?

*

It was not long before Christmas, bitterly cold that year of the national fuel crisis, the snow cleared from the walkways but stretching like a pale lake across the open spaces of the park. There were fewer girls than usual. Those there were were bundled in heavy coats, distinguishable at a distance from passing men only by the pale blur of their stockinged legs as they neared the lamplight.

My search for Shirley had by now become an obsession. I was convinced she was working in the park. This was the fifth or sixth Friday night I had been looking for her in the last three months and I now realised that the girls came and went on an unpredictable basis. Some nights I would recognise most of the faces, others practically none at all. One night, I was sure, I would see Shirley's flowing red hair as she stepped under a lamp.

And then what? And then . . . what?

That night just before Christmas I was walking, muffled in a scarf, hands deep in my pockets, the snow beginning again, drifting through the lamplight, when I saw her on Serpentine Bridge. She was leaning against the parapet smoking a cigarette. She flicked it over her shoulder on to the ice of the frozen lake and began to walk slowly away. She wore a dark coat and a scarf draped high on the back of her head. That red hair tumbling beneath the dark scarf was unmissable as she passed each light on the bridge. I hastened my step. When I was about ten feet behind her I called her name: 'Shirley . . .'

She turned in shadow. 'Shirley?' she said in a foreign accent. She stared at me, then her face relaxed. 'I am not your Shirley. See?' She lifted her head under the light. She was tall like Shirley, a young woman in her early twenties with large wide-set eyes, her hair more fair than red. I think she was pretty but she dropped her face back into shadow before I could see more.

'I'm sorry. I thought you were Shirley,' I said. 'A friend of mine.'

She didn't believe me, didn't care anyway. 'In my country we don't have girls called Shirley. You know Switzerland?'

I nodded.

'I'm Swiss.'

I didn't think to ask her what a Swiss girl was doing working in Hyde Park in post-war London. Or perhaps she wasn't Swiss at all. Austrian, Latvian, a refugee . . . She made no attempt to turn away. 'Well, so I am not your Shirley.'

My head was aching from the cold, even more from the tension.

She saw. 'You have money? You want to come with me?'

I had two pounds from my dog racing earnings in my pocket.

'Make up your mind,' she said. 'What does it matter if I am not Shirley? You have a pound, we can go over there.' She nodded ahead. 'It's quiet under the trees.'

I closed my eyes. 'OK,' I said.

She took my arm, guiding me until we reached the nearest in a stand of leafless trees. She held out her hand and I took a pound note from my pocket. She took the money and made it disappear somewhere inside her coat. The tree she had chosen was striped with driven snow. She brushed it away and rested her back against the trunk, methodically removed her gloves and undid her topcoat.

I watched her, my mouth dry; an almost intolerable tightness in my head; a swishing in my ears. A large part of me wanted to turn and run.

'Come closer,' she said. 'You can't do much from there.'

Two or three minutes only passed while she clasped me to her, my frozen breath pumping out over her shoulder. In these moments, urgently needed, desperately awaited, God knows what I felt. I was shivering, but at least the swishing sound in my ears had come to a stop.

'Such a young boy,' she said as I shuddered.

Should I say thank you? I said thank you, my chin on my shoulder.

'Goodnight, young boy,' she said. 'It's better we did this than you become one of them.' She nodded over my shoulder.

'Who?' I turned my head. Ten or a dozen men stood there in a half-circle behind me, watching me impassively. As I looked they moved and began to shuffle nervously away, their shoes swishing through the snow.

The Swiss girl broke from me and, facing away from the wind, she began buttoning her coat. Without turning back to me she lifted her hand in a finger-fluttering wave then, pulling on her gloves, she strolled back to her place under the lamp on the bridge.

The men had disappeared. I glanced once towards the Swiss girl. She was looking in the other direction, fumbling a cigarette from her pocket. I crossed the park to Marble Arch and bought a tube ticket back to White City. On the journey I had made so often, through Lancaster Gate, I sat pierced by guilt. But slowly forming beneath this was something else. For all the regret I felt, I realised I would not have it otherwise. It was a hurdle of my own making (like most perhaps) but it was still a hurdle cleared.

I was no longer a virgin.

TWENTY ONE
A Suitable Opponent

If I try to draw out the main strands in my life they are, I think, four in number: family, birthplace, a certain sexual anarchism, and the French experience. This last, the impact of France, came to the surface cumulatively during two or three visits to La Frette sur Seine following that first time just after the war when I stayed with Julien Lelong.

Although Harry Little, the Sloane middle-school French master, maintained a thriving, and I suppose profitable, part-time tourist business taking groups of Sloane boys to Paris, I never went as one of his party. By now I was well established with the Linquier family whom I had met on that first visit the year after the war ended. Monsieur Linquier's original plan had been for exchange visits to London by his son Daniel and to Paris, or rather La Frette sur Seine, by me. It didn't entirely work out like that.

Daniel came to London once and didn't like it one bit. He found the city battered and ugly compared with his beloved Paris, and English food, except for baked beans, dull and uninteresting. All true. But his real problem was a serious Gaullist contempt for the Anglo-Saxons, a conviction that they had stolen credit for victory over the Third Reich from the French Resistance.

Although I had become familiar with Julien Lelong's Gaullism on my first visit to La Frette, in my schoolboy way I had understood his anti-American feelings as simple economic envy. This attitude was certainly not unknown in Britain. But Julien's understanding of the vast scope of the conflict was unusual for a Frenchman in that he had fought throughout as a British-based submarine captain, read British newspapers and listened to the BBC regularly throughout the war. Most French people, trapped in an occupied land, saw France as the hub of the world war raging around them. They tended therefore, and still do, to exaggerate the importance of France as a theatre of the Second World War, and the role of the Resistance in particular. General Eisenhower had unwittingly helped this process along by generously calling forward General Leclerc's French 2nd Armoured Division to lead the American forces into Paris. De Gaulle, naturally, seized the opportunity to expand the myth of a France 'liberated by her own efforts'.

So, surprising as it seemed, it was politics that came between two fourteen-year-old boys when Daniel Linquier first came to London on exchange. I found him already embittered by France's treatment at the hands of the Anglo-Saxon world. Britain, he insisted, had a long history of imperial theft. Had they not stolen India from France?

What?

'And Canada? Why is Canada not still French? Stolen.'

'When?'

'At Quebec. In 1759.'

'That's history.'

'So, in the eyes of the English, Time justifies Theft?'

'Well . . .'

And then there was Syria, and British and American plots to steal Algeria, a department of Metropolitan France itself. How these dull, pedestrian British (*les Rosbifs*) and these naïve, self-indulgent Americans (*les Ricains*) managed to outwit the inestimably more intelligent French at every turn, Daniel never explained.

He was better prepared than I was with the details and dates of the expulsion of France from India and Wolfe's battle for Canada on the Plain of Abraham. When it came down to staring at a Persil advertisement in the Underground and Daniel airily claiming further British exploitation of a French possession – '*Voilà*, India, Canada and now Persil!' – I didn't realise he was leading me on.

'Persil!' I said. 'That's made by Unilever. British. Or Anglo-Dutch anyway.'

As I protested our right to Persil his mouth twitched into a smile of infinite superiority. This was one round France had definitely won.

We sparred like this throughout the time he stayed in London. There was no real truce. Yet no overt unfriendliness. We just didn't get on well.

Nevertheless I continued to stay with the Linquiers at La Frette. Monsieur Linquier was a man I greatly admired for his enthusiasm for French history and his impressive honesty about the recent past. Madame Linquier was mildly amused by me, I think, as an eccentric English boy who had never seen artichokes, asparagus or courgettes. But she was kindly and an impressively good cook and, like her husband, made me feel as much at home as she possibly could. Of course she never knew that I didn't get along with her son, unless she knew it from him. But in any case the theory was that we benefited from being together, speaking both English and French to each other. Except that Daniel, at least at this stage of his life, had no real wish to speak English. He's probably a distinguished Professor of English at the Sorbonne by now.

Days at La Frette were spent less and less with Daniel. Most of the time I think I was simply a burden for him to have around when he might have more enjoyably spent the time with his girlfriend, Monique. I was certainly envious of his relationship with her but by now I was accustomed to going into Paris by myself and, on a summer visit, would sometimes meet up with some of the boys on one of Harry Little's Commando Paris Trips.

Best of all was the summer when Kit was one of Harry's party. This trip had a different purpose from the others, not different in that the object was to make Harry a profit, or at the very least get him to his beloved Paris at a much-reduced cost, but this visit was essentially a football trip.

The Sloane School football teams had by then a reputation throughout south and south-west London. The school was fifty or sixty yards from Chelsea football ground and the management had, since the war, taken a real (commercial) interest in the school's unusually high standard of football, enough to supply one of their first-team players as a coach for our First Eleven. I was certainly not a member of this august company. I had played one season with Kit in the second eleven when he was on his way up to the top but I was never more than an average player. Kit, however, was of a quite different standard and had been asked by Harry Little to join the Sloane team going out to play in France, even though he was just a month or two past his fifteenth birthday.

It was to be a short stay, just over a week, and Harry had promised to arrange two matches for the team. Everybody assumed this would be with the Paris equivalent of grammar schools about the same size as our own. But Harry had upped the ante.

In his deep growl he admonished us, 'Remember, best behaviour, boys. No chopping down the referee. You'll be playing against the cream of the French education system. The Eton and Winchester of Paris.'

As Kit and various friends have since told me, Harry's Commando Trips were as unlike today's school trips as you can imagine. This one was no different. Kit and his friends were housed in a 'doss-house' hotel on the Rue du Bac. They had been given instructions on the quantities of goods they were each to bring before they left. Kit remembers he was detailed to bring sugar and tins of Nescafé. On the first evening they arrived at the Rue du Bac, Harry called all the boys together with their luggage into his room and repacked the sugar, coffee, soap and probably other goods into the two biggest suitcases. He had then selected two of the older boys as porters. 'Foller me, boys, and I'll show you something of French culture you won't forget in a hurry.'

He had set off with his quick, rolling gait, the two boys struggling with the weight of the suitcases behind him. His destination was a basement brothel on the Place Pigalle. There the goods were displayed on a table. The two 'porters' understood nothing of the rapid bargaining that followed with a figure out of a George Raft gangster movie. Music played and half-dressed girls floated through the basement pulling on flimsy costumes. None of this deflected Harry from his table-banging demands for an improvement in the gangster's offer. When he was content with the deal struck and the money handed over, he had advanced a couple of thousand francs to the boys and told them to go off and spend it wisely somewhere else. He himself would be staying on a while.

In fact, Kit said, they hardly saw Harry after that until the morning of the first match. This, I learnt from friends who had been on others of Harry's trips, was standard. He would disappear on the first evening and reappear only sporadically in the next ten days. Most nights he seemed to spend away from the hotel. To give Harry credit I suppose he had never specified *who* was to 'enjoy the cultural experiences that Paris has to offer' but a closely supervised school trip to Paris it certainly wasn't.

The morning of the first football match I travelled into Paris to meet up with the team. To my astonishment the match was to be played at the huge Stade de Colombes. The team were impressed, more than that, intimidated.

'Wembley or Wormwood Scrubs, boys, it's all just grass,' Harry reassured them.

It was an August morning of sapping heat. The concrete seating where Harry and I finally settled ourselves was at least partly in shade but on the pitch the hot air shimmered across the grass. The referee and linesmen came out from the tunnel below us, all properly turned out in black shorts and black alpaca jackets. In red shirts, the opposing team followed.

I looked at Harry in amazement. 'They're grown men! And . . .' I pointed 'they've got bare feet!' I could have added that they were all North Africans but that wasn't uppermost in my mind.

I was thinking of Kit at barely fifteen playing against these powerfully built, unsmiling men. I was thinking that with bandages as their only protection against the heavy football boots our players wore, things could turn nasty very quickly.

I turned to Harry. 'So what happened to the Eton and Winchester of France, sir? It's a long time since this lot's been to school.'

'If ever,' Harry said with equanimity.

I was not going to get an answer. 'What about boots?'

'Unobtainable in France at the moment, my boy. Gold dust.' He paused and took out his notebook. 'Yes, must remember that for my next trip.'

'But our team has studs! They could tear the others' feet to ribbons.'

'Just watch the match, my boy. You'll see they're very worthy opponents.'

They were. Nobody's feet were torn and their ability to kick the heavy leather ball of those days seemed unimpaired by the absence of boots. Perhaps they had the advantage in the extreme heat but the Blues (our first team were wearing their Chelsea shirts) played the Reds to a standstill. At full time the score was 1–1 and the North Africans, suddenly friendly and smiling, clapped the school team off the pitch.

There was a rumour among the boys when they got back to London that Harry had only got the North Africans to play us by passing off the Sloane team as Chelsea (even then one of the most famous teams in Europe) Reserve Eleven.

But there was still a second match to play. The day before the match I went to see Kit at the Rue du Bac. Harry had put in a rare appearance. 'On your toes tomorrow, boys,' he admonished. 'This match is to be played at Billancourt, a sort of suburb of Paris. The RAF bombed the Renault factory there to smithereens during the war, so the locals aren't naturally friendly. But the Renault people have kindly allowed us the use of their own pitch.'

'And who are we playing?' one of the team asked.

'I've made special arrangements for an excellent team, one of the best teams in the land . . .'

'A school team?'

'Perhaps more college age,' Harry conceded ruminatively, and would be drawn no further. 'Don't worry, you can handle it. I've got real faith in you, my boys.'

The following day (it was to be an evening match this time) Kit and our centre-forward came to the Linquiers' at La Frette for lunch. First they had news.

'You're going to have to play tonight, Dee,' Kit said. 'Jackson's down with food poisoning.'

I was appalled. I knew I wasn't anything like up to standard. Even my second eleven days were now long behind me. If I ever played for a school team now it was as a fill-in for the third or even fourth.

'We'll carry you,' Kit said. 'At least it'll be better than playing with ten men. Just.' My younger brother did not think highly of my skills as a footballer.

Tomkys, the centre-forward (who incidentally was playing for Queen's Park Rangers first team immediately after leaving school), was more encouraging. 'Harry says tonight's game should be a walk-over . . .'

'What? He told me it was one of the best school teams in the land. More like a college team.'

'When we told him we'd have to get you to play, he said different. He said you'll probably even get a chance to score.'

But Harry's statements, promises or estimates were no longer likely to impress me.

The Linquier parents were as friendly and welcoming as ever. Kit already knew Daniel from his trip to London that Easter and, in any case, has always had that rare ability to get on with people that transcends language difficulties.

It was a normal Linquier Saturday lunch in the garden. We began with a home-made fish pâté, accompanied, because Monsieur Linquier was a Norman, by still cider. Kit and Mike Tomkys enjoyed the cider. For the main courses we moved to red wine. Lamb and vegetables served separately intrigued them both and probably made them forget how much red wine they were drinking. Monsieur Linquier had played football as a young man and poured liberally to toast the Sloane team's success against our unknown opponents.

The alarm bell rang for me when I caught a flash of sunlight on Kit's hair as he rocked back and hit his head on the tree-trunk behind him. It was less than three hours to the match and the centre-half was incapably drunk. I took a quick glance at Mike Tomkys. The centre-forward was well on the way.

Madame Linquier put Kit to bed; Mike Tomkys fell asleep in an armchair. It looked as though our opponents for which Harry had been moved to make special arrangements were going to be the ones to get a walk-over.

Two hours later, on the train to Paris, both Kit and Tomkys looked as fit as fiddles. I was the only one with a knot in my stomach, fervently hoping that Harry's later estimate of a walk-over was closer the truth than his earlier estimate of our opponents as one of the best college teams in the land.

We drove in a team bus supplied by our opponents out to Billancourt. There was still daunting evidence of the big RAF raid on the Renault factory in 1944. But, past the factory, lay the undamaged sports ground. Not as impressive as the Stade de Colombes, of course, but impressive enough.

We changed into our white shorts and blue shirts in the visitors' large changing room. Harry strode up and down giving pre-match tips like the manager of Chelsea or Manchester United. But even when pressed, the name of the opposing team seemed to escape him. 'They're a good quality local team,' he said. 'All young lads from Billancourt.'

Outside the dressing room we assembled in a broad hallway to have a team photograph taken. While we were being positioned I looked around. The walls were covered with pictures of the trophy-winning Renault Works team. In those days companies recruited talented footballers and gave them virtually work-free employment to train and practise their football. In the French Works League, Renault with its 60,000 men to choose from was a regular winner. The cup-holder captain in all the most recent winners' photographs was a black-haired, hard-faced man with a sardonic and triumphant smile. An unsettling thought crossed my mind.

We were first out on to the floodlit pitch. Only when we heard the roar of voices did we realise there were several hundred spectators. I looked round. The roar was for our opponents being led out on to the pitch just behind us. Led out on to the pitch by the same black-haired, hard-faced man, now wearing a grim smile, that I had seen in the photographs. Harry Little had fixed us up with the Renault Works Team, professionals in all but name and playing before a home crowd!

There was nothing else to do but get down to it and play. They were a notably hard-elbowed team with a hostile, aggrieved manner of playing. By half-time we were 0–1 down but it wasn't, for the Renault team, anything approaching a walk-over.

Kit, Mike Tomkys, Peter Tribe and others played their hearts out. At half-time we went in to examine our bruises and suck on our slices of orange. Criss-crossing the wide dressing room with his fast, rocking, bandy-legged walk, cigarette in one hand, segment of orange in the other, Harry Little was complimentary. To himself. 'A well-chosen opponent for you, boys,' he pronounced in his rapid, slightly cockney speech. 'A truly suitable opponent. I knew you could do it.'

Somebody reminded him that we were losing one–nil and that only because Kit had cleared twice off the line.

Harry shook his head, again ignoring the score. 'You only *seem* evenly matched. But I've been having a word with the French coach. He's a very worried man. Very worried indeed, my boys. Now go out there and worry him a great deal more.'

In the second half there was a glut of goals.

Renault were left reeling, beaten by an English schoolboy team, 4–1.

Kit and the team left Paris in triumph a few days later. I was to stay on at the Linquiers' another two or three weeks. Harry, I've no doubt, was well pleased with the results for both the team and himself. The name of the Arab team the school played at the Stade de Colombes was never disclosed.

TWENTY TWO

Reds under the Beds?

At Sloane, as we entered the recently created sixth form, we all watched American films, we listened to Glenn Miller, Frank Sinatra, even the Andrews Sisters, and we began to take to the flavour of jazz. We read American novels, often the abandoned pocket books of GIs found on second-hand bookstalls – *A Farewell to Arms*, *For Whom the Bell Tolls*, *The Great Gatsby* and *Light in August* . . . Strangely my more left-leaning friends were the most admiring of American popular culture. Strange, because it wasn't difficult to see, as the Cold War polarised the world, that a very distinct left-leaning anti-Americanism had become a reality.

National Service hung over some of us as a threat. As our sixth-form years passed we became more and more divided by the prospect of military service. There were those inclined to pacifism among us, like my friend Larry Naughton, who simply wanted nothing to do with any military organisation; there were some, like brisk, efficient Fred Alsop, who welcomed the thought of the two years to come; then there were others like Ted Simon who genuinely wished to avoid military service because he did not believe in the cause for which we were to be conscripted. Others were quite simply unable to conceive the possibility of a Stalinist threat and spoke scornfully of the undecided as believers in 'Reds under the Beds'.

For those like me, the majority, in the uncertain middle, among all our doubts about Soviet intentions there still existed a parallel inclination to consider the possibility that many Soviet actions were simply reactions to what they saw as the menace of American power.

But the Kravchenko issue was clearly different. It was, at its root, a simple issue. It was black and white. If Kravchenko were recounting the truth, then all who felt any sympathy for the Soviet system or Soviet ideals had been victims of a grotesque deception. It meant the reality was that Soviet government was backed, made possible even, by a huge string of concentration camps (the term Gulag was yet to become fashionable). That millions of Soviet citizens had been murdered in the deliberately created Ukraine famine. That, in the workers' paradise endlessly depicted in Soviet propaganda, and Western pro-Soviet articles, hundreds of thousands of innocents were in fact dying every year in the intolerable conditions of the camps. And it meant that the Red Tsar was a man of a gross and casual brutality to match Adolf Hitler's.

At Sloane argument raged round this issue. To some the duplicity of the CIA was to be seen in every sentence of *I Chose Freedom*; to others it was the duplicity of the Soviet Union.

So, sometimes stormy, sometimes well-argued, it became a central issue among us: was Kravchenko telling the truth?

The Saturday morning two men knocked on the door of our house at White City and showed Metropolitan Police warrant cards was a bad shock for all of us. While still being careful with friends and secretive with neighbours about the family bookmaking, both the legal and illegal side of the business, we had all come to believe that trouble was unlikely. All except my father, that is. He maintained the need for caution.

That Saturday morning my mother was white-faced as she hurried from the front door to fetch my father. Moments later she returned, suddenly composed, and smilingly invited the two policemen in.

'You gave me quite a fright,' she said. 'I thought it was bad news.'

'Just a few questions for your husband, love. I'm sure he can clear it up.'

'He'll be with you in a moment. Cup of tea while you wait?'

She made them tea and chatted to them for a few minutes until my father came downstairs. Through the open kitchen door Kit and I heard one of the CID men: 'A drunk and disorderly charge was laid last night against someone named George Robert Simpson. You know him?'

My father's voice: 'George? Known him for years on and off. Why?'

'Stack of betting slips on him when he was arrested. All neat with a rubber band round them.' There was a long pause.

'Go on.'

'The top one had your telephone number on it, didn't it, Mr Wheal? Quite unusual to have your own phone. Simpson wasn't phoning those bets over to you, I suppose?'

The kitchen door closed. Kit, my mother and I looked at each other in alarm. A charge of illegal gambling would lose my father his legal bookmaker's licence at the track. It would inevitably lose him his job at Whitelands as well.

'If they go upstairs,' my mother said, 'your father's ledgers are all over the bedroom table. There's a pack of slips too.'

We held our breath. Five minutes later we heard the front door close and my father came into the kitchen. He went straight to my mother and hugged her.

'What did they say?'

'They said what a nice, sensible woman your wife is. Gave one of them some advice about his daughter, apparently.'

'He was a bit worried about her boyfriend. I said my dad had been a bit worried about you . . . that sort of thing.'

'Had he?'

'Of course not. So . . . George got picked up with a pocketful of slips?'

My father nodded. 'Our number on the top one, five bob each way My Love for the Derby.'

'What did you tell them?'

'I said that top one was mine. Put my number on in case I had a big win. Knew nothing about the other slips.'

'Was that all right?' I asked.

'Funnily enough, it's not illegal to *place* a bet. Only to accept one.'

'What will happen to George?' my mother asked.

'He'll get something for the drunk and disorderly and I'll pay his fine for possessing betting slips. It won't go any farther.'

'Thank God they didn't search the house,' she said. 'The bedroom's full of slips. And the ledgers.'

'Was. I got rid of them while I was upstairs.' He opened the back door. A pillow case was hanging on a string out of Kit's bedroom window. Though it was puffed with betting slips, you could still see, from the sharp angles, the outline of the weekly ledgers.

In these years immediately after the war the success of the book-making, both legal and illegal, was moving my father up the income scale. This had consequences for all of us. I remember he was always urging my mother to spend her clothing coupons on a more expensive outfit, and Kit and I gradually lost our drab wartime look. My father was a generous man. He never visited his sister Alice, who still lived in the World's End, without a five-pound note slipping between them, although he knew that most of it would go straight back to the local bookmaker. I suppose he felt a similar sense of resignation when we visited his mother. Intensely dislikeable as she had always been, in her advanced years she had become ingratiating, even cringing, towards her youngest son. Possibly not uninfluenced by the white fivers, tightly folded, that were transferred, hand to hand, as we left.

He spent very little on himself. As energetic as ever but beginning to take on a distinctly portly shape, he decided he needed well-tailored suits of a quality he probably couldn't afford. He had therefore made one of his mysterious deals.

He had already organised a supply of white shirts from America for himself, Kit and me via one of the American tenants at Whitelands and, of course, to avoid overburdening my mother, a laundry service. No doubt the Mayfair Laundry was repaying some unspccified favour by producing daily laundered shirts for the three of us.

He was understandably proud of his suits. They were at the very least the equal of those worn by the best-dressed tenants at Whitelands House. When he stood in the pink-carpeted hall you could easily imagine he owned the building – until he leaned forward to open the glass door and a seven year old sailed in, head held high, with a sideways: 'Thank you, Wheal.'

I remember asking him where the suits came from. We might still have been in clothes rationing, or possibly just at the end of it. Even so, most high-quality cloth was being exported. I had noticed that his suits (two pairs of trousers to each one) had a double flap built into the trousers to keep his stomach trim, or at least trimmer. He laughed about this when I asked him about it.

'Think of the shape of the Aga Khan.'

'Yes, he's a bit weighty . . . You don't mean your suits were made by the Aga Khan's tailor?'

'Why not?'

'What! They must cost a fortune.'

'I've plugged into a very useful line, Dee,' he said. 'The Aga Khan throws away a suit after he's worn it a few times. One of the tenants buys them second-hand, no coupons necessary, from a posh West End tailor. For another five the tailor'll make any adjustments needed. So I made this arrangement. I said to the tenant, you know, joking but serious, "Put me down for a couple." And he did. Now here I am – the best-dressed head-porter in London. Shame you and Kit can't put a bit of weight on.'

TWENTY THREE
Kravchenko's Paris

Our new comparative prosperity, our step out of the working class, into some limbo we each now had to define for ourselves, meant among other things that my father actively encouraged me to visit France. He saw it as part of the concept of escape which I believe, in fact, dominated his own life, and has probably gone a good way to dominating mine and Kit's. To learn a foreign language, to become familiar with another country, was, he knew, not for him. But for his sons it was another means of differentiating themselves, of distancing themselves from the life he had grown up in.

I think he felt the fragility of the progress we had made so far. We depended on gambling, on his success at making the weekly book. He had very little backing. Three or four bad weeks in a run could have caused the business to crash. And illegal bookmaking is not open to pleas of bankruptcy or supportive bank loans. He was also, as the recent police visit had showed, in constant danger of prosecution. A heavy fine would have ruined him. So our newfound prosperity was built on still insecure foundations.

The further away we all got from there, the less chance there was of slipping back. Going to France was definitely part of his plan for his sons. First me, then later Kit. These visits had at the same time become an important source of income for the Linquiers; the exchange element between Daniel and myself had been quietly dropped. He had no real interest in further visits to London and I was paying board and keep in sterling which seemed, at least for a little longer, proof against devaluation. This was much appreciated by the Linquiers.

I found France excitingly different from the greyness of Britain. There were so many public crises. I remember how the French people I knew felt in these chaotic times with one premier following another with dizzying speed. Staring angrily at the morning's headline, a deeply humiliated Monsieur Linquier could stand it no longer. 'Go to the window, Daniel,' he cried to his son one morning. 'Watch for the special messenger. They've been through everybody else. They'll be calling for me next!'

He got up and left the room, wiping tears from his cheeks. It was a moment of more than embarrassment to me. In Britain, politics was not played out before your very eyes in the same way. You saw no tears running down the faces of honest men.

Monsieur Linquier's arm-waving passion took me into different political territory. When he talked about the possible Communist takeover of France, he did so in the light of his recent experience of the savagery of the Communist revenge during the post-war purges, as well as the earlier terrors of occupation – the memory of the German klaxon van parked on his own corner of the Rue Aristide Briand, its revolving detector seeking out Monsieur Linquier himself crouched in his bedroom, listening to the BBC.

I was full of admiration for this short, good-humoured, volatile Frenchman. His honesty was impressive. When he talked about the defeat of 1940, he never once tried to lay the blame on British perfidy or any of those theories of London's betrayal of France that still swirl around French dinner tables today. In May 1940 he had been, as a conscripted private soldier, serving just behind the front at Sedan in Eastern France. It seemed to him as if every second soldier in his company was a defeatist, a pacifist or a Communist.

'You must remember, Donal, that Russia was Germany's ally at that time,' he said. 'We had Communist agitators moving among us distributing leaflets, whispering in our ear the question, "Why fight for the English?" The moment the Germans attack, these agitators said, the English will be back on their island.

'Then one morning after six months of waiting, of playing football and writing letters home, a motorcyclist came round the bend in the road, driving with one hand and waving us away with the other. "Run for it. They're coming," he shouted. "The Panzers are coming."

'We were an army,' Monsieur Linquier said. 'The French Army. What had happened to the spirit of Verdun? We should have been prepared to fight. Instead we ran. The whispers of the agitators had undermined the Army's will. Forward troops, French infantry, were in tears, throwing away their weapons, some of them even throwing away their *money*. Believe me, Donal, they were throwing away their money. It seemed true, what the Communist agitators had been telling them – the old France was finished. That was the day I understood we could be defeated by whispers as effectively as by machine guns.'

Monsieur Linquier played a large part in my teenage education, not least because, now that Daniel had removed himself from the equation, spending much of his time at Monique's house, night after night his father and I would stay up talking and sharing a further litre of wine when the rest of the family had gone to bed. Drunk almost every night, I struggled with my inadequate French to follow the labyrinths of French politics. I don't think Monsieur Linquier realised how I fought to keep my Anglo-Saxon *sang-froid* as I finally made my way up to my room, reeling against the sides of the narrow staircase or sometimes, I have to admit, crawling up, with exaggerated care, on my knees. Drinking wine, I learned, can be handled sitting down with no more than a few speech slurs and unfortunately timed remarks. Getting up – and mounting stairs – is a different proposition.

Each time I returned to England my mother would be aghast as she hugged the pale, drawn-featured son who got off the train at Victoria. 'My God,' she'd say. 'Is French food that bad? Those poor French people.'

Hand-printed posters and graffiti covered the walls as my train steamed into the Gare St Lazare for the Easter holiday of 1949. Paris was in tumult. Victor Kravchenko, author of *I Chose Freedom*, had arrived in the city.

'Furthermore,' Monsieur Linquier announced, waving his arms in excitement, 'he is here to fight for freedom. For the truth. Have you heard of Kravchenko, Donal?'

I told him I'd even read the book.

He let out a shout of delight. 'You've read it. This is wonderful!' Madame Linquier sent us out into the garden where we would not get in the way of the far more important activities of the kitchen. Outside, we sat with a glass of Normandy cider. Monsieur Linquier opened the newspaper and beat it down in the slight breeze coming off the Seine.

Kravchenko had come to Paris to fight a court case against one of the most respected magazines in France, *Les Lettres Françaises*. The magazine had published an article condemning *I Chose Freedom* and crucifying Kravchenko. The author of the article was Sim Thomas, a recently retired CIA man who had, he said, seen the light. He was now ready to denounce Kravchenko as an illiterate, a drunk, seriously unbalanced, a defector to the West who had sold out to American Intelligence in order to pay the debts accumulated by his drinking and womanising in New York. He had written no word of *I Chose Freedom* – and no word of the book was true. The CIA, as was their practice, refused to comment.

'What do we know about this Sim Thomas, Donal?' Monsieur Linquier cried, fighting the wind for possession of his newspaper. 'You don't know. I don't know. And *Les Lettres Françaises* won't tell us. Why?' He beat the newspaper into submission. 'Because he doesn't exist!'

Kravchenko was furious at the attack on him. The charge of being an American dummy is potent in leftish circles even today. In the mid-eighties I wrote a novel called *The Fall of the Russian Empire*. Its central theme was the prediction that the Soviet Union would fall in 1989, a forecast I considered totally plausible. But when the French translation appeared my book was widely believed to be CIA-funded, or even totally written for American Intelligence, despite my protests that I had never knowingly met a CIA man in my life. I specifically denied any connection with American intelligence in a number of interviews with and on French radio. Even so, the Russian-born political correspondent of *Le Monde*, when I told him during an interview-lunch that I had never been to Russia, put his index finger to the side of his nose and said in his heavily accented English: 'Except . . . under cover, heh?'

If you want to believe . . .

My session in the garden with Monsieur Linquier was the first of many such. The case, Victor Kravchenko v. *Les Lettres Françaises*, received tens of thousands of column inches throughout France. Kravchenko's book had appeared in French some time before to a paper snowstorm of denial from Communist Party and intelligentsia alike. Nevertheless, 500,000 copies were sold within a year. This astonishing volume of sales was an open challenge to the French Communist Party. *Le Monde* was one of the first journals to suggest an American Intelligence ghost-writer. Communist newspapers condemned the book automatically. Had not many a Trade Union delegation visited Russia before the war and since, without seeing a sign of a concentration camp?

As Monsieur Linquier had predicted, the case immediately developed into a wide-ranging trial of the Soviet system. Soviet and American governments both recognised this as a key moment in the struggle for hearts and minds. From this trial the Soviet Union would emerge – Guilty or Not Guilty.

I remember an evening, or probably several evenings, stumbling up to bed, drunkenly muttering and mumbling to myself, 'The Soviet Union – *Coupable ou Non-Coupable*?' before reaching my room and throwing myself on the bed fully dressed and passing out until woken by the first light of dawn.

The days would normally pass quietly. Head throbbing, I would try a game of tennis with Daniel and Monique, wobbling towards the net with little chance of any real alignment with the ball. Strangely enough, no one in the household seemed to be aware that I was either permanently drunk or permanently hungover.

Each evening Monsieur Linquier would bring in the newspapers, the Communist *L'Humanité* and the right-wing *Figaro*. Sometimes one or two others. In the small kitchen it would be chaos. Madame Linquier would be trying to cook with the help of her ancient Italianate mother. Cooking in France requires much banging of pots and discussion *à haute voix*. The piping voice of Marie-France, aged seven or eight, would join the culinary debate. Before dinner in the kitchen Monsieur Linquier and I would drink Normandy cider and discuss the course of the trial. The truth or otherwise of Kravchenko's position was vitally important to me, of course, but I also began to understand Monsieur Linquier's viewpoint.

He was angry, proud, ecstatic, voluble and enthusiastic by turns. He saw the trial as a chance for events in Paris once again to hold the attention of the world, a chance for a democratic France to demonstrate that it was governed by the rule of law. The United States and the Soviet Union had thrown their prestige into the ring. What had fallen to France was the opportunity to hold its head high and to pronounce an impartial verdict in a Paris court.

Banished by Madame Linquier to the garden after dinner with a litre of red wine and a thick fold of newspapers, sometimes joined by Daniel, we studied the day's court report by one small light set in the apple tree and rehearsed refutations of the claims of the Communist Party witnesses. When the wind chased pages of newsprint into the dark corners of the garden Monsieur Linquier pursued them, returning triumphantly from the darkness with his pale curly Norman hair rumpled and the papers crushed and torn. '*Voilà!*' he'd say. 'See how the Communists try to steal the truth from under our noses!'

Bitterness reached new heights, even for French politics. There were daily demonstrations in Paris and in the small towns around. One Sunday morning the *affaire Kravchenko* came to La Frette sur Seine. Hearing bugles and kettle drums, I hurried down the street. A line of Moroccan troops held back the enraged onlookers as a flag-waving Communist Party march paraded through Gaullist La Frette. Vying with the shouts and threats from the sidewalk were complex chants from the marchers that I couldn't understand, though the focal meaning was clear: *Kravchenko à la lanterne!* The old Revolutionary cry: *Hang him!*

The crowd seethed at what they saw as clear provocation. But the Moroccan troops effectively discouraged scuffles from either side with their extraordinary stillness and menacing indifference to the issue at stake.

In Paris there was both chaos and elation. It was, I have since realised, the sort of show Paris loves. Fashion, outrage, politics and an intellectual gloss on the whole. Film stars and intellectuals came to the trial, members of the Paris bar, leaders of the Communist Party and ministers of the government. The arrival in Paris of Zinaida Gorlova, Kravchenko's first wife, created intense interest. She was surrounded by journalists at the airport before being whisked off to the Soviet Embassy, but her story was being kept for the court. Nobody doubted her evidence would be crucial.

In court Zinaida was a round-faced, attractive blonde, thirty-six years old with a full figure taken full advantage of by photographers as she entered and left the courtroom. 'She's a very beautiful woman,' Monsieur Linquier said glumly.

But the evidence she gave was harsh. Kravchenko had beaten her during their married life. She confirmed what Sim Thomas had said in his article: her husband was a liar, a womaniser and a drunk. The anti-Soviet incidents Kravchenko described in the book, Zinaida insisted, had never happened. Monsieur Linquier was cast down by her evidence but sympathetic to her nonetheless. 'The poor woman,' he said, smoothing the paper on the garden table. '*La pauvre!* With her father and daughter in Russia, what choice does she have but to blacken her ex-husband's name?'

But the retaliation by Kravchenko's lawyer matched her evidence for harshness. She denied she was lying in a French court because her father was being held hostage in a Soviet prison camp. She denied she feared for the life of her daughter, held by the authorities in Moscow. The cross-examination was chaos. Kravchenko was shouting across the court at her. Attempts to restrain him were inadequate. Was there really a Gulag awaiting her if she didn't perform? Or was that simply another of Kravchenko's lies?

Zinaida had made an impression. *L'Humanité* praised her to the skies. Communist Paris was jubilant. Then, suddenly, the bubble burst. Under strain we can't conceive, she broke down in court.

During the next days, in the anti-Communist press, we read how Zinaida Gorlova stood, tense and dark-eyed, in the witness box. Her hair was unkempt, her hands shaking. Kravchenko, late as it was, took pity on her. Uncontrollable in his pity as he had been in his anger, he cried out to the court: '*The world knows she did not come here voluntarily!*'

Zinaida stood there totally distraught as he made promises across the courtroom that he would look after her if she defected, but first she must tell the whole truth. The judge and the ushers were unable to control him.

When Kravchenko finally sat back, the court went silent. This very ordinary woman, impossibly torn by the two great political systems that ruled the world, stared at the judge in wordless reply to Kravchenko's questions. Their child *was* still in Russia? Her father *was* most probably already in a camp?

She fell back into her seat, unable to speak.

That night she was hurried off to a Russian aircraft waiting at Orly airport and from there back to Moscow.

'*Voilà!*' Monsieur Linquier said grimly, with a wave of the back of his hand across the newspaper headline.

In Paris, the last days of the trial were as sensational, as moving, and as deeply significant as the opening had been. Kravchenko's task was to prove that the appalling Soviet cruelty he claimed to have witnessed in the Ukrainian farmlands in the 1930s had in fact taken place, that Stalin had indeed contrived the murder by starvation of uncountable millions of people. So casually accepted today, the issue burned fiercely in 1949. For Western Communists it threatened not only their political theology but the social networks of their lives. Not to be a Communist like every friend you had was unthinkable. Not to be a Communist if your wife maintained the faith meant divorce. For non-Communists like myself, who nevertheless felt that the left, on many issues at least, was on the side of the angels, it was a choice less charged with personal pain. Even so, I was deeply disturbed. If Kravchenko were proved a fraud, a plant by the Americans, I knew I would have to learn to march to a very different drummer.

'Today the judgement,' Monsieur Linquier said as he left for his work, checking water standards in the Paris *banlieues*. I walked down to the café and ordered a *vin blanc*. There were several people there, some like the local Mayor and the gendarme I knew quite well by then. They shook hands and made the usual comments on the weather but nobody was talking about Kravchenko. I paid for my drink and walked back to the house. Daniel was just going out, to meet the lovely Monique no doubt.

'The result of the Kravchenko trial today,' I said.

He nodded. 'The world looks to Paris for a verdict.'

Did he care about the result; was he perhaps jealous of the amount of time his father spent with me? I think he was just pleased that the trial had not taken place in London or New York.

I went into the house. Madame Linquier was out shopping, but she wasn't interested in Kravchenko anyway. I couldn't really talk about it to the old *grand-mère* because I couldn't understand her Italian accent. I began to feel my own interest in the case, in the whole issue, was somehow unhealthy, isolating. I should have been with Daniel, taking out one of Monique's friends. Or else in Paris outside the courtroom waiting for the result.

Then Monsieur Linquier returned home. He could barely control his excitement. The verdict had been announced. For Kravchenko! The court had upheld the case against *Les Lettres Françaises*. (Many years later Claude Morgan, editor of the magazine, admitted that there never was a Sim Thomas of the CIA. The article had been written by a French Communist.) From the day of the verdict, though many on the Left still contrived to ignore it, the social democratic tendency at least felt it dishonest to indulge a convenient myopia. From that day the Soviet Union was revealed, as Mao's China (born that same year) was later to be described, as a land ruled by the poet scattering rose petals before the long shadow of the executioner.

At his kitchen table in La Frette sur Seine Monsieur Linquier sat for a long time staring at the headline in the *Figaro*. Tears brimmed in his eyes. His wife and mother-in-law watched him in silence. I think for him it was revenge at last against those political agitators he believed had destroyed and dishonoured his beloved France in 1940. Then he lifted his head. Slowly this time, deliberately, he struck the newspaper with the back of his hand. '*Voilà*,' he said.

And in case there was any doubt remaining, '*Voilà! Enfin, la France a gagné.*' At last, France has won something.

He lifted his glass and drank to us all.

TWENTY FOUR

All things Bright and Beautiful . . .

Inspired perhaps by stories of Whitelands House and the people who lived there, I asked my father one day during the war what class we were. It was sometime during our stay at Windsor with Joe and Jinny, I was twelve and I doubt if I knew anything of the possible options which, for us, lay between working and lower-middle class. Anything else was outside our aspirational range.

When I put the question to him my father and I were helping Joe with the strip of vegetable garden he had in front of the cottage. Joe himself was just leaving on one of his mysterious errands.

'There's a question for you, Joe,' my father said, perhaps playing for time. 'What class do you think *you* are?'

A convoy of American trucks hurtled by on the road to Windsor. Joe watched it and turned back to my father. 'What class is that you're talking of?' He began to clean off his flat-bladed digging fork with his boot.

'Working class, middle class, upper class, that sort of thing,' my father said.

Joe put up his fork, handle on his shoulder. 'Now let's see, young Bob. I'd say . . . if asked . . . that I was one of that there upper poaching class meself, best I can tell.'

He gave me one of his sly grins, pulled his cap sideways and sauntered off somewhere to help a neighbour get rid of his rats or deliver a hare or two to his friends at the American camp. My father leaned on his garden fork. 'You see what Joe meant,' he said.

'No. He was just joking, wasn't he?'

'He was joking. But it wasn't *just* a joke. I think what Joe meant was that his life had given him no choice but to be a poacher, and not just a poacher of hares and rabbits.'

I stopped and looked at him. 'Even poaching them's against the law.'

'It is . . . But keeping to the law is easier for some than others. Some people say it's only the rich that can afford to be really honest. I think Joe meant something like that. I think he was saying it doesn't matter how hard he works, there's nothing he can do to improve life for him and Jinny. Except for a bit of poaching. And it's his poaching that raises him up that bit over the other Emmet workers. He takes pride in that.'

Perhaps some of that went over my head at the time. I didn't realise, for instance, that Joe's answer might just as well have been my father's.

'We're working class', I remember him saying just before we moved to White City. 'For the moment anyway. It might not look it but we're on the move. I think this war has got a lot of people on the move.'

'Because they've been bombed out?'

'I'm talking about the way people are beginning to think now. The different classes have all rubbed shoulders in this war, because of the bombs and evacuation, much more than they did in the last one. We'll all come out of this a bit different to what we were when we went in. The working classes have seen that upper-class people can be scared or brave, bright or dim, same as anybody else. And the upper classes are beginning to see that if the working classes *are* sometimes found keeping coal in the bath, they don't do it by choice. They do it because the way they live, there's nowhere else to keep it.'

'Does that mean all these different classes are coming together?'

'It's a nice thought, but it's a lot to hope for.'

'Do you have to have a lot of money to be upper class?' I asked him.

He shrugged. 'Not necessarily. Some people at Whitelands can hardly find enough for a Christmas tip for the porters. It's more than just money. It's a generation or two of education that kicks it off, Dee. Then it's the way the upper classes live. The way they dress, the way they talk. And then there's masses of customs, ways of saying things, for instance, that people like us don't know anything about. If you don't say the right thing, or don't say it in the right way, then you're not one of them. They laugh up their sleeves at you. I've seen it at Whitelands.'

'Is that how you know about all these things?'

'I don't.'

This shocked me. 'You mean, *you* make mistakes?'

'Dozens, I expect,' he said. 'But I don't know when I'm doing it. And if I tried too hard not to, I'd just make a fool of myself. That's the other catch – you mustn't try too hard.'

'I think it'd be better if we were all just one class.'

'It's never happened anywhere in the world yet, Dee. And it's not likely to. Class differences are here to stay. In themselves they're not important. It's the senseless part of class discrimination that hurts people.'

In the twenties and thirties were was no choice for people like my father but to accept the humiliations of the class system. But after the war, people, especially many young people of my own age, were very much less willing to concede a natural inferiority they did not feel. Perhaps this was one of those massive silent changes made by six years of war. It was certainly one of the most positive results of

Attlee's Labour government. And perhaps more than anything it was the increasingly liberating influence of the grammar schools.

But grammar school or not, for young working-class people your world was still the post-war world of the streets. Having somewhere to go where you could sit around and talk was the problem. We had homes but they were the preserve of parents, grandmothers and siblings. There were pubs when you were old enough, but most London pubs were unappealing places for the young. Spilt beer, ancient Scotch eggs and a bar dominated by the middle-aged is my memory of most pubs in the White City area. Shepherd's Bush and Hammersmith were not much better.

And restaurants? Well, if you've grown up going to restaurants the whole idea of being intimidated by the waiters or your fellow diners seems ridiculous. But if you had never been to a restaurant, if you considered Lyons Corner House too intimidating a place to enter, as we did, then the idea of going to La Bohème on the King's Road, even if you had the money, was out of the question. In the decade after the war, voices, clothes, social mannerisms still overwhelmed the working man. I find it immeasurably sad that my father, even when able to afford it, never felt able to take my mother to a restaurant by himself in his whole life. Exclusion, of course, even self-exclusion, was the key feature of class. Still is, probably.

I don't know if it was an early awareness of class or something more complex still, but I think many of us at Sloane kept parts of our real lives hooded, even from close friends. Certainly Ted no longer proclaimed himself a Communist in so open a manner and kept his mother's allegiance to the Party from anybody who didn't already know. In the late forties that was perhaps understandable enough. Another good friend lived in Newport Dwellings, a late-nineteenth-century block of Industrial Dwellings off a narrow alley in Soho. He was an intelligent, gifted young man but I think ashamed of the Soho alley he lived in or else of the very small cramped flat which was the home of his parents, sister, elder brother and himself. Yet another friend, Larry Naughton, was always strangely reluctant to talk about his father's profession when he was in fact a writer who had already published a volume of autobiography and a novel and was on the way to a national reputation. Perhaps the word 'autobiography' was the clue. Perhaps Larry felt the memoir would disclose too much of his past.

I was equally secretive, even more so after the visit of the police. But, although working at the Dogs was by now legal, I was still anxious to draw a veil over the fact that I was a Stamford Bridge tick-tack man on Saturday evenings. I also remember equally vividly that, at school, I seldom mentioned that we had lived in Guinness Trust Buildings, never talked about the fact that we had spent our early lives in what was being rebuilt from the ruins not two hundred yards away, although there were plenty of boys there who knew anyway.

Why we as sixteen or seventeen year olds adopted this class-conscious attitude to each other is difficult to analyse. In the grammar schools of London I'm sure the Sloane sixth form was not alone. It might have been a form of working-class snobbery, such attitudes certainly exist, but I think we were rejecting, not all authority, but the automatism of 'know your place', the status quo hymned at Ashburnham Elementary in the school song: 'All Things Bright and Beautiful':

> *The rich man in his castle, the poor man at his gate,*
> *He made them, high or lowly,*
> *And ordered their estate.*
> *All things bright and beautiful . . .*

Through my father's job at Whitelands I probably had more contact with the upper-middle class, as it was then known, than most pupils in the Sloane sixth form, but still this contact never amounted to much. I never spent time talking to the tenants as anything other than the head porter's son. I had never been into any of their flats.

I'd stoked the boilers for their hot water, I'd even emptied their dustbins when the Ghost was mysteriously absent, but I had never shaken hands with any one of them, never really knew them even when they were boys or girls of my own age.

Yet for most of us 'class' remained a marginal concern, far from a preoccupying factor. It would not become so for me until I reached the Army.

TWENTY FIVE

Travels with Larry

By the end of my first year in the sixth form Guy Boas had pretty much retired to his study to write, it was said, a book on Churchill. Before this he had agreed to a request on the part of the sixth form that the prefects should have the power to elect the School Captain. Of course he retained the right to veto the election of a totally unsuitable School Captain (we were not keen on the Head Boy terminology of the public schools, reminiscent we found of a senior servant in a colonial household). At the 1949 election, the first I think at which the prefects elected the School Captain, Guy Boas made his own wishes clear. It was that we should elect a good friend of mine named Bernard Cousins. In fact the electors voted narrowly for me. Guy Boas was markedly displeased but felt, to his credit, that he could not declare null the result of the first-ever election for School Captain.

Not as a result of my election, I'm sure, but what he subsequently did all the same was to spend even more time in his study. I would meet him to report on school discipline and activities every Monday morning. I would make requests. He would deny them. I eventually learnt to ask Cousins in with me whereupon Boas would usually accept our jointly proposed reforms.

I wouldn't want to malign Guy Boas. He was in so many ways, and for most of the years I knew him, the best headmaster I ever came across. (I myself taught for a brief while a few years later and saw at first hand how disastrous an impact a bad headmaster can have.) Guy Boas took a ramshackle post-war World's End secondary school and lifted it up by its bootstraps. But he had that bit of the bully about him, and a sense of Divine Right hovered about his decisions. Perhaps I was fortunate that by the time I was appointed School Captain the last five years had, in all probability, taken their toll on him.

Almost simultaneously with my elevation, Kit was voted Football Captain. Football was God at Sloane. It meant that within a short time my brother and I ran every important activity in the school outside the actual teaching. My father was so puffed up with pride that the tenants of Whitelands House heard virtually nothing else from him.

In our last year at school I had begun to spend more and more of my time with Larry Naughton. He was my age, between seventeen and eighteen, good-looking, bright, and with a sense of anecdotal humour much influenced by the Irish literary associations of his father, Bill Naughton, at that time a struggling writer. Larry came to Sloane very late and carried a slight but intriguing air of mystery with him. Without setting out to mislead, he was inclined to be sparing with the facts of his own background. A strong sense of loyalty to working-class Lancashire, and Bolton in particular where his father had grown up, left me and I think others at Sloane with the belief (until just last week, in fact) that Larry had come to London straight from Lancashire, whereas in fact he had lived in the south of England most of his life.

He had a sister, Marie, of whom he was obviously very fond. Marie was in her first year at Oxford and, as Larry's father supplied him with the latest Dublin literary gossip from writers like Frank

O'Connor, his sister supplied him with another string to his bow, the latest Oxford gossip. I had no idea what Marie looked like but I absorbed from Larry a strong sense of sheer personality. Oxford, the Naughton looks, a stream of good stories, all added up to an acutely romantic picture. Unsurprisingly I made several attempts to get Larry to introduce me to her when she was back home for the vacations. But I felt some protective barrier would rise, some reluctance to connect his best friend and his much-admired sister. At the time I simply didn't understand it.

We soon found, however, that he and I shared a good many interests, interests in trying to educate ourselves. Stoically we endured Fauré recitals at the Wigmore Hall or the hideously uncomfortable cheap seats from which it was impossible to see the stage at Covent Garden. We failed, too, to fall under the spell of the Albert Hall although the Sunday afternoon concerts were, I seem to remember, exceptionally cheap for students.

The problem was that we had received no musical education during the war or the years following, and neither of us had heard any music at home. With literature, even modern literature, we had no such problem. It was, I suppose, our principal cultural interest. Books were enthusiastically puffed and lent by friends; some of the younger masters in all subjects would recommend authors, and Larry was always a good source of enthusiasms acquired from the many Dublin writers his father had staying a few nights at his flat in Plimlico.

The other interest I shared with Larry was France.

Hitch-hiking was adventure. It was the Grand Tour of the late 1940s. We had toured Britain on the back of coal and furniture lorries, in limousines and army jeeps. We had slept in mining villages in Yorkshire, a ruined castle in Dorset, a Tudor manor house in Shropshire, a graveyard in Warrington, by a monks' fish-pond at St Albans, on a deserted airfield, in innumerable barns and shop doorways and railway sheds. We had met hundreds of our fellow countrymen and women, some cranky and bad-tempered, most good-willed, angelically kind even. Now we set out for France.

We stumbled through the darkness. Somewhere, far too close, a big dog barked. If there'd been a church clock to strike it would have struck midnight. We had left the main road down to Dover to find a barn which would take us out of the freezing wind. The shape faintly outlined against the dark sky might have been a barn, a house or a large chicken coop. Larry was confident it was a barn. I was for staying on the road to get a last lift into Dover where we could find some all-night café to doze the night away down by the docks. Hitch-hiking in pairs like this is all about give and take. Tonight I gave. We stumbled on towards the dark shape.

It was a barn. But with black-painted corrugated iron sides, big sliding doors and padlocks. Trucks lumbered along the road towards Dover about a quarter of a mile away. We were balancing the idea of exploring another dark mass against the sky or returning to the main road when we were flooded with light from an open door. A woman stood in the doorway with what looked very much like a shotgun lifted to her shoulder.

'Come forward,' she said, voice shrill with nervousness. 'Into the light.'

We walked forward very slowly. I think we might even have had our hands up.

I started explaining when we were about twenty feet away. She was in her midthirties, dressed in a dark blue dressing gown and pink pyjamas. I finished my explanation. Larry said: 'Yes, that's right,' in fairly unconvincing confirmation of my story about hitch-hiking to France. We stood in the light spilling from the door about ten feet away from her, heavy rucksacks slung on one shoulder.

She stared at us then burst out laughing. 'Gypsies,' she said.

'There've been a lot round here lately, but I've never seen fair-haired ones before. D'you want a cup of coffee?'

'Thank you,' I said, surprised by the rapid change in her welcome.

She put the gun up. 'Come in. This is the back of a hotel. Did you scramble in over the field? You can only see the sign from the side road.'

She took us into the kitchen and introduced herself as Eileen Taylor, the manageress. 'Make yourselves comfortable. It's cold out there tonight. Now, food,' she said. 'Are you hungry? Fried egg on toast?'

We unslung our rucksacks and placed them beside our chairs. While she bustled about putting the coffee on, frying eggs and making the toast, we talked about where we were from, and what we hoped to do in France.

'You can stay here tonight,' she said casually. 'There are a couple of unoccupied rooms. We specialise in comfortable beds.' When her back was turned we exchanged glances of bafflement, eyebrows raised. Such extraordinary hospitality to two young men who had been strangers blundering into her backyard only five or ten minutes ago!

When she served us the fried eggs and I thanked her, calling her 'Miss Taylor', she laughed. 'Call me Eileen,' she said. 'I'm not that much older than you, am I?'

We were talking, finishing our eggs and coffee, when there was a roar of aircraft engines taking off nearby. She checked her watch. 'That'll be Johnny Maxwell,' she said. 'He's Flight Leader B group. Largefield is on the 0100 flight tonight.'

The thunder of four engines was joined by those of a second, third and fourth plane hauling themselves into the air.

'Airlift,' she said. 'Berlin, Tempelhof. They do a week of nights, a week of days. Lucky for you they're on nights or all the rooms would be taken. Not that there's much sleep to be had anyway when the boys are here.'

I could see that she was intensely proud of this effort being made by the RAF and the US Air Force to keep Berlin alive.

'The whole airfield system in this part of Kent is signed up to it,' she said. 'Some operated by the Americans and some by ourselves. Then there are a good half-dozen Yankee bases in East Anglia. We're providing coal. The Americans are flying rations and oil across the Atlantic to load it here for Berlin. It's an astonishing effort. A plane lands at Tempelhof, taxis off runway, is unloaded by German handlers and has taken off again before you can say knife.'

'You know a lot about it,' I said.

'Heard it from the pilots living here since the lift began. They're a jolly fine lot. The best.' There were tears streaming down her cheeks by now. 'Here, join me in a glass of wine?' she said. She jumped up and poured three glasses without listening to our answer.

Larry and I exchanged glances. She walked up and down the room, pushing tears away with the back of her hand. 'It's no good,' she said. 'Can't keep it to myself . . .'

She turned her back on us. 'One of the planes went down at Tempelhof last week. Perhaps you saw it in the papers?'

She didn't wait for an answer. 'He was the pilot. My . . . my lover, I suppose I shall have to call him, since he was already married and had two children.' She drank, a large gulp, and took a deep breath before turning to face us.

'I shouldn't have allowed it to happen. But no sense denying it now. Things like this happen in war. No excuse perhaps, but it's painful when you can't go out to bring him back. When you can only go to the funeral as the manageress of the little hotel near the airfield where he stayed.'

'We could drink to him,' Larry said. We lifted our glasses.

'That's nice of you,' she said, and burst into tears.

Small adventures like this one peppered our time in France. Most, not all, were with women. We met a man in the Loire who could not stop singing the praises of Balzac and Rabelais and descanting on the delights of Loire wines. When we left him near Tours he gave us a bottle of Vouvray and said: 'France is the most beautiful country in the world. It was necessary to pay a price to History for such good fortune.'

I fell for it. 'What was the price?'

His face set. 'The price, young man, was to have been placed by God between the two most predatory Anglo-Saxon nations on earth – the Germans and the English.'

Larry, who considered himself Irish when English matters arose, smiled broadly. There was nothing I could say. He was our host, this man who had just driven us fifty miles and given us a bottle of wine. A good man at heart, I think. In the backwash of a great war his view was perhaps understandable, but in the next half-century it was to be a view that was only half-adjusted, and perhaps rather surprisingly that half in favour of the German enemy (who I admit has behaved impeccably since the war) rather than the British ally.

We were given a lift by an Algerian doctor somewhere outside Poitiers, a woman of about thirty-five, very tall and darkly beautiful with a mixture of French, Greek, Jewish and Arab blood. She was on holiday for ten days. In Poitiers she bought us lunch and talked about the Arab advance into France and the medieval epic poem, the *Chanson de Roland*, about the Occitan language that had preceded French in the whole of this area of France; and about the English victory here at Poitiers in the Hundred Years War. She was formidably well read and when she left the table for a few moments I remember the movement of her very pale flowing khaki dress as she walked. We drove through the afternoon towards the Dordogne river and stopped at Limeuil, at a café under a network of vines. Below was the confluence of the clear waters of the Vézère and the silt-bearing Dordogne, linked by a double stone bridge. She took a few moments to feed her dark hair through a ring of bright blue and red beads and spread it out across her shoulders.

'I have a proposal,' our new friend said.

Larry and I sat staring at one another, stunned into sobriety. When I changed the direction of my glance I could look down at the tall and elegant Frenchwoman as she reached the middle of the bridge and stopped to peer down at the drift of sparkling Vézère water into the heavy Dordogne flow.

'Well?' Larry said. 'Jesus Christ.' He looked back at me. 'You think she's serious?'

I nodded. 'She's serious.' We sat looking at each other.

'It's the end of the holiday if we do it,' Larry said.

'She made herself clear enough.'

Neither of us had come across anything like it. A very suave, beautiful woman more than fifteen years older than us had laid out her proposal quite calmly and bluntly: she had five days more before she had to start back for Marseille to catch the boat to Algiers. She would like to spend that time, day and night, with one of us.

But only one of us. It didn't matter which.

I don't need to describe the plus side of the proposal. The idea of being paid for in a French hotel for five days to make love to this spectacularly beautiful woman . . . Well! It was the stuff of fantasy. Yet there was also something about the proposal that I'm not sure Larry and I ever articulated but was there all the same. I think we both realised that if we went ahead, or rather one of us went ahead, it would have left us permanently divided. The end of our friendship as we had known it.

She was waiting for one of us to go down to the bridge. After a few minutes longer she ceased staring down at the strange confluence of the rivers and turned to rest both elbows on the stone balustrade. She arched her back, looking up at us now. Men didn't turn down such offers from beautiful women. I felt it was ungracious and, I don't know why, tremendously sad. I didn't know where to look.

She waited for a few moments more, her large, dark eyes fixed on us. Then she pushed herself off the balustrade, turned a shoulder to us and walked with long strides towards her car.

We arrived back in Paris having discovered that, despite our early successes, hitch-hiking in France was not as it was in Britain. Many days were spent on the roadside and we would camp in the same spot we had slept the night before. Those who gave us a lift talked a great deal of bandits, people who get into your car when you stop and hit you over the head. Russians who had fought for the German Army in France and had escaped rounding up by the allied armies were most often accused. Gaullists tended to blame former members of the Communist Resistance. I suppose there might have been some shreds of truth in these stories and recent French history had certainly shown France to be a more lawless country than Britain, but nobody recounting these tales had ever experienced roadside banditry themselves, nobody had so much as met a Russian.

For us it simply meant we never managed to get down to the Mediterranean. Money was short – we were forced to turn back to Paris in plenty of time. We arrived back on the evening of the Fourteenth of July having 'guided' a diminutive, septuagenarian Bordelais in an overloaded and totally ramshackle lorry round the *boulevard extérieur*. As every British visitor to Paris knew, even then, that what was to become the *périphérique* is both a ring-road and a twenty-four-hour race track where the French take historic revenge on the nerves of all foreigners. We found Parisian drivers none too fussy about our tiny Bordelais either, especially when he insisted on stopping in the middle of the road as traffic raced by on either side, to shout for directions to a motorcycle cop. The policeman couldn't understand the Bordeaux accent; our driver couldn't understand the Paris accent. Larry and I hung off the back of the truck, shouting at the motorcyclist a re-phrasal of the question, and after a hundred sets of screeching tyres, drivers hooting like madmen, vehicles criss-crossing in front of us as the Bordelais began a U-turn in the middle of the most dangerous road in Europe, we got our driver moving straight ahead, though still insisting it was the wrong direction.

We discovered as he dropped us off with the present of a bottle of still-fermenting wine that our Bordelais had had no idea that the *boulevard extérieur* was a ring-road. Indeed he'd never been on a ring-road in his life. When the motorcycle cop had pointed backwards as the direction we should be heading, our driver had seen a U-turn as natural enough.

The Rue St Severin is just off the famous Boulevard St Michel, church on one side, Hotel St Severin on the other. The hotel is today a rather fine and (I emphasise for legal reasons) perfectly respectable establishment. Then it was rather different. We took an inexpensive room with a bed and sofa and squabbled in a friendly manner about who would have the bed that night. We took a shower and went downstairs to see what would be going on in Paris on the Fourteenth of July.

'*Mais les événements*,' the broad-beamed madame behind the desk said, her eyes sliding towards the top of her head as her memory glided back to *événements* of her youth.

In each district, she told us, the *pompiers*, the firefighters, would hold a dance, a Bal des Pompiers. There was to be a parade, fireworks, a great celebration . . . Her descriptions were vividly provocative. We said we would be investigating one or two *bals*.

'Then what time will you be back tonight, Messieurs?'

'Late,' we said.

'How late?'

'Is there a time the hotel shuts?'

'Not on the Fourteenth of July.'

We thought at first we had not understood.

'The purpose of my question was to see if I might perhaps offer you a little reduction on your tariff – if you can guarantee not to be back before midnight.'

'Not to be back *before* midnight? You mean, after?'

'I mean before, Monsieur.'

'For that there's a reduction?'

'Of one hundred francs. And clean sheets guaranteed.'

It took more than a moment for it to sink in.

'I think they want to use the room,' Larry said in English.

'I think they want to use *the bed*. For purposes other than sleeping. For the local girls to bring their clients.'

'Thus the clean sheets,' he added.

We stood for a moment.

'Well, what do you think?'

'Disgusting,' I said. 'But as it happens we're not made of money.'

'We shall be living on the profits of prostitution,' Larry mused. 'The bed still warm, a trace of cheap perfume lingering in the room . . .'

'True enough,' I said.

It was decided. I turned to the woman. '*D'accord*, Madame. Midnight at the earliest.'

She nodded enthusiastically. 'And the afternoons,' she said. 'Is there an arrangement to be made there also?'

'Undoubtedly.'

'A further one hundred franc reduction might be possible. Will you be seeing the monuments of Paris between, *disons*, two o'clock and six?'

'We certainly shall, Madame,' we said without hesitation. 'Wouldn't miss the monuments.'

'Thus a total of two hundred francs reduction.'

'And clean sheets each day,' Larry added.

She inclined her head. 'Of course, Messieurs,' she said. 'Clean sheets. That goes without saying in a hotel of this quality.'

TWENTY SIX

Odds On?

The Labour government was debating a massive increase in the defence budget to counter growing Soviet hostility. National Service was on every young man's mind. There was the prospect of even more austerity, more rationing, fewer goods in the shops, even prescription charges, it was rumoured, for the new National Health Service. There were those, of course, who opposed the whole idea of serious defence. They contended that defence budgets were rising in the West solely to satisfy the demands of the United States armaments industry.

Pacifism was strong under the leadership of Bertrand Russell who had refurbished the pacifist views he had abandoned in the Second World War and was by now, very persuasively, back on the stump. I had some experience of Bertrand Russell's pacifism at first hand when, a few years later in a crowded train, I stepped on his tiny foot with my large Army boot. He seemed to see it as a premeditated attack, a pre-emptive strike to use the atomic terminology of the day. He was, literally, hopping with rage – and, possibly, pain. The greatest philosopher of our age certainly did not reason with me.

NATO was coming into being while, in some sections of the

electorate, anti-Americanism was growing stronger. When I look back I see the campaign in Britain to undermine National Service had only a marginal connection to pacifism. Monsieur Linquier would have recognised, in many cases, the same motivation as among the 1940 agitators in France. The themes used by the Communist Party were, in fact, barely polished up. This time National Servicemen were being conscripted to fight for increased profits for British, and particularly American, capitalism. Scorn for the naïvety of anybody who believed differently was a powerful weapon when employed against young people. Even at school there was quite a lot of sneering. 'Waste of time.' 'Just playing soldiers,' was the confident assessment of those opposed. But it was only four years since the war had ended and for many of us against whom these comments were directed there was a strong sense of continuity with the military service of all those who had joined up since 1939. Nazi Germany was dead but Kravchenko and those who followed him in further documenting Soviet barbarities had stripped Stalin, for those prepared to listen, of any last shreds of anti-Nazi credibility.

For myself, I could now see no reason to think of Stalin as any less a fascist than Adolf Hitler. I was one of those, not alone, but not numerous among the young, who insisted that you didn't have to be a supporter of Senator McCarthy in order to fear Stalinism. But of course moral relativism, that brilliant tactic of the extreme Left, preached the opposite. If you opposed Stalin, you must, *relatively*, support McCarthy. This relativism was the most successful and dangerous dialectical element of the times we lived in.

Most of our arguments with friends were good-natured but it's undeniable that the differences ran deep. For many people the division created then has remained throughout their lives.

From time to time we had a visit from friends home on leave. If they were officers they were mostly second lieutenants in the Service or Ordnance Corps. I remember talking to Fred Alsop about what he did and receiving the strong impression that it was mostly administration in a smart uniform. This wasn't at all what I wanted to spend two years of my life doing.

I was going out with a girl named Marianne at the time. She prided herself on being 'perky'. 'So what do you want to spend two years doing?' she asked.

'Not sitting at a desk.'

'It's not so bad. I don't even get a desk to sit at.' She was a saleswoman at Harrods.

'But listen, I have a chance to do something new. Something I probably won't be able to do again in my life.'

'You're just a big I-am,' she said. 'You want to be different.'

'Why not?'

'You got to do it, so do it. Two years playing soldiers. Why not just do it, no questions?'

In those years many young men found they deeply resented girls for this 'just do it' attitude. There were many young women who felt quite differently. But there were plenty of naïve girls too who viewed two years as worth no more than a shrug of the shoulders. They of course were not the ones who were going to have to 'just do it'.

That month the results of our A-levels (or Higher School Certificate as it was then called) came through. We were only the third year to take them since the war and were all pleased enough with ourselves, although the lack of straight As would have bitterly disappointed any reasonably ambitious sixth form today. I was given an A in spoken French, three Bs and a C. Ted Simon, I recall, got an A in Chemistry, the only full subject A that year.

I had talked with my father about going to university. He was as keen for me to go as I was myself. A-levels were not so important a consideration in university entrance then as they are now. London University could be applied for straight away and entrance was granted or refused on the basis of a rigorous series of interviews. Oxford and Cambridge required further examinations which would mean staying on another few months at school because their entrance examinations took place on either side of Christmas.

I didn't even consider London University, impressive institution as I now know it to be. I suppose it was some reflection of our World's End background that for my father and me university meant either Oxford or Cambridge. When I was young I doubt if I knew that London University existed, and even Oxford and Cambridge meant no more to me than the Boat Race. Suddenly they had become much more.

It also meant getting the backing of my school, and in particular of the headmaster. My History master, Leslie Berkeley, was enthusiastic but he infused the task ahead with a sense of his own modesty and caution. A man who constantly reminded his pupils that he had received no more than a third-class degree from Keble, Oxford, was overawed on my behalf by the thought of the competition. 'You will,' he said, 'be put up against the very cream of Eton and Winchester. The quality of teaching at the best public schools is very high indeed. It's my duty to warn you of that.'

He was totally well-meaning and in many ways was an excellent teacher but he did not inspire great confidence. Nor did he by his further, and alarming, warning that he did not feel qualified to coach me. He would read my essays, but I would have to understand that his comments were likely to be too superficial to help me very much. Since History was the subject in which I was hoping to gain entrance, this was, Fatty the Yid would have said, a bit of a poser. In fact when I next saw Fatty at Stamford Bridge and told him what I was hoping to do, he was delighted. 'Learning History at Cambridge, eh? Become one of the nobs? Bowler hat and umbrella? "*Strollin' down the Bois de Boulogne with an independent air* . . ." Yeah, I like it.'

Darkie Evans was less taken by the idea. 'History? Don't they teach you Latin there at Cambridge?' he asked suspiciously.

'It's part of the entrance exam, Darkie. You have to do Latin to get in.'

He brightened up immediately. 'That's the place to go then. You go there, Dee.'

'It's not easy to get in, Darkie.'

'Nah. Don't you believe it. You're odds on,' he said, and whipped in a quick hook that barely stopped short of my ribs.

Guy Boas came through reluctantly. I don't think it was personal, although it's true we'd never got on well. Standing in his room, I watched him as he stood behind his desk, one hand in the pocket of his pinstripe trousers, the other fiddling with his watch chain. His head was turned towards the window, his whitening Hitler moustache glittering tobacco-gold in the sunlight. 'Do you have any idea of the standard of entry Oxford and Cambridge demand?' This was the bully in him coming to the fore – of course he already knew I didn't.

'I imagine it's very high, sir.'

He made his characteristic throwaway movement with the right hand. 'You don't just walk in, you know,' he said irritably. I knew he felt I had 'just walked in' to too many things already. 'You must know that the school can't afford a bad failure.'

I was furious. 'Then I'll have to do my best not to fail, sir.'

He glared at me and turned back to the window. 'History,' he said, pulling out a bandanna-like handkerchief and flicking it under his nose. 'I'll think about it.'

I think he considered anyone reading English should be given preference over all other applicants. For a week he said neither no nor yes. Leslie Berkeley pressed him in his diffident manner. Guy Boas repeated that he was concerned about the school's reputation. 'On this school's reputation dozens of other boys' futures will depend,' he said, not unreasonably. He repeated his argument: Sloane should not be allowed to fall by the wayside with the first candidate it had sent up for Cambridge entrance since the war. (In fact, I was to be the second.) Berkeley loyally pressed him some more. A verdict was finally promised.

Together Leslie Berkeley and I went to the headmaster's study. Berkeley made a cautious but effective case for my taking the Cambridge entrance but Guy Boas had already decided. He cut Berkeley short then responded as he did so much in that year, with a grumbled, 'Very well, then. If you must.'

There was one final decision. Oxford or Cambridge? As very young children in the World's End we'd always pledged ourselves to Oxford or Cambridge and worn their colours on Boat Race Day. My choice as a five year old had been Cambridge. At home I talked to Kit about it. 'Go for Cambridge,' he said. 'You've always been Cambridge.' So on the basis of an ex-boxer's endorsement, a five year old's boat-race decision and some pale blue ribbons tied to an orange-box cart, I chose Cambridge.

TWENTY SEVEN
Marie

By now I'd met Larry's father often enough not to be in awe of him. Bill Naughton, soon to be author of the long-running West End success *Spring and Port Wine,* and the novel *Alfie* on which the Michael Caine and more recent Jude Law films were based, was a little over forty at this time, not tall, already balding, but with a smile that really would affect everybody in the room. Born in County Mayo, he was taken to Lancashire as a child and lived in Bolton for the first thirty years of his life. Today Bolton Public Library holds his voluminous notes, work unfinished and the full, unpublished version of the journal he wrote for much of his life.

Though he had left Ireland as a child, Bill Naughton always saw himself (as indeed did Larry with as much relish but perhaps rather less justification) as Irish. Though his accent was the softest Lancashire and he had barely lived in Ireland, he was markedly Irish in so many ways and particularly in his literary interests. He maintained a network of contacts with Irish writers and it seemed usual rather than exceptional for me to find he had a writer over from Dublin staying with him for a few days. In those early times before *Alfie* or any of the stage plays were written, Larry's father was already recognised as a writer with a future. Frank O'Connor visited; Samuel

Beckett was a correspondent and enthusiast for Bill's work. Other writers and painters were frequent visitors.

He was by now writing full time and was best known for his short memoir, *A Roof Over Your Head*, and a novel, *Raef Granite*. Each book was more a *succès d'estime* than the sort of bestseller which might lift a writer into wealth. But he did, as he recounted it, really think things were looking up when to his surprise one day he received a phone call from the Soviet Writers' Union official (later author of *The Thaw*) Ilya Ehrenburg, inviting him to the Soviet Embassy to celebrate the publication of *Raef Granite* in Russia. At the embassy there was smoked sturgeon, vodka and caviar and much talk of vast printings, but when Bill asked about royalties Ehrenburg fell silent. Pressed further, he pointed out that he thought Bill would be proud to be contributing to the Soviet people's understanding of the tyranny of capitalism. But that isn't even what the book's about, Bill told him. And, he pointed out, his need for royalties at least equalled his fervour for educating Soviet people. As a celebration it didn't go well. Ehrenburg, who was himself doing very well in the Soviet bear-pit at that time, made it clear that there would be no royalties forthcoming. Bill Naughton, who like almost all other writers, would sooner be published than not at all, conceded with as much grace as he could muster.

At this time Bill, who was divorced, lived with Larry in a small flat in Pimlico. Larry's sister Marie stayed there during university vacations from Oxford, although I had not yet met her. Most evenings I was there Bill or Larry would cook some variant of spaghetti and the current visitor or house guest, a painter or writer over from Dublin, would provide a couple bottles of Spanish Burgundy. The talk, of books, plays and paintings, was pretty consistently above my head. It took me some time to realise that this was, at least in part, because the essence of the talk was Irish-anecdotal. And that I, at just eighteen, had nothing like the breadth of experience from which to draw or embroider anecdote. Nor, frankly, the talent to do it.

*

With frightening speed, anti-Americanism was coming into vogue on the Left. Republican Senator McCarthy was beginning to create a stir among liberals in America and Western Europe with his almost entirely unfounded accusations of widespread government subversion under FDR and Truman.

I saw myself as a supporter of the Labour Party, an enthusiast, as I still am, for its introduction of the National Health Service. But the automatic anti-American reaction of so many of my friends began to acquire a comforting completeness which couldn't be challenged. If the problem were Britain's inability to increase wages or the meat ration, the answer was American manoeuvring, American economic bullying or American insistence that we should increase the size of our armed forces. On the farther bornes of the Labour Left Senator McCarthy was seen as a more threatening figure than Stalin. Kravchenko, for example, was too likely to be dismissed as a simple CIA set-up: 'You don't believe the Yanks can't fix anything in France? Offer a few more million dollars. Or unload a few thousand tons of surplus wheat. Easy.'

I didn't have the answers to this blanket anti-Americanism. I only knew that I would shortly be going into the army for two whole years of my life. I had come to believe that it was an important thing to do, that there was a West European frontier to be defended by NATO against the Soviet Union. I believed that those who saw Stalin and his Praesidium as somehow irrelevant rather than menacing were not taking Stalinism seriously enough. The truth is I believed that opposing Stalinism was more important than writing books. But at eighteen I didn't have the courage to say that to Bill Naughton's friends in the flat at Pimlico, or to those like the painters, desperate to imitate Chagall's fabulism, that I used to meet occasionally in the cafés of King's Road. I argued against the actions of the USSR at school, of course, but often felt uncomfortable, even among friends, as a Labour Party supporter endorsing American actions.

Of course I recognised the justification for their distrust of America. As 1950 progressed McCarthy was becoming responsible for the ruin of hundreds, later even thousands, of lives. America seemed to be on the point of succumbing to anti-Communist hysteria. It took too long for McCarthy to be censured by the Senate for breach of constitutional privilege. Years later, when I was writing for television in Toronto and New York I would work with a number of black-listed writers, people like Ian Hunter who had been cut off from all Hollywood work for refusing to testify that his friend, Paul Jarrico, was a Communist. It so happened that Paul, with whom I became particularly friendly, *was* a member of the Party but Ian Hunter saw that as an irrelevance in the issue before him. Ring Lardner Junior and *The Producers* star, Zero Mostel, whom I later met with Ian in New York, were among others in this tight-knit group of friends. Some survived and even prospered later. Some, like Ian Hunter, suffered greatly for their loyalty.

So in 1949 I recognised the illiberalism of aspects of American political life – but I also believed that, despite the brutality and the menace to the personal freedom of thousands that McCarthy represented, the Soviet record left no case for moral relativism. I believed, in fact, that America was strong enough to recover from McCarthyism; I had no such optimism about the USSR while Stalin was alive.

As ever when I thought about these things in my later teenage years, the approach of National Service was the spur. As it became increasingly obvious that some sort of conflict, hopefully limited and non-nuclear, with the Soviet Union was possible, I wanted to be clear what I believed in.

I knew Larry's sister had come back from Oxford for the vacation. Larry had told me that she would be staying at the flat. He wasn't looking too pleased about it as he told me so I assumed, as I had before, that he was trying to avoid my meeting her.

I rang the bell to the flat in St George's Square one late summer afternoon and a girl of about nineteen opened the door. 'Hi,' she said. 'I'm Marie, Larry's sister. I know who you are. I can see straight away.' Whether that was the way it was intended, I took it as the most extravagant compliment.

It's easy to say I was bowled over. So perhaps I'll say it. She was not tall, but well shaped without being dramatically so. She wore a black pleated skirt and black pumps, a dark blue sweater and white shirt. But it was her features which were unforgettable. She had her father's extraordinary illuminating smile and hooded blue eyes under dark blonde-chestnut hair. You felt you were spot-lit by her glance. I did.

'Before we go in . . .' She put her hand on my arm. We were standing together in the dark hallway of the house. Their flat was entered through the door off the hall, into what would have once been the main reception room. 'I've something to tell you,' she said.

I watched her as she pursed her lips. 'Oxford,' she said. She grinned, very even, white teeth in the half dark. Then quickly grimaced. 'I've been sent down.'

'God, I'm sorry.' And after a moment. 'How's your Dad taking it?'

The hooded eyes almost closed. 'Furious,' she whispered.

'Larry said nothing about it.'

'He wouldn't. He's mortified.'

Mortified. That was Oxford for you.

'Should I push off?'

She grabbed my hand. 'No! Please. Dad likes you. And you're Larry's buddy. They won't keep up the black faces while you're here. I need your help.'

She led me in.

We had a great evening. A young Austrian woman, Erne, a friend of Bill's, came in a little later. She had brought schnitzel and cheese from Soho. The lights were turned low. A candle or two was lit. We had *terrine de canard*, schnitzel and Camembert. Red Spanish Burgundy, and a liqueur of mixed Drambuie, Avocaat, and Scotch and Irish whiskies which Dublin Customs had confiscated, mixed in a vat and then sold off at auction (so I was told). We were all singing drunk by nine o'clock.

I was sitting on the sofa with Marie. Under cover of candlelight and a gingham cushion, she took my hand as we sang 'Danny Boy'.

My father's medical emergency was a shock but no surprise. At the age of seventeen he had narrowly escaped death from peritonitis. He had been rushed to St Stephen's (as it then was) and operated on. The operation had saved his life but the suturing of the wound had been badly bungled, knotting various layers of muscle in his groin. He had always known that these would at some time have to be separated. Despite this, he continued to do the stoking at Whitelands if the regular stoker was off for any reason. Now, nearly twenty-five years after the operation, the muscle had finally been torn, almost certainly by the last bout of stoking. The tear quickly became infected. Treatment was necessary right away.

We were not used to my father being ill. It was, for all sorts of reasons beyond the obvious one, an alarming prospect. It seemed likely that there was no serious danger if he were treated quickly enough, but he kept so many balls in the air, both at Whitelands House and in his bookmaking businesses, that to keep things going while he was confined to bed was going to be difficult.

My mother was worried on both counts, his health and the responsibility of maintaining the business. But she was supremely capable in a crisis. On the business side she advised all the runners and customers that the pay-in/pay-out was going to be delayed over the week my father was expected to be in hospital. This must have been the first known example of a World's End-based bookmaker accepting bets without taking the money on the spot. Normally credit betting was just not done.

My mother was also taking care of the phone bets. There would be no Mick Burns stand at Stamford Bridge that week, and Kit and I were going to handle my father's current problem at Whitelands – the absence with 'flu of the stoker. I suppose some head-porters would have sat back and said that if a new stoker hadn't been employed, the tenants of Whitelands would have to content themselves with cold baths while their maids boiled kettles for washing-up water. But that was not the way my father ran Whitelands House.

When we were younger Kit and I had helped with the process of raking out the furnaces and refilling them, but we had never carried out the whole process by ourselves. We knew, however, the size of the task. So it was with a good deal of trepidation that we let ourselves into the boiler room the day my father was taken to hospital. Of course we knew this vast underground area well. We had spent a large part of the Blitz sleeping down here and had come to hate the coke-dust-laden atmosphere, the low lights, the vast hillocks of coke and the temperature permanently approaching 100 degrees.

We imagine everything encountered in childhood looks smaller to the adult eye. But none of the stoking tools looked smaller to me on that day. There were still the same great iron pokers twelve foot long; the rakes of the same grotesque length and rendered more unwieldy by the great claw on the end; the shovels with elongated handles, their scoops twice the size of a normal shovel. The whole panoply of stoking instruments seemed to have been made for giants. It was of course designed to keep the stoker as far as possible away from the angry heat of the furnace when the iron door was opened.

Our task was to rake the red-hot crust of coke out of two of the huge furnaces and use it to light two clean furnaces. Then to take out the remaining white-hot 'canker' and let the two clean boilers cool down. Ideally this was done once a day but my father had decided that it was acceptable for us to tackle the clean-out every other day for the week or so Whitelands would be without a stoker. When Kit and I had finished, the easier part of the stoker's job, keeping the furnaces topped up, would be done by the porters, none of whom was fit enough to have handled the clean-out.

Stripped to the waist, we approached the first boiler. Kit lifted the handle with a hook poker and swung open the iron door three foot wide by two high. Flame leapt from the mouth of the monster; the hot air hit our bare chests like boiling water. Kit swung the door closed with a clang. 'God Almighty,' he said.

We realised now why stokers always wore those filthy singlets when they worked. There were two torn undershirts my father kept in a locker in the stoker's room. We put them on, thick with sweat and coke dust as they were, and went back to face boiler number one.

The next hours came close to a medieval descent into hell. My father, working alone, could handle the change-over of two boilers in well under two hours. Two hours into our shift and Kit and I had a huge pile of white-hot cinder in front of number one and number three had gone out. We had thrown in too much coke and extinguished the glowing base that should have given us a merrily burning boiler. This mix of dead cinder and fresh coke had to be raked out before we could start again.

I don't know what I looked like but Kit looked as he had the night we were bombed in Guinness Trust. Coke dust covered his face and hair. His eyes seemed to stare like a maniac's. I suppose I looked the same. We were weak with effort and even weaker with laughter.

We knew the porters upstairs would be checking the time and having a good laugh at the idea of the two of us struggling away in the depths, but we consoled ourselves with the thought that they were too old and decrepit to have taken on the job themselves. Welsh Wally and Long Tom wouldn't have lasted fifteen minutes down here. Exhausted, with blackened faces and coke dust crunching between our teeth, we made sure we avoided the porters when we eventually crept stealthily up from the boiler room a record five hours later.

My father was still a young man, in his late thirties. After the acute danger of the few hours before he was operated on, his recovery was more or less assured. Within a week he was in bed at home, calculating winnings and entering them in the ledger on his lap. Another week and he was walking about only a little less energetically than usual. My mother smiled her pleasure. Kit and I were almost as pleased to hear from Whitelands that the stoker had recovered from his 'flu.

I was seeing Marie regularly by then. She had a part-time job with a Jewish refugee friend of her father's (or perhaps of Erne's) who was now running an Austrian travel business on the corner of Shaftesbury Avenue and Macclesfield Street. There was not much holiday travel about in those days so perhaps the bulk of his trade came from Jewish Austrians who had fled to London before the war and were now going back to trace any family who had survived. The job gave Marie a welcome salary and a chance to work up her German.

De Hems is a pub a few doors down Macclesfield Street where Larry and I used to go to meet Marie after work. Her smile and bubbling intelligence gave her a ready audience from the moment she entered the saloon bar. Even the edgy, almost violent brand of older homosexual who used to frequent the place with their 'chickens' seemed captivated by Marie.

But her future was uncertain. I seem to remember that there was some possibility that her college, Lady Margaret Hall, would relent and allow her to return to Oxford but nothing came of it. To her father, I believe her being sent down was an acute disappointment. Winning a place at Oxford or Cambridge was seen as an extraordinary achievement in working-class families like ours. It was a ticket into another life. I never knew the details of his reaction but I think her father felt that Marie had thoughtlessly torn up the ticket and thrown it away.

A gifted and immensely likeable man, there was, I believe,

probably far below the surface, some of that Catholic Irish puritanism in Bill. Marie's debacle at Oxford was probably enough to bring it to the surface. He was, and I must say again that this is only my impression because he never discussed it with me, determined Marie should not leave university for a London life spent flitting from party to bright party given by her Oxford friends.

But he had not yet made up his mind what should be done about it.

Nothing had really happened between Marie and myself since that first night of holding hands under the cushion and singing 'Danny Boy'. I remember being very unsure about Larry's reaction to the possibility. Certainly I felt in him some resistance to anything developing between myself and his sister. I seldom, for example, seemed to get the opportunity to spend any time alone with her. Perhaps he was just unaware that I wanted to be. I wasn't sure.

Nevertheless, Marie and I were coming closer together. I suppose on my side I was feeling less overwhelmed by the fact that she had actually been to Oxford whereas I was just taking the first steps towards Cambridge. But we enjoyed the same sense of humour, and when she mentioned them I rapidly read poets I had only heard of before, Auden, Spender, Louis MacNeice. I even read the sad and crudely propagandistic Mayakovsky because I'd heard him being praised by a visitor of Bill Naughton's. Most enjoyably I dipped deeply into Joyce since no one would have been able to stay the course of an evening at the Naughton flat without some familiarity with *Ulysses*.

Marie and I were by now cautiously becoming more open with each other about wanting to spend some time alone together. Mostly left unexpressed, it was clear to both of us all the same. The fact was that, intentionally or not, Larry was always there. We went out together as a threesome, enjoyed being all three together – but I still felt the need, and I was becoming sure she did too, for us to spend time alone. I felt snared: I couldn't tell Larry what Marie and I wanted before I'd talked to Marie – but then I had no opportunity to talk to her. And Larry was a good organiser, full of suggestions, quick to propose ways of spending the evening. I could readily sympathise. It's an awkward and disagreeable moment when your best school friend and much-loved sister start coming together.

Even worse was an impending sense of disaster that I had. I'm not normally subject to these feelings from *outre monde*, which made my forebodings all the more alarming. Perhaps it had something to do with the way Larry and his father both seemed *not* to recognise that Marie and I were drawing together. Only Erne, Bill Naughton's wife-to-be, seemed to be aware of what was going on. I called round one day when Larry was taking a shower. Marie, she told me, was at the corner shop buying vegetables for soup. 'The soup can wait,' she said with a quiet smile. 'Go and meet her.'

I did, but a busy greengrocery in Pimlico on Saturday was not the place to tell Marie what I was feeling about her. I had just discovered seventeenth-century love lyrics and we talked about Sir John Suckling as we walked back to St George's Square. She knew of him but had never read his poetry. 'I'll get you a copy,' I said.

'And will you write something in it?'

'If you want.'

'What will you write?'

I thought of one of his poems. 'How about:

> *"Out upon it, I have lov'd*
> *Three whole days together*
> *And am like to love three more –*
> *If it prove fair weather."'*

She laughed. 'Not entirely reassuring to a girl.'

'A pretty clumsy choice. But I have this feeling,' I said, taking my courage in both hands, 'that we don't have months. We have to take it a few days, or maybe just a few weeks, at a time.'

She looked at me, her smile fading. 'Perhaps you're right,' she said. We had reached her door.

'Let's walk on a bit,' I said. 'We can talk.'

'Uh – no.' She shook her head, lifting the string bag of carrots and parsnips. 'Erne's waiting for the vegetables to make the soup.'

Erne had said the vegetables could wait but she fumbled her key in the lock all the same.

One day we went to the Tate Gallery. With Larry.

'We're not going to all stand gawking at the same picture, are we?' Marie said. She was slightly behind Larry and raised her eyebrows at me.

'No,' I said. 'Let's split up and meet downstairs in the entrance hall.'

Marie was already moving away.

'See you downstairs in about fifteen minutes,' I said.

Marie and I met up almost straight away on the floor above. There were no more than half a dozen people in the gallery. I suppose it was the chance we'd been waiting for. We came together in the middle of this huge ornate room among flaming Turners and kissed.

'That . . . was wonderful,' she said. 'Do it again.'

A few people turned and smiled indulgently.

We met Larry downstairs a few minutes later. We didn't say a word about the exhibition. The truth was I couldn't stop looking at Marie.

I'm sure Larry knew the dam had broken. Within no time, I think Marie's father knew too.

TWENTY EIGHT

A World of Difference

Of course it was a very different world then. Boy and girl didn't announce to their parents, as they drew breath from their first kiss, that they would from now on be sleeping together among the teddy bears and Beatrix Potter pictures of the girl's bedroom. Fear of pregnancy was acute for parents and young lovers alike. So finding time to be alone together absorbed us both. We spent an hour here, an hour or two there. Once we managed the darkness of a film together (*Annie Get your Gun*), and we met a couple of times by ourselves in a corner seat in De Hems. It was very little.

I was due back at school the following week. Marie was still working at the travel agency. It seemed to me her father was less his smiling self than usual but he still treated me with great friendliness. As indeed did Larry. It was difficult nevertheless not to feel that I had committed some serious *res non grata* as far as two-thirds of the Naughton family was concerned. And there was something else too. My feeling of vague foreboding had metamorphosed into a growing certainty that Marie had not told me something which affected us both.

When I look back I find it extraordinary how difficult it was to find the time to talk to her about it. Once or twice I asked her directly if she was holding something back but she shook her head in reply. I spent a lot of time thinking about that shake of the head. I was sure there was something.

There was a moment when Bill's friend Erne was going back to Austria. Bill and Larry left with her to carry her bags to the bus stop.

I waited for the front door to bang and watched them go down the street to the stop. I turned to face Marie. She came to put her arms round me. I held her away. 'Tell me,' I said.

'Tell you what?'

I could see from the window that a bus had already pulled up at the stop. Bill and Erne had got on. He would be taking her to Victoria station. Larry would be back in minutes.

'I don't know,' I said to Marie. I put my hands round her waist. 'But there's something, isn't there? Do you want me to stop coming round?'

'No.' She pulled away, but she said it with so much vehemence I couldn't doubt it.

'OK. So what is it? There is something, isn't there?'

She looked at me. 'Don't ask,' she said. 'Not yet.'

I took my Army medical examination in Hammersmith and was duly passed fit. I remember little of the detail except the voice of a young man in the next cubicle being interviewed. If the Army doctor was asking about shortage of breath, he suffered from it. Eyesight was an acute problem and, no, he couldn't read any of the letters on the card. Barely see the card, matter of fact. Sense of balance? Appalling, daren't get on a bike without risking a fall at the first bend.

In my cubicle the doctor examining me smiled. 'Infantry,' he muttered to himself. 'That's where he'll end up.'

I saw the man who was being examined as we came out of our cubicle. He was big, strong-looking . . . 'Hear that? A push-over. The

Doc swallowed it whole,' he whispered. 'Just watch, it's a Grade Four for me. Exempt service. I feel sorry for chaps like you.'

Afterwards I was interviewed by a selection officer. 'What do you want to do in the Army?' He was looking at my school record. 'Apply for officer training? Or languages? You've the qualifications to apply to do a Russian course at Cambridge.'

Two years learning Russian, three years reading History (if I was successful). I wondered if the delights of Cambridge would sustain me through a whole five years. 'No,' I said to the interviewing officer. 'I was thinking of the infantry.'

'Were you?' He lifted his eyebrows in surprise. *Cannon fodder*, he seemed to be saying. *If that's what you want . . .*

On one of those few occasions when Marie and I were alone we'd dreamed of going away somewhere together. It was desert island stuff. We had neither the money nor the time to do anything as exotic as hitch-hike to Paris and our preferred destination was very much more distant than that: the virtually (at the time) undiscovered paradise of Ibiza. We played with the idea, neither of us anxious to let it drop. It was something to share – but we both recognised a complete fantasy.

Then something happened, I no longer remember the background, obscured I suppose by the brightness of the foreground. Marie and I were to be able to spend a weekend together. We would have to be back late Sunday afternoon, but it was enough. Paris or Ibiza were reshaped as Brighton. Our shortage of money meant we'd be camping.

We spent an afternoon wandering round the Prince Regent's magnificently bizarre Pavilion, then took a bus. For that one night we stayed on the cliff-top at Rottingdean. Sex was out of the question. They were indeed strange days. A young man with serious feelings for a girl would never have produced a condom and announced that

that was the pregnancy question settled. Just wouldn't. I think the girl, even Marie who was a good deal more worldly wise than I was, would not have been at all happy about that. So, wrapped near-naked in a double sleeping bag, we made less than love until the dawn came.

It was a cold early-September morning. The sea was bucking white patternless waves and the wind came hard off it, scouring the cliff top. On our primus stove we brewed up a cup of breakfast tea and warmed our hands and drank it with the sleeping bag round our shoulders. Our eyes locked. It was the first time in my life I had consciously thought: *I am really in love with this girl.* It obviously showed. After a few moments Marie looked away and smiled a disconcerting, rueful sort of smile. The last hour we had spent together in the sleeping bag had carried a presage of this. 'I must tell you,' she said. 'It can't wait any longer.'

I blew on the tea. Since we'd last spoken about it I had thought of little else. Was she going to tell me that she was pregnant by some undergraduate at Oxford? In my worst moments I thought that was the secret she was nursing.

'You don't seem that interested,' she said.

'Of course I am. It's bad news, isn't it?'

'Yes.' She drank some tea. She was looking past me to the line of the cliff top. 'Dad wants me to go to Vienna to stay with a friend of Erne's. Apparently I can get a job with the Control Commission there.'

It was a body blow.

'Is it because of us? Is that why he's sending you away?'

She shrugged. 'Partly because I made such a mess of things at Oxford. He thinks I've thrown away the chance of a lifetime. He knows you've got the Army then Cambridge . . .'

'If I get in.'

'I think he doesn't want me to ruin your life as well as my own.' She spoke without bitterness.

'So it's all over almost before it began.'

'The Army . . .' She brightened with a falsity that was just too obvious. 'I suppose you could be posted to Vienna.'

'Or Malaya.'

We put our tea down and hugged each other.

'Better pack our things and hitch back to Brighton,' I said. 'Sunday trains.'

She nodded.

'When?' I asked her as I packed the rucksack.

I was crouching to do up the straps. She stood looking out at the sea. Then she turned back towards me. 'This week,' she said. 'The ticket's booked. Wednesday.'

TWENTY NINE

Pembroke College

My last months at Sloane were the autumn term at the end of which I was to take the entrance examination for Pembroke College, Cambridge. Leslie Berkeley had written for copies of past papers and I was able to get a measure of the questions at least. I never did get a measure of the standard the college expected from candidates' answers because Berkeley felt it his duty instead to remind me constantly of his own inadequacy and the fearful nature of the public school competition – the dreaded Eton, Winchester and Marlborough trio in particular.

My last months at Sloane were also a time of missing Marie badly, of counting the days until I would take the entrance examination and until I would see her again when she came back for Christmas. Meantime the dark blue airmail letters arriving regularly from Austria kept my spirits at a tolerable level. But Christmas was what I was really waiting for. By then the examination would be over – and Marie would be back in London.

The letter with the Pembroke College crest on the envelope laid out the format of the week-long examination. You arrived at the college on Monday evening and left late Friday afternoon. There was to be a three-hour essay on the first morning. The General Paper on politics, arts and public affairs took up the first afternoon. The following morning, Wednesday, was free, with the Language Paper in the afternoon: compulsory Latin with one other language, in my case French. Thursday there were the two crucial History papers, British and European. On Friday there were interviews in the morning and the Science Paper in the afternoon. You could sprawl, glassy-eyed, across a seat on the six-thirty train back to London if you hurried. It was a rigorous test of nerve and stamina.

It was already growing dark as I left Liverpool Street Station on the train for Cambridge. I carried my pigskin Gladstone which I had not learnt to love more than the first time I took it to France and, in my inside pocket, a still-unopened letter from Marie which had arrived that morning. In a compartment by myself, I opened it.

Now I remember nothing of what she said but for the first sentences: her father had decided he and Larry should go out to spend a few days with her in Vienna. Marie would not be coming back to London for Christmas.

What it really meant went much deeper. With my Army service coming up in a matter of weeks there was every chance we would not see each other for another two years. I wasn't a fool. I was a bookmaker's son. I knew how the odds stacked up. It was the end of the road.

Even so, on the train to Cambridge I had re-read the pages of the dark blue airmail letter with the close attention of a code-breaker. Was she acknowledging that it was over between us? Or was she somewhere suggesting we could overcome the seemingly insuperable problems? Of course, I knew in fact that I had no need to be a code-breaker. She was free to say in clear whatever she wanted to say. But she'd chosen not to.

I read Marie's letter yet again. And this time I did see something in it that I hadn't seen before, hadn't wanted to perhaps, something like an acceptance of her new life in Vienna. I thought back over her earlier letters and remembered the sense of turbulent unhappiness I'd received from them. Love is savage. The unhappier she was in Vienna, the happier I was in London. But, studying this letter, I saw there was no longer any solace to be derived from that direction. Today's letter made it clear she wanted to come back to London for Christmas. But, as I read between the lines, I thought I saw how her feelings had settled. I thought I saw that she now felt at home in Vienna.

Pembroke College is an ancient stone-fronted building with an arched doorway on to Trumpington Street. Left of the archway is a chapel licensed by the Pope in 1357, a few years after the college was founded by the widowed Countess of Pembroke. It is now deconsecrated and known as the Old Library.

I arrived on Monday evening for the week-long examination. At the porters' lodge was a list of the rooms candidates had been allocated. In the screens, the area outside the darkened dining hall, there was, I was told by a porter, a list of times and places for examinations and interviews for candidates in History. I went first to check the screens. I had an interview at 10.30 on the free morning, Wednesday, with Anthony Camps, the Senior Tutor. I nervously noted it down. There would be two further interviews with History supervisors on Friday evening at six o'clock, after which I would be free to leave.

Friday evening seemed half a century away. Lights attracted me. I walked forward through the screens and stood in a part Tudor, part seventeenth-century, ivy-covered court. I remembered from the handbook I had looked up in Hammersmith Library that the rooms on the first floor of J staircase had belonged to William Pitt. Gray, writer of the 'Elegy in a Country Churchyard', had also lived on the same staircase. That night, light from the ivy-fringed windows was filmed with droplets of mist. A few young men carrying valises walked through, stopping at each staircase to check the numbers of the rooms they had been allocated. One or two raised voices to greet another candidate. They actually knew someone else who was here putting themselves through this torture! The Eton, Winchester, Marlborough connection that Leslie Berkeley had warned me about, no doubt.

The court emptied. Behind me chandeliers suddenly came on. I turned. Gothic windows ran the length of a nave-like Hall. Above two lines of heavy oak tables running towards a raised High Table, the walls were hung with portraits of former masters and notables of the college. A medieval master here, Elizabethans like the poet Edmund Spenser and Lancelot Andrewes there, William Pitt, of course, and a dozen nineteenth-century figures. Places were being set at the long tables.

I was overwhelmed. Most of all horrified at the possibility of unknowingly making some appalling social blunder. My immediate problem was where I should eat that night. In hall? Never having been in a restaurant in my life, I just didn't want to add this to the barriers I would have to begin hurdling tomorrow. Today it seems an almost unrecognisable problem – but this was 1950. Instead I walked down to the pub on the millrace of the River Cam and bought a Scotch egg and a pint of beer.

I walked slowly back to college. But I was also thinking how badly I wanted to be part of this as I retreated to the rooms I had been allocated beside the Wren Chapel.

Old Court, the original extent of the college, was empty. I stopped under a yellow lamp and leaned against the stonework. I recovered my balance as I often have throughout my life by summoning up an image of my grandmother Eliza, in moth-eaten coat and Eliza Doolittle hat, this time dancing irreverently across the central lawn of Old Court vigorously singing her favourite soldier's song of the First World War:

Mademoiselle from Armenteers, parlez-voo,
Mademoiselle from Armenteers, parlez-voo,

Mademoiselle from Armenteers,
Gotter get out of this Vale of Tears,
Won't be back for a thousand years.
Inky pinky parlez-voo . . .

It almost worked.

The first examination next morning, the three-hour essay, was a disaster. The night before I had looked at the bookshelves in the rooms I was allocated with the idea that I should read something not too taxing, something light but distinctive enough to take my mind off the morrow. I had hit upon Damon Runyon.

I don't have to remind anybody that the two significant characteristics of Runyon's style are the first-person singular and his favourite present tense. 'I am taking my usual mid-morning stroll down Broadway when I spot Bulldog Bagshaw standing outside Mindy's in a black snap-brim fedora, and a faultless tuxedo with the trouser legs rolled to the mid-calf over bare, wet, very cold feet.' That sort of thing.

Thirty or forty pages of Damon Runyon is relaxing but can make a big impression on a susceptible young mind. It can even carry over its neuro-imprint until the next morning. Installed in the Examination Rooms I opened the paper in front of me. Six essay titles, none of which even remotely appealed. I chose one, 'Melodrama', and nevertheless set to work with a stylistic vigour Damon Runyon would have approved. Very much approved, I'm afraid, since it was a dead ringer for his own.

I wrote for the full three hours, fighting Damon Runyon all the way. In the last half an hour other young men (undoubtedly from Eton and Winchester) got up and strolled casually over to the invigilator's desk to deposit their papers. I was the last to leave, a wet rag, with the rhythms of Runyon still unexorcised.

Nothing that followed was so bad. I was comfortable with the

General Paper, more or less taking it in my stride, I thought. I had dinner in hall that night and, locked in common adversity, found I got on well enough with my neighbours from Marlborough and Winchester.

Wednesday morning at 10.30 was my first interview. I had been to the screens at least three times to check I'd got it right. It was a dark December morning as I skirted Ivy Court and entered the Tudor buildings I had first seen on Monday evening. With absolutely no idea what I would be asked, I climbed the winding timber staircase up to the Senior Tutor's rooms. He opened the door to my knock, a tall, thin-shouldered man with an enormous head that seemed to float above his shoulders. It might have been a balloon on a string. But his smile was genuinely welcoming. I introduced myself and with extreme courtesy he introduced himself to me (as if it were necessary) and gestured to a chair. On his desk I saw a pile of examination papers he had been marking.

It was a long beamed room with windows on either side. Oak furniture gleamed by the light of table lamps. For the next hour we talked, I about the Russian novels I was reading at the time. He prompted me by affecting to know little about Russian literature but declared his interest in it. Since he seemed interested in everything, I also talked about Auden and Isherwood, Spender and MacNeice. Pouring me a glass of sherry, he seemed to be quite happy to let me run on into the time I had spent in France. It was only when I took a covert glance at the clock I realised I had been there almost an hour. But he had given no sign that the interview was over so I ploughed on.

Finally he stood. It was clearly time for me to go. 'I have someone to see before lunch,' he said, walking me to the door. 'Very good of you to call. I really have enjoyed our talk. Now let me look at my list. I shall be seeing you, I see, at ten-thirty tonight, will I not? Awfully late, I'm afraid.'

The Turkish carpet could have swallowed me up. Rolled in it, I could have been dumped by Janissaries unsung into the Bosphorus. The terrible social gaffe I had feared had been committed. I had taken up half the Senior Tutor's morning rambling on about Kravchenko and hitch-hiking in France!

I missed lunch and went down to the Anchor on the river and bought myself two glasses of red wine. I felt deeply miserable and angry with myself. But who would have guessed I would be called for interview at 10.30 at night! Perhaps if I'd realised that he actually lived in those rooms, I might have studied the times of interview with more care. But I still imagined that all senior members of college lived in their own homes with wives and children. I didn't understand what a bachelor society Cambridge was.

The wine helped. As I looked down at the millrace my stomach settled slowly and I made my way back to the Examination Rooms for the Language Paper.

I took a long time to put the Senior Tutor sufficiently out of mind to tackle the paper. When I did I saw that, for the French, it presented a passage from de Gaulle to translate, which was not a problem, and a difficult piece of Tacitus which gave me trouble but not too much. Darkie Evans would have been proud of me I estimated as I handed in my papers. Unless, I thought ruefully, he heard the full story of the day. 'You put up a right ricket there, Dee,' he would have said. 'How d'you expect to become a doctor now?'

Yet, when I went back to the Senior Tutor's rooms at 10.30 that evening, he asked me no 'interview' questions at all and we sat there like old friends, comfortably talking about college history, with a glass of port and biscuits.

A strange place.

The Thursday morning History papers were crucial. British History enabled me to concentrate on my favourite period, the seventeenth century. I was quite pleased with my essay on Cromwell. I argued that the Protectorate had been necessary to resolve the pressing issues of sovereignty which Charles I had raised, and had made impossible a reversion to the claims of the earlier part of the century by any restored monarchy. A perfectly tenable point of view, I would have thought.

For the European History Paper I produced four dull, workaday answers, then on Friday morning tackled the Science Paper. Or failed to tackle it as I struggled to explain the workings of the jet engine and offer a definition of Nuclear Physics.

I had lunch in hall and watched the other candidates, laughing and relaxed. My neighbour said he'd seen me in the History Examination Room and suggested a glass of wine to celebrate the end of the inquisition. He signalled a college servant and ordered a half-bottle of Burgundy. 'Looking for an award?' he said.

'Award?'

'Scholarship or Exhibition.'

'I'm just looking to get a place,' I said. 'What's an Exhibition?'

He looked at me amiably. 'You don't know a lot, do you? Scholarship's the top award. Exhibition very nearly as good. That's the field – Scholar, Exhibitioner . . . or Commoner if you just scrape in as I might just. I shall need a fair wind, though.'

The Burgundy arrived and was poured. We finished the first glass and he took the bottle to top us up.

'We still have this afternoon's interviews,' I said warily.

'Not for me,' he said cheerfully. 'I have a party on tonight. I told Tony Camps I just had to catch the 2.30 train to Liverpool Street and he squeezed me in before lunch yesterday. I was out in five minutes.'

Five minutes?

'Cheers!' he said. 'Army first?'

'Yes,' I said. 'Best of luck.' I raised my glass.

'Where are you posted?'

'Winchester,' I told him.

'Ah, the Green Jackets. R.B. or 60th Rifles?'

Gibberish. I had no idea what he was asking.

'The Green Jackets have two regiments,' he explained patiently. 'The Rifle Brigade and the 60th, also known as The King's Royal Rifle Corps. Good friend of mine at Eton's just been commissioned in the King's Royal Rifle Corps. Adam Butler. Son of Rab, the ex-Education Minister. He's coming up next year.'

'Here to Pembroke?'

'Yes. You'll like him. He's a training officer at Winchester. You could well end up with Adam as your platoon commander.'

My companion left to catch a train to London to prepare for his party. Unfortunately, I never saw him again.

I passed into New Court to my interview with David Joslin, supervisor of History candidates, still bemused by the easy manner of my lunch companion. The Eton connections – Green Jackets, Adam Butler, R. A. Butler, Sir Montagu Butler, former Master of Pembroke . . . And he had risked putting forward his interview because he had had to get back to London for a party! But perhaps it was no risk at all if this was the sort of place that gave you port and biscuits with your interview. Perhaps you just asked. And if they could do what you wanted, they did it. Well!

David Joslin was small, rounded, with an air of intimidating intelligence. When I approached to shake hands he leapt up on the brass fender in front of his fireplace and invited me to sit.

I remember a few of his opening questions.

'What do you think happened to the sales of domestic coal and margarine in the depression of the early 1930s?'

Coal? I thought of the coke we used to collect from the gas works to sell in the World's End. Coal cost twice as much. 'Coal sales down,' I said, 'in favour of coke.'

'Margarine?'

My grandmother used to say a dab of butter was better for you than a thick smear of margarine. 'Margarine down,' I guessed wildly. 'Butter up.'

'Why?'

A deep breath. 'A belief, right or wrong, in the nutritional value of butter.'

'Would you like a glass of sherry?'

Here we go again. 'Thank you,' I said.

'You upset John Dickinson with your paper on Cromwell, you know.'

God, had they read it already? I only wrote it yesterday. 'John Dickinson?' I said.

'He teaches History here. Devoted to the memory of Charles I. Member of the Society of Charles the Martyr.'

'No!'

He smiled broadly. 'I thought you'd done it on purpose.' He handed me the glass of sherry.

On purpose? I wanted to shriek at him. How could I have done something like that on purpose?

I couldn't grasp the relationship he seemed to be offering. I'd expected it to be that of schoolmaster and pupil. This was adult to adult. With a glass of sherry thrown in. Look, he seemed to be saying, if you've got a party on in London tonight, you should have fixed your interview earlier.

It was all something of a shock.

A brief knock and the door was flung open by a tall, grinning man in a gown and dog collar. He grasped my hand. 'You don't leave anyone in doubt about what you think of Oliver Cromwell, do you?'

'If I offended you . . .'

'Much the best thing,' he said. 'Strong views. We'll fight it out.'

We talked about Cromwell for the next twenty minutes. Then David Joslin took over and we talked about the emergence of Economic History as a discipline. When I was leaving John Dickinson held open the door. He shook hands: 'See you in two years' time . . .' he said.

I walked slowly down the staircase. Two years' time? Did he say that? Did he *really* say that? That's what I *think* he said.

To the clatter of the train's wheels on the track the questions came: See you in two years' time? Did he mean it? Did he even say it? Hadn't he added '*I hope*'? Being polite? Parson's version of a glass of sherry? I tortured myself with that sentence all the way back to London.

My father was desperate to hear how it had gone. We had agreed I wouldn't try to phone home while I was taking the exam. Now what was I to tell him? That I thought, was virtually convinced, I had failed – but for that extraordinary valediction: 'See you in two years time.'

And did even that mean, quite simply: we'll know when we've read all the other candidates' examination papers?

THIRTY

Act of Indecency

What did I think about Cambridge? How did I think I had done? I could answer the first question easily enough. I wanted to go there. More than anything, I wanted to take part in that life. It wasn't an overwhelming intellectual need to study at Cambridge. It was a desire to take some part in, to savour, this new socially tolerant background, this existence where the acceptance of faux-pas was so laid-back the offer of a glass of port or sherry would smother any gaffe. Beyond that I knew enough to realise that a degree from Oxford or Cambridge could erase parts of my past, or at least the parts that, at that time, I felt I needed to erase. And it could do the same for my parents, for my father especially who had early seen there was no future for us in the World's End and now viewed his sons' successes as a confirmation of the steps he had taken since.

My world so far had been one where these small deviations from the expected counted as intensely important. The working-class life, even less the lower-middle-class life into which we had graduated at White City, is not as forgiving as it likes to imagine.

'You'd think he'd have the decency to . . .'

'The brass neck of her . . .'

'The bare-faced cheek . . .'

'And who does she think she is?'

These and others, less polite, were the oft-heard, heavily empha-sised reactions of people around us to quite minor misdemeanours.

My mother had always fought against this running paranoia, explaining people's intentions, trying to brush away others' imagined insults. But offence could so easily be taken on the most banal basis. Sensing a slight, women would not speak to each other for the most trivial reasons. Feuds often developed, sadly between neighbours who needed each other. The World's End was as riddled with them as any medieval Italian city state. My two grandmothers, living a few hundred yards apart, never spoke together once in their lives.

What seemed to be on offer in Cambridge was a different set of possibilities. An ease of manner, an imperviousness to the unintended slight. Life, of course, wherever you experience it, soon teaches that the difference is less in the substance than the presentation. Bitter childishness is as prevalent among politicians, film producers, judges and Oxbridge dons as it is among working-class grandmothers. It is simply one face of humanity. But my first real contact with that other world was undoubtedly appealing.

I guessed, of course, that waiting for the Cambridge results was going to be hard, at least as hard on my father as on me. Kit and my mother took things more calmly, my mother saying that there were other universities besides Oxford and Cambridge (though I don't know how many she could have named) and Kit reminding me (his idea of humour) that if I failed, I could always make a career in football. With all this in mind I had made arrangements to do a short hitch-hike with Larry Naughton, just to kill the time before the results arrived.

I consulted Leslie Berkeley at school but no one seemed to know when this was likely to be. Not before Christmas was the best guess any of the masters could offer – so I set off with Larry on a cold December afternoon to hitch to Oxford, which I was anxious to examine now that I'd experienced the architectural splendours of Cambridge. And not to be denied, of course, was the fact that I had a strong sentimental attachment to this university I'd never seen because Marie had spent an evidently happy year there, *avant le déluge*.

We trudged with our backpacks from White City perhaps four or five miles up that long rise towards Northolt and even stopped in a pub on the way for a pint of bitter before we were lucky enough to get a lift on the back of a lorry carrying steel tubing. Thereafter it was an easy, familiar ride to Denham roundabout. Our plan was to walk a mile or so beyond Denham and then start serious hitching for a lift to Oxford that night. There, Larry assured me, we would find innumerable nooks and crannies in which to unroll our sleeping bags and sleep through the night to the melody of Oxford's bells.

That was the plan. We jumped off the lorry at Denham roundabout and thanked the driver. Before setting off down the Oxford road we both felt the need to relieve ourselves of some of the beer we had drunk. We slid down a bank. Except perhaps for head and shoulders, we were out of sight of any cars using the simple grassed roundabout that existed at what is now the frenetically busy M4–M25 link.

Glancing over my shoulder as I zipped my flies, I saw a policeman's helmet sailing round the green mound which formed the middle of the roundabout. I assumed that under the helmet was a policeman and under the policeman a bike. It never occurred to me to be alarmed. We picked up our rucksacks, swung them on to one shoulder and began to climb the bank. The first thing I saw was a bicycle parked against a wooden post. I remember thinking I hadn't seen it there as we scrambled down. I looked a little to the right. A large police sergeant stood waiting for us.

He wasn't friendly as most police had been over the years we'd spent hitch-hiking. But he had a fairly neutral manner as he asked us what we had been doing down the slope. Larry, who as I've pointed out had a natural hostility to authority, said he would have thought it was pretty obvious.

Instead of showing some sign of irritation he nodded. 'I see,' he said. We were asked for our National Service registration cards. We'd left them at home. He took our names and addresses and instructed us to deliver our registration cards to Oxford Police Station by six o'clock the next day.

We achieved this with a good deal of phoning to parents. Explaining what had happened to the sergeant at the Oxford desk, we watched him barely glance at the papers. 'Old Benton get on to you, did he?'

'Sergeant Benton?'

'That's him. Used to be at this station. Eighteen stone and not always the best temper on him.'

'He was all right.'

He laughed. 'You were lucky! Stay out of that ditch on your way back.'

We enjoyed Oxford. I thought it was magnificent, but it didn't blend with the mists of December as Cambridge did. Summer, I could see, was Oxford's season of the year.

I arrived back at White City. I was still reaching for the handle when my father dragged open the door. 'The results came yesterday,' he said, before I could speak. 'A telegram. I had to open it, Dee. I wouldn't have slept a wink if I hadn't.'

I could see by his face, red with excitement, and my mother's just visible by his shoulder, that it wasn't bad news. 'Have I got a place?'

'A place? Stone the crows!' he said. 'A place? Better than that.'

'Well, what then?' I urged him.

'Stiffen the Prussian Guards!' he exploded. 'They've given you a Scholarship!'

THIRTY ONE

The King's Shilling

The train arrived at Winchester station on a dark, sleeting afternoon in January. It was the day the government, Attlee's second short-lived Labour administration, had announced the massive increase in the defence budget they had been debating for the last three months. In those days even popular newspapers carried news. Britain, impoverished by the second great war of the century, was to spend a full ten per cent of its total budget on defence. This huge amount of money was not going to be spent on training parade-ground soldiers. The government had decided the country needed more fighting units. The significance of this was not lost on most of us joining the Army that day.

I had seen one or two men of about my age wandering the corridor at different moments in the short journey from Waterloo, but had made no contact with them. I thought that could wait an hour or two. I knew that for the next two years I would be living together with them, or young men very like them. I didn't object. But I was going to take a few more minutes to myself before it all started. I suppose I was, in a sense, taking a deep breath between two phases of my life. I had no real idea what lay ahead, where I would be sent after training. There was a war in Korea with hundreds of British National

Service infantry already dead or injured there, and a bloody anti-guerrilla conflict in Malaya. National Servicemen were serving in half a dozen trouble spots across the globe. There were 60,000 of them serving in the Rhine Army, holding a major section of the German front against a possible Russian attack. An attack which, clearly, the Labour cabinet thought eminently possible.

I spent my last half an hour of freedom wondering whether I would ever see Marie again, wondering whether I would ever actually make it to Pembroke, wondering where in the world I would spend the next two years. It was, I suppose, a reverie balanced equally between nostalgia and a not unpleasant sense of anticipation. A reverie shattered as the train was still drawing into Winchester Station by the sound of the Army in full cry: 'Look in, there! Move, move, move! At the double . . . Move, you idle man!' Six corporals and a sergeant ran along the platform, banging with the flat of their hand on the side of the carriages, screaming at the top of their voice as we stood by the open doors. And the train hadn't even stopped.

I knew it was a calculated pantomime. I think we all did. But, pantomime or not, I was still out of that train, jogging along the platform, scrambling on to the back of an Army truck, and on the road to Bushfield Camp trailing the shreds of my reverie, before I was even sure what was happening. These next two years of my life, I thought, were definitely going to lack poetry.

The first few hours after arrival at Bushfield Green Jacket Training Brigade, a wooden encampment on a hill near St Cross, had the atmosphere of entering a prison camp. By the fading light we were hustled into the stores. There was a brief moment of reverence when we were issued with our green berets and black Cross of Malta cap badges. Then in short order we had thrown at us khaki denim trousers and jackets ('Don't fit? Don't fit? Listen to me, with this kit, if it fits good, you're deformed!'), boots, gaiters, mug, knife, fork, spoon, two blankets and a mattress. Struggling to hold all this in our arms, we were 'chased' (ordered to do everything at the double) uphill to a wooden hut furnished only with pairs of iron cots one above the other and rough timber hanging-cupboards.

Beds were assigned by a corporal. One of the boys threw himself down on his cot springs with a broad smile of contentment. 'Home at last, Corporal,' he sighed.

But life was hell.

We lived in 'spiders', six wooden huts arranged spider-legged to meet washrooms at a central entrance point. The huts were thin, bare-walled, board-floored, about fifty foot long. Heating was by two pot-bellied stoves not to be lit before six o'clock at night. Beyond the stoves, no sign of creature comforts.

We were introduced to our new routine. At the double to the cookhouse. First use of our new eating irons. A terrible meal which might have been fish. I hoped it was because nothing else should taste like that. Back at the double. Put to polishing the boots and the impossible brasswork on belts and packs by our two corporals, one from the Rifle Brigade with a silver cap badge, the other from the King's Royal Rifle Corps with a black Cross of Malta badge against a red background. We soon learnt that corporals and sergeants (almost all regulars) were the back-bone of the Green Jackets. I am not exaggerating when I say that they were selected with more care than the subaltern officers who commanded them.

That evening we sat on the lower level of our double bunks with, before us, the pile of boots to be polished, a tangle of belts and webbing backpacks to be blancoed and their brasses shone by the morning. We stared disbelievingly at the corporals' impeccably tailored uniforms, at the glittering belt brass and the just-so set of their berets as they moved among us, making clear the standards they expected to be achieved – or else. I don't think any of us got to bed that night before one or two o'clock.

At 5.30 next morning we were quick-marched (at 127 paces a minute) to the cookhouse, along a path glittering with frost and with the moon still high in a clear black sky. We wore our rough, shapeless khaki denims and heavy ammunition boots, as they were called. Our pint tea mugs (it was the British Army after all) and 'eating irons' were in danger of falling from our frozen hands. We were exhausted, dark-eyed and apprehensive. We had been in the Army twelve hours.

As our boots snapped on the frozen cement pathways the short, strongly built cockney next to me whispered something I couldn't catch. But the corporal in charge had heard words. He brought us to a halt.

'What was that, Rifleman Snelling?' he barked. 'Did I hear you say you'd sooner be dead?'

'Not before breakfast, Corporal,' Snelling replied, straight-faced.

There was a long pause. 'Very wise, lad. Though most clever lads find they don't have time for breakfast by their second day here. You're not a clever lad, are you, Snelling?'

'Dumb as they come, Corporal.'

I thought the skies were about to fall in on Snelling but he had the measure of our new life far quicker than I. The corporal (turned out for the parade ground at 5.30 in the morning) stepped back a pace and grinned. 'I tell you what I like about you, Snelling . . . that's your air of quiet resignation. I'll spread the word.'

Breakfast was burnt eggs, burnt toast, burnt bacon and burnt baked beans thrown into our mess tins by Army Catering Corps cooks. The pint mug of tea was thick with condensed milk – but I thought of Ron Snelling and the corporal and decided I'd probably survive the Army after all.

Two and a half million young men between the ages of eighteen and twenty-six were drafted into the Army, Royal Navy and RAF between 1949 and 1962. Not all of them went unwillingly. Not all found it 'a laugh', as it has been so often represented. In the infantry and armoured units nobody found it 'a long exercise in boredom'. Yet this is how it has often been described – as a misguided and complete waste of time. In Korea or Malaya, National Servicemen didn't see it as a waste of time; nor those in the Armoured Divisions in Germany in 1951 and '52, especially as evidence mounted of a mentally unstable Stalin weighing the chances of a successful breakthrough into Western Europe.

The two and a half million young men who gave two years of their lives to National Service deserve more to mark its passing than *Privates on Parade* or *The Virgin Soldiers*. I find it hard to think of any account of this massive event in British social and military history that has accurately recorded what it was like for those hundreds of thousands who didn't lie on their beds all day with only a waking dream of Betty Grable to prevent them from succumbing to a mind-deadening boredom.

There were of course those, particularly those who stayed in Britain with the RAF, who suffered legitimately from a sense of a totally wasted two years. But even there a few were able to carve their own path through National Service. Like my friend Ted Simon who managed to parlay his service period (in the post-Stalin years, admittedly) into devising and editing a magazine, to be distributed first to Padgate recruits and finally throughout all RAF training camps. His last days as a serviceman were spent negotiating with an Air Vice Marshal to sell the magazine to a commercial organisation in the hope of recovering some of the vast sums of RAF money he had spent.

Throughout the period of National Service there was also strong opposition to conscription from outside the Army. Moscow understood the significance of the fact that 97 per cent of the British Army was now conscripted. If conscription had been abandoned, or even run down, Britain would have been totally unable to fulfil its NATO commitments. And if Britain had failed to maintain the Army of the Rhine in NATO, it is inconceivable that France, Holland, Italy, Denmark and others would have been prepared to support an American presence in Europe. It follows that without Britain's National Service Army, the US government would have withdrawn

its forces to a fortress America. I am far from certain that all senior
Soviet politicians would have been anxious to take on the massive
logistical problem of occupying Western Europe, but I have no doubt
that Stalin himself and the European Communist Parties would have
found an undefended West an extraordinarily tempting bait.

During the first morning of our service we were taken out on to the
parade ground to be introduced to Green Jacket drill. This has the
advantage of a good deal less stamping than the Guards drill used by
most other regiments in the British Army. It requires, however, a
speed of co-ordination which it took our drill sergeants less than
three minutes to discover I somewhat lacked.

'Like bloody Beethoven,' his voice swelled indignantly. 'Slow in all
his movements.' Insults flowed my way, but never insults you could
take seriously. Only the most thin-skinned would see these
comments as anything but another part of the serious pantomime we
were all embroiled in. And the insults were seldom reinforced by real
anger. Frustration, mock-despair and simulated rage were the
training NCOs' stock-in-trade. All the same, it wasn't comforting to
discover I was a nanosecond slower than my fellow recruits.

This first drill session lasted an exhausting hour. As the drill
sergeant stood us easy, a corporal I later discovered was from the
company commander's office came on to the square and whispered
something in the drill instructor's ear.

Sergeant Wilkinson came forward, his two-pronged measuring
stick flicking across the asphalt. 'Rifleman Wheal . . .'

I knew enough to come to attention.

'I don't know what you've been up to, Rifleman, but it appears
there's a police constable awaiting you at Company Office. Not only
a police constable but the company commander himself is looking to
have a word with you.'

I blanched. There was a shuffle of interest in the ranks.

'Not been giving away our little secrets to the newspapers, have you, lad? No? Had your hand in some young lady's till, perhaps? No? Bad luck. So a bit of a mystery, is it? Right . . . double away. Company Office.'

I was baffled. The corporal who had delivered the message could tell me nothing. The policeman in Company Office would, it appeared, only speak directly to me.

A policeman's bicycle with the owner's identification number painted in white on the black mudguard stood resting against the wooden wall of the Company Office 'spider'. That was reassuring. If they'd planned an arrest they'd have sent a car. I entered the main office and was marched into the commanding officer's room and halted. A young policeman stood next to the desk. Seated at it, a King's Royal Rifle Corps captain glanced up at me. 'Very well,' he nodded to the policeman, 'let's see what this is about.'

The policeman pulled stapled sheets of paper from his breast pocket. 'You,' he said, 'are Donald James Wheal of White City, London?'

'He is not, Constable,' the captain interrupted firmly. 'He is Rifleman Wheal, D. 22448635.'

'Yes, sir.' The policeman drew a deep breath. 'You are charged that on December the twentieth of last year you did commit and were apprehended in an act of indecency.'

'What!'

'Silence!' roared the corporal in the corner of the room.

The company commander raised his eyebrows. 'Interesting,' he said. 'We often enough get the odd housebreaking charge in the first few days of a new draft. A hangover, I always think, from the Riflemen's civilian occupation. Nothing like this, though. Yes, very interesting. Any details?' He leaned forward encouragingly.

The police officer consulted his sheet. 'The charge reads that the said . . . hmm . . . Rifleman Wheal did commit on the said date an act of indecency to the annoyance of passengers passing.'

'That's less than a detail, Officer. What was he actually *doing*?'

'Nothing, sir,' I said.

'Quiet!' the corporal yelled in my ear.

The policeman was in genuine difficulty. 'The actual nature of the act is not specified in the charge, but I believe it relates to exposure, sir.'

The company commander looked at me. 'Been out flashing, have you?'

I recoiled.

'Stand straight,' the corporal bawled.

'I have no idea what this is all about, sir,' I said.

The corporal was about to silence me again when the captain raised his hand. 'Now where is this act of indecency supposed to have taken place, Officer? That might help us.'

'Denham in Buckinghamshire.'

'Ah!' I said.

'Silence!' the corporal yelled.

'So do we have the answer to the mystery?' The captain nodded to me to speak.

'I was . . . relieving myself in a ditch, sir. A police sergeant came round the Denham roundabout at that very moment.'

The captain nodded sympathetically. 'There but for the Grace of God . . . Could have happened to any of us, Constable,' he said. 'Young man gets out of his old sports car. Overcome by the last half-pint of ale. Takes discreet pee in ditch. Seen by overzealous member of the noble arm – and ends up charged with an act of indecency. Where's the court hearing?'

'Beaconsfield, sir. Buckinghamshire.'

'Very smart of you, Rifleman,' the captain said. 'Skipped Basic Training for a couple of awful days on a trumped-up charge of indecency. Well done. Shows initiative. Please serve the summons, Constable. I'll sign a thirty-six-hour leave pass. Give you time to have a night in your own bed and a quiet dinner after the hearing. One or two nice little restaurants in the Beaconsfield area, I believe. Friend of mine swears by the Orange Tree.'

I left Company Office in a daze. The company commander seemed to be quite content to see me go to court on an indecency charge. The Army, at least in its more senior ranks, was revealing itself to be a stranger institution than I'd ever imagined possible. Not so very different in tone from my experience at Pembroke. I wouldn't have been entirely flabbergasted if the company commander had offered me a glass of sherry.

I had spent the night at home. Perhaps taking my cue from my company commander, I was not really taking the indecency charge seriously. My father was. 'If it's on your record nobody's going to know you were peeing in the ditch,' he said. 'Indecency . . . you can guess what that brings up in most people's minds. Stone the crows! You could even lose your Scholarship to Pembroke!'

I could? I didn't know that. He didn't either but he had shocked me into thinking seriously about what was to happen the next day. I managed to argue him out of getting a barrister through somebody at Whitelands to represent Larry and myself. I knew he couldn't afford that sort of expenditure. But I also knew that Larry and I were going to have to perform well the next day.

We got to Beaconsfield with nearly two hours to spare. I do believe my father had never been late for *anything* in his life. A few minutes of the time we spent wandering up and down the main street to find a paper for my father to check the runners that day. An old man with a brown-spotted bald head stood behind the newsagent's counter. My father slipped him half a crown. 'You know the police sergeant here?'

'Benton? 'Course I do.'

'What's he like?'

The old man shrugged. 'You up for the court?'

'They are.' My father thumbed towards Larry and myself. 'So this Benton . . . well liked, is he?'

'I wouldn't say that.'

'What would you say then?' Another half a crown hovered under my father's fingers on the pile of *Daily Heralds*.

'People don't like him much in the village. He's a troublemaker. Brings a lot of silly-arsed cases. Retires next month. Most of us say good riddance.' He glanced down at the silver coin under my father's fingertips.

The half crown stayed there. 'Go on,' my father said.

'He's just not liked that much, that's all. Especially at his own station. He'll not get much of a send-off, I can tell you.'

The half a crown, newly minted with George VI's boyish features uppermost, was exposed on the *Herald*.

'Throws his weight about, does he?'

'That's about the size of it.'

'What about the magistrates?'

'The chairman's a decent chap. Old soldier, you know the type. Wounded in the First World War.' He looked at me in uniform. 'You should be all right.'

We left the shop and walked down the street. 'There you go,' my father said. 'You got the patter? You had no idea you were going to be summonsed. You were not cautioned in the required manner. You were first informed during infantry manoeuvres . . .'

'It was drill.'

'Infantry manoeuvres. When seen by Sergeant Benton at the Denham roundabout, you were doing nothing wrong. You took your National Service card to Oxford as you were told. You just can't see why the sergeant should have brought this charge.'

'It's the truth. I can't think what he's up to.'

'No,' he said. 'But just let the magistrate do the thinking.'

Our court case was already set for farce. Larry looked clean-cut and honourable; I was in uniform. An unhappy police inspector was prosecuting. The chairman of the magistrates asked me so many pre-match questions about Bushfield that I thought he must be an old Green Jacket. 'Are you enjoying the Army?'

'Yes, sir.'

The police sergeant's evidence was heavy with innuendo, but distinctly muddled with a suggestion of homosexuality (a prison offence in those days) in one sentence and of flagrant exhibitionism in the next. I could see his inspector was getting angrier by the minute.

When the inspector cross-questioned Larry, he pretended that he had not understood the implication of a homosexual act and concentrated on the improbable idea of exhibitionism from a ditch on a day of driven sleet on an almost empty roundabout.

The magistrate nodded to himself. The inspector gave both Larry and myself a token cross-questioning bordering on the apologetic.

Suddenly the magistrate stopped proceedings. 'I don't really see these young men have a case to answer, do you, Inspector?' he enquired.

'No, I don't, sir,' the inspector rather surprisingly replied, and glared at the sergeant. 'Frankly, I don't.'

'Then I'd like to be assured that Sergeant Benton will be reprimanded for wasting a good part of our morning?'

'I can assure you of that, sir.'

'Thank you. An absolute discharge seems appropriate. Case dismissed.'

THIRTY TWO

Pride comes . . .

There were two parts to the draft which arrived at Bushfield Camp on our freezing first day in the army. There were the mainly short, stocky, highly motivated Londoners from the Green Jacket main recruiting boroughs of Deptford, Shoreditch and Bow. Totally different in background, education and very often physically (taller certainly but usually less well-muscled), there were also those from Eton, Winchester, Marlborough, Harrow, Haileybury and Ampleforth, who hoped to obtain a commission in the Rifle Brigade or King's Royal Rifle Corps. As the only grammar school member of the intake, I stood somewhere in the middle.

You'd think this division between cockney East London and the country's best known public schools was the simplest cook's recipe for trouble. All in the same barrack room, glottal stops and strangulated vowels criss-crossing the bed spaces after Lights Out, how could a clash be avoided?

Yet somehow it produced no problems. Public schoolboys made bad Hollywood imitations of East End accents, cockneys responded with equally poor simulacra of the fashionable upper-class drawl. Perhaps because our real enemy was the system which enveloped us, it was all done in good humour. I'm not claiming that the two groups fell into each other's arms on sight but I certainly never saw class difference develop into a clash between public school and cockney Riflemen.

In that first six weeks at Bushfield we were truly run off our feet. In retrospect you can see the object of the madness of induction. Sixty young men, from backgrounds as diverse as could be imagined in Britain, were to be de-civilianised, taught that if the Army says do it, you do it. Only afterwards could personal initiative be allowed to flourish. I can't imagine there's any more effective way of breaking in young men than a six-week induction of the sort we suffered at the Green Jacket Training Brigade, Winchester.

My impression is that most National Servicemen undergoing similar severities in the Guards, Armoured Corps and the county infantry regiments responded much as we did to Basic Training. Many who in general had an easier (more boring?) time in their two years persuaded themselves that such madness was unnecessary, even aimed at them personally. They were certainly unhappier for it.

Everything depended on your attitude. If you snivelled, you had a very bad time indeed. If you saw the deadly seriousness and the mad humour of those days, you still longed for them to end but you took the opportunity to enjoy this unique sense of force-fed community and comradeship, stronger than any of school or class.

Of course there were young men for whom separation from the known world was impossibly difficult: those who had already married, for instance, one or two of whom had children. There were also men who had been the only ones around to visit their widowed mothers or provide financial support. There was not much evidence of military humour if one of those went absent for a weekend. There was such a thing as compassionate leave but getting it took nothing short of a death in the close family, not just an anonymous letter to say your wife was seeing someone else. For some young men National Service was a long sentence and the Army its prison. Some were by no means as free and easy as I was, trailing only the painful memories of Marie. Although we had by now ceased writing letters I still thought about her in a confused but painful way. Mostly, of course, my head was filled with the shattering experience of this new Army world; hers (no doubt more agreeably), by life in Vienna.

Regimental indoctrination was high on the list of the days' activities. From day one we were told that the two Green Jacket regiments, The King's Royal Rifle Corps and its sister regiment, The Rifle Brigade, were incomparably the best in the British Army. The Guards, while similarly elite, were nevertheless stiff, slow and inflexible. The Green Jackets, raised in America before the War of Independence as the Royal American Regiment were not redcoats. Their uniforms were green, their buttons not brass but black bone, their drill quicker. At the time I joined the regiment we were the only fully motorised infantry in the British Army. In the battalions in Germany we would be trained to operate in small units, carried in our own armoured vehicles ahead of advancing tank formations.

The psychology behind creating an elite self-supporting community in just six weeks was interesting, if at times baffling. The excessive physical demands, the calculated madness of Basic Training was balanced by a barrage of historical truth and fable (delivered by our platoon officer) designed to convince us that we had been allowed to join a unique regiment in the British army, the best in standards of training and appearance. Perhaps the hard times themselves played a part in convincing us. Accepting the myth was the only thing that could justify the suffering.

My platoon instructor in all this was, incidentally, 2nd Lieutenant Adam Butler, KRRC.

After six weeks together our intake was split into two groups, one for immediate dispatch to Germany for continuation training, the other to go before the three-day War Office Selection Board, WOSB – pronounced Wosbee – for selection as officers. I applied and was accepted as one of those to be sent before the selection board. I was confident of passing. I wasn't the best parade-ground soldier in our platoon by any means. But I was good in the classroom, and my hitch-hiking days meant I took to any sort of infantry field training they'd subjected us to. I'd got on well with both sides of our original platoon, the cockney side whose resilience echoed my own World's End past, and the public school group who were new to me and were indeed from a different world – but were far from the daunting strangers that Leslie Berkeley had pictured.

For the last four weeks of the full ten-week induction our training in the Potential Officer platoon was of a slightly different order. It moved from a heavy emphasis on drilling, weapon training and physical exercise, to slightly more cerebral studies such as map reading, leadership, and military knowledge. But drill, kit inspections, cookhouse fatigues and exercise were far from forgotten. One morning our platoon sergeant came round with a clip-board. The Brigade Cross Country and Boxing Championships were to be held in three weeks' time. We were all expected to volunteer.

I had no love of cross-country running. Who has? But although I'd known plenty of playground fights in my early youth, I'd never boxed before and I suppose I was curious to see how World's End life and my staged clashes with Kit and my father would serve me in a ring, boxing to set rules. As there were a lot of lads there from a very similar background to mine, albeit in Deptford or Bethnal Green, I was interested to see how it might work out. I put my name down as a light-heavyweight.

WOSB now beckoned. A pass there meant four months' training at Eaton Hall Infantry Officer Cadet School in Cheshire and a posting to a battalion which might, in theory, be any one, anywhere. Most prized, of course, was a recommendation for a commission in the Green Jackets. I suppose I knew this was not likely to happen to me. At the beginning of the 1950s class distinctions were, on the surface at least, still as strong as they had been before the war. All my companions in the Potential Officer platoon were from major public schools. Battalion officers bristled with names like Lieutenant Lord Lennox and Captain Lord St Aubyn. But somehow I thought the distinctions just might not apply to me. Or at least I still thought there was some chance of my being selected for the Green Jackets – until the day we were asked to hand in our birth certificates. I had never seen mine before. I sent for it from home.

Looking at it for the first time, under father's profession – where all the other candidates' certificates would have had inscribed judge, barrister-at-law, company chairman, Peer of the Realm or Minister of the Crown – mine read, journeyman plumber. It was a shock. I thought ruefully that this isn't going to crack the ice.

I felt then, and still do, a great distaste for self-pity. The most perfunctory glance around showed me I had no cause to bewail my lot. Pride, vanity maybe, wouldn't allow it. I suppose in fact my nature is deeply, maybe subterraneanly, competitive, though super-ficial competition doesn't attract me. I don't care who wins at draughts.

But I wasn't inclined to back down. I had a week to decide. Perhaps things had changed since pre-war days. Perhaps the Green Jackets *were* now taking the odd plumber's son.

I doubted it, but it was true that I had not so far in the Army come up against issues of class. Here at Bushfield, cockney and public schoolboy were in the same boat. At the end of most days we were an indistinguishable huddle of mud-covered, exhausted young men. Class denominators were dissolved in military uniformity, regi-mental haircuts and khaki denim . . . Only accent and education remained. In education I had a head start with my Pembroke Scholarship. My accent by this stage of my life was no longer World's End. It was probably mildly Estuarian, as we might now say.

I spent as much time with the boys from Shoreditch and Bow as I did with the Marlburians and Etonians. The two groups seemed to me to share the same qualities in more or less the same measure.

They accepted the rigours and calculated folly of Army training with roughly the same degree of resignation, grumbling or cheerfulness as the case might be. They all supported each other with a sense of humour that, as I've said, was quicker on the cockney side, more considered on the other, but still largely accessible to each other. There were almost no superior airs exhibited by the public school group. And the only item that might have been stolen in six weeks, or might simply have been lost, was a single cracked white china mug.

Yet there were obvious class differences. The first purpose of the training we were undergoing was ostensibly to subordinate all individual differences to the regimental sense of community, the wonderfully unifying effect of hard times. The next stage, when some were selected for Potential Officer training, was paradoxically to open up that class gap again. Certainly the British Army at this time was one which consciously manipulated its recruits to achieve a structure of discipline and authority based on class differences. At the same time it united officers and non-commissioned ranks by a sense of self-esteem rooted in a shared regimental identity. I think, at least in the infantry, armour and artillery, this fine balance was successfully maintained.

When I began to realise that this was the case, and very much the case in the Green Jackets, I wondered where I myself was going to fit into this jigsaw. I might have opted for a commission in one of the corps, the Army Ordnance Corps or the Service Corps. Most of their officers were from Grammar School and I knew I could fit in easily there. But that seemed what my father would have called dodging the column, dodging the challenge of class distinction. My week of indecision was over. I applied for a Green Jacket Commission.

I can't think of anybody I seriously disliked in my intake. But there was one man whose manner seemed to me impossibly aloof. He was, I think, the only member of the intake with whom I hadn't, at some point, sat around the pot-bellied stove chatting and cleaning boots and rifles. He seemed to spend all his spare time lying on his bed with a book of Latin verse. Rifleman Richard Rougier was from Marlborough, as indeed were several others in the intake. I knew little or nothing about him except that he had a sharp tongue which I'd seen demonstrated on one or two of the other Marlburians who seemed to follow a fundamentalist Christian line. And somebody had once told me that his mother was the novelist Georgette Heyer.

But I had decided in the first few weeks that I got along a lot better with someone like Reggie Bosanquet, later the high-living ITN newsreader, or even languid, sleepy-eyed Mark Tennant, than I ever would with Richard Rougier.

Sometime after midnight one night not long before we were due to complete our Basic Training, I found myself crammed in the back of a canvas-sided three-ton truck as we left the frosted hillsides of Winchester where we had been practising night attacks. We were cold, hungry and tired out with three hours of crawling over icy fields at the end of a long day of parades, physical training and small arms instruction. The man next to me, hands in a priestly fold across his chest, was Richard Rougier. There was no room to move. We were crammed into the truck, our legs tangled with rifles, steel helmets, webbing. I closed my eyes and tried to catch a few minutes' doze before we reached Bushfield. But it was not to be. As we turned off the hillside tracks my neighbour began to sing. In Latin!

I couldn't imagine anything so irrelevantly pompous given our travelling conditions.

> *Odi profanum vulgus et arceo.*
> *Favete linguis . . .*

And then I realised. He was singing a Horace Ode: 'I hate the vulgar crowd – and ward them off. Grant me your silence . . .' Given our cramped, noisy conditions, *not* so inappropriate. I laughed.

'I thought you'd like it,' he said. 'We who are destined for Pembroke must stick together.'

I looked at him in surprise. 'You're going to Pembroke too?'

'If I survive.'

'I expect you will. How did you know I was going?'

'You're a Scholar,' he said.

'And you?'

'A mere Exhibitioner.'

Exhibitioner. At the time I thought that was pretty appropriate too.

'Shall I ask the Dean to get us rooms on the same staircase?'

I had to laugh at the sheer improbability of the idea. 'He's not going to do that.'

'Why not? When we get there we'll need someone who knew what we went through in this Vale of Tears. We can celebrate with a glass of excellent port and a Bath Oliver.'

More port and biscuits. He obviously knew the ropes. The only problem was that I thought him completely mad. 'It's a date,' I said as we slowed to enter Bushfield Camp. 'A glass of port and a Bath Oliver in two years' time.'

From such a Curzonian young man, I didn't believe a word of it. It was merely something to shrug about, to recognise as a friendly gesture and dismiss. Anything more seemed impossibly distant. The present was the hard truck-bed of the lorry, the tangle of webbing equipment, the sodden boots, the ridiculously blackened faces making us (as I now see it all these years later) look like something out of the cast of *Cats*.

I was by this time slowly working my way through the eliminating bouts for the Green Jacket Training Brigade Boxing Championship. My semi-final match was against the amiable Reggie Bosanquet. He had boxed at Winchester College and was at that time a fit, heavily muscled young man an inch or two shorter than me. It was a close match but I passed on to the Final, to be held before the whole Training Brigade the following weekend.

The Championship was well staged at Green Jacket headquarters in Winchester. It opened with Ron Snelling, the man who'd braved the training corporal on our first morning's march to breakfast, fighting as a lightweight. I don't any longer remember his opponent but he hadn't much chance against Ron's Bethnal Green Boxing Club skills. My opponent in the Light-heavyweight Division was a Rifle Brigade training corporal, a man of about twenty-six, roughly my height but with an unusually long reach. I had watched him in some of the eliminating bouts and saw his opponents had difficulty getting close enough to him. I was equally wary of his reach in the first round, but if he was harried I soon realised he didn't exploit his advantage. He went down just before the final bell. My hand was raised and with a rush of blood to the head I realised I had won the Green Jacket Training Brigade Light-heavyweight Championship.

I phoned home that night. My father was jubilant, my mother merely relieved it was all over. Kit was due to be called up in six months. For her it would be another three years before both sons had passed the last milestones in their long trek to safety at the end of National Service.

We lined up nervously outside Company Office. It was a few days before leaving for Aldershot where the War Office Selection Board (WOSB) would test us on our suitability for officer training.

At the end of officer training we would be allocated to a regiment. Everybody in the Potential Officer platoon at Bushfield Camp had of course applied for a commission in the Green Jackets. Now we would discover who among our platoon of twenty would be selected. Alphabetically we were called into Company Office and handed an envelope. In this was an acceptance or rejection of our request to be commissioned in the Green Jackets.

On the card inside the envelope there was no written assessment, no reason why, simply the result: 'G-J' or 'Not G-J'. Of the twenty or so in the platoon, perhaps six or eight were recommended for the regiment if they passed WOSB. The rest would receive a card marked 'Not G-J' and, after WOSB and officer training, be assigned to county infantry regiments.

I think Adam Butler, my platoon officer, chose my result with care – and, in the circumstances, a good deal of consideration. My card was marked ambiguously, 'Not yet G-J'. He was well aware of things I had hardly thought about – that I would never be able to afford the level of mess bills or the elaborate dark green and silver dress uniform a Green Jacket officer had to pay for himself. I would guess he was also acutely aware that he could not have recommended the son of a journeyman plumber. It was still a blow.

WOSB came and, for me at least, went. I failed. The intelligence test left me completely baffled. Much of it seemed crossword-based. I had never done an anagram in my life, and even now I find it hard to understand why anyone should want to.

A quite sympathetic colonel said I had done well on the practical and leadership tests but my intelligence test . . . he looked down at the papers on his desk and pulled a face. My intelligence tests, he began again, had recorded Educationally Sub-normal which, glancing at my CV, he was happy to accept was unlikely to be the case. Was I playing the fool?

'No, sir,' I said, aghast.

'And your lecture on Plato's *Republic*.' He grimaced and shook his head. 'Bad choice.' He closed his eyes. 'Very bad choice.'

There was nothing I could say. I suppose I had taken it for granted I'd passed. It was a far worse blow than not getting the Green Jacket recommendation, the reasons for which I think I understood.

The colonel looked at me and shrugged in a friendly enough manner. 'Come back and see us in four months' time. In the meantime, do the *Times* crossword,' he advised. 'Put Plato aside until you get to Cambridge. Give your lecture on the Battle of Waterloo,

Collecting Militaria, Dan Dare if you want. But "Beware the Greeks . . ."'

It wasn't quite a fail but, by God, it felt like it.

Back at Bushfield Camp all the members of the Potential Officer platoon had passed except me. Richard Rougier, Reggie Bosanquet, Michael Mosley, Mark Tennant, all passed. I knew I had to resist the temptation to explain this set-back to myself as a simple case of class discrimination. The 'Not yet G-J' almost certainly was (with, I accept, some rationale); the failure at WOSB was my own. It would have been all too easy to blame it on the system, but the system was there to be beaten. You can't change a birth certificate but you can change other things. Crosswords, for instance. And no more thoughts of Plato for the next two years. OK. It was what is now known as a steep learning curve.

Within two days of returning to Bushfield I was given my posting. I was to be sent to the 1st Battalion, King's Royal Rifle Corps, in Germany and given two weeks' embarkation leave. My father was deeply disappointed, I think shocked, by the WOSB result. He couldn't understand how I could have failed the intelligence test so badly. The label Educationally Sub-normal which I had not (nor indeed had the colonel) taken seriously, was something that really angered him. I gave him one of the questions in the test which I remember to this day. It was unadorned with any interrogative trappings. It simply read, 'Question 14: Trocune-catkat.' Apparently the crossword devotee would have seen that immediately as an anagram for *counter-attack*. I had looked at it in deep bafflement. No less my father. He was outraged. The Plato lecture, he conceded, was a poor move. But the intelligence test . . . 'Trocune catkat? Stiffen the Prussian Guards! What sort of question is that? What does that tell anybody about the sort of man you are?' I was really touched when that weekend he bought himself a book of crosswords.

My mother and Kit took it all much more calmly. Not the end of the world was my mother's comforting reaction. 'Perhaps if you're not an officer they'll send you somewhere not so dangerous.' Her ambition for both Kit and myself was a safe job as company storeman at Bushfield.

But I was deeply disappointed with myself. I had worked hard on my lecture on Plato's *Republic*, though I knew exactly what it was – a piece of pure showing off. A defence of grammar-school against public-school standards I had been taught to fear, and no longer did.

But there was, at least, another WOSB in four months' time . . .

THIRTY THREE
Sennelager

The military train from the Hook of Holland passed through Eindhoven and I could see the machine-gun bullet holes criss-crossing the corrugated iron engine shed. Ours, I wondered, or theirs?

Once in Germany the signs of bombing were visible in every town and city we passed through . . . Krefeld, Duisburg, Essen, Dortmund . . . and due east towards the Russian zone. There were frequent stops for no discernible purpose. At one I leaned out of the window to talk to two red-capped British Military Police. I wanted to know if they'd ever been to our destination, Sennelager. One of them had. He was a tall, lugubrious-looking corporal but seemed to lighten up at the name of Sennelager. 'Know it well,' he said. 'Small town, village almost, not exactly the bright lights but a few nice quiet *gasthauses* where you can get a drink and a meal, and very friendly inhabitants. And, of course, some very pretty girls.'

I thanked him, feeling considerably cheered. Not immediately by the thought of the very pretty German girls. Marie was still very much on my mind. But I saw her in my imagination going to parties at the American and Russian Control Commission in Vienna, attending concerts, visiting art galleries . . . I made a serious effort to tell myself it was a young persons' romance. It was over.

I went back to the compartment and told the other members of our draft that Sennelager was probably not a bad place, and saw from the change in their faces that they too had been feeling apprehensive about where they were heading, none of them having been abroad before, let alone to the country we had all spent most of our younger lives hating.

We continued our long slow journey, lightened by occasional visits to the bar in the end carriage. From time to time we would make our way down the carriages packed with a dozen different units, to enjoy the selection of German beers. Slowly most of these units, Royal Signals, Service Corps, Catering Corps, Infantry and Armoured Corps units, were dropped off at unrecognisably named stations along the route. After several hours of travel from the Hook of Holland, Ron Snelling and I left our equipment in the care of the rest of our draft and set off down the train for another visit to the bar. Once there we ordered a half-litre of the excellent German beer and bought a sort of Frankfurter heating in a tin of hot water. The German barman who served us had a crooked smile as he cleaned up, covering the bar-top with great sweeping movements of his cloth. He didn't seem to want to talk even though there was no one else to be served.

Ron Snelling and I speculated about what life in Sennelager would be like. A small German village, a bar on the corner. Music, dancing perhaps on Saturday nights. I had a pleasant buzz in my head from our last visit to the bar as I imagined the weekends in Sennelager. Learn German, get to know some of the locals, a friendly greeting from Gretchen or Traudi or whatever the name of the innkeeper's daughter was going to turn out to be.

The train had stopped in a town of some size and we ordered another beer to while away the time as we listened to the pleasing clink and puff of shunting steam engines and watched the German railway workers going about their day-to-day tasks. Occasionally they would glance up at us in the bar carriage. Neither friendly nor unfriendly.

Germany, I said to Ron with the portentousness of a young man with two or three litres of beer inside him, was going to be a place where we'd have to work to be liked. But we'd do it.

'Too true,' Ron said sagely. 'Too fuckin' true.'

We finished our beer and sausage, thanked the barman and started back, only a little unsteady on our feet. Ron reached the end of the bar carriage, opened the door into the next one and turned back to me, frowning. ''S funny thing,' he said, a deeply puzzled look on his face. 'Somebody's nicked our fuckin' train.'

He opened the communicating door wider. No train.

This took me more than a few seconds to absorb. Ron was no quicker. I lifted my eyes to follow the line of the track. Our train was steaming round a bend about half a mile ahead.

Behind us the barman lifted both hands in an apologetic shrug but his crooked grin said he wasn't sorry not to have warned us we were being uncoupled. I just about restrained Ron Snelling. He was not tall but I'd seen him in the ring at Bushfield and I didn't want assault on a German barman added to whatever other offence we had committed by missing the main train.

As we clambered down into what was obviously the marshalling yard of a sizeable town it felt strange to be crossing rail tracks, hearing German voices shouting to each other. There were still signs of heavy bombing. I wondered if we were in the marshalling yards at Hamm which had been reported so often by the BBC as RAF bombing targets during the war.

'What's a marshalling yard, Dee?' Kit used to say to me as we snuggled up in bed together (with my grandmother).

'It's a yard with . . . It's one of those yards where . . . I'm trying to go to sleep, Kit. The good thing is, the RAF's bombing 'em. So they're important for the German war effort. And they're getting a pasting.'

'The more the better,' Kit would agree, and fortunately abandon his interrogation.

As we crossed the tracks it occurred to me that Ron and I were technically AWOL, absent without leave. This is a serious military offence, especially on an overseas posting. But I thought we'd be given Brownie points for initiative if with fewer than a dozen words of German, and without a single German mark in our pockets, we somehow made our way to our destination, which may have been five or five hundred miles away for all we knew.

Ron Snelling was a cheerful companion with unlimited confidence in my knowledge of the German language (the result of my ordering *zwei bier, bitte* in the bar). Even so our journey was a nightmare. Unaware that British occupation personnel were allowed to travel free on German trains and buses, I tried to negotiate our fare with station masters in the most inadequate of pidgin German. When they showed us on to trains without asking for money, I tried to press a written IOU on them. They thought I was out of my mind.

Long after nightfall, travelling on small branch lines, sometimes waiting an hour or two for a train but receiving a great deal of friendliness from Germans we met on the way, we arrived at Paderborn. I had vaguely heard of the town as the birthplace of Charlemagne, or perhaps the site of his court. More friendliness from an amused station master and I was on the phone to 1st Battalion, King's Royal Rifle Corps, Dempsey Barracks, Sennelager. Home at last. I remembered one of the boys saying that while throwing himself down on the bare springs of his cot when we first arrived at Bushfield.

On the phone I asked the Regimental Police sergeant, in a fashion I didn't think too lordly, to send a car to Paderborn to pick us up. 'Yes, sir,' he said. I thanked him and put down the phone. I looked at Snelling, he at me, and we grinned triumphantly at each other. We'd made it.

Fifteen minutes later a green-painted battalion Volkswagen pulled into the station forecourt. The driver got out and opened the back door. Perhaps he raised his eyebrows at us as we climbed, hatless, into the back seat, but he said nothing. I tried to ask him what the village (*dorf*, wasn't that the word?) of Sennelager was like.

'*Dorf?*' A long pause. But his shoulders began to lift. He was chuckling as he drove.

We were driven through darkened countryside with increasing numbers of regimental signboards to different barracks in the Sennelager area. We were, I slowly realised, headed for no chintzy little German township. Sennelager was obviously the name of a huge ex-German Army barrack area. Bleak military buildings lined the road. 'Is this Sennelager?' Ron Snelling said, unbelieving.

'*Ja. Hier ist Sennelager,*' the driver said.

The gates of Dempsey Barracks, *1st Battalion KRRC* inscribed across the arching signboard in the familiar dark green and red, were opened by two members of the guard. Our car pulled up at the Guardroom steps. A tall sergeant with a Regimental Police armband came clattering down the steps. He was lifting his arm in the direction of a salute when Snelling and I, dishevelled, capless and beltless, clambered exhausted from the back of the Volkswagen.

Sergeant Johnson's scream of rage was real. The tic above his left eye was real. The shuddering fury as he got the words out was more than real. 'Absent without leave,' he screamed. 'Impersonating an officer, improperly dressed, misappropriating battalion transport, wilfully abandoning Ministry of Defence equipment while on active service . . .'

I tried to speak but his incomprehensible scream silenced me. I heard, 'Under arrest. Before the colonel tomorrow morning . . .' I was doubling up the steps before I knew it. The heavy steel-barred doors of the Guardroom jail crashed closed behind me. Ron Snelling winked at me through the bars of the neighbouring cell.

I took a deep breath. There was nothing else for it. First night in Germany and behind bars. I threw myself on the single-planked bunk. 'Home at last,' I said to Ron Snelling through the bars.

THIRTY FOUR

The King's Commission

The Guard Commander marched us to the cookhouse to collect tea and egg on toast at 5.30 the next morning before we were set to scrub floors. No floors were ever cleaner than this Guardroom's even before we started, but when a Regimental Police corporal arrived at 6.30 he cursorily inspected my work, kicked my bucket of soapy water over (and partly over me) and ordered me to start again. 'Both hands on the brush, lad – both knees on the floor!' Half an hour of that and knees, shoulders and back were telling me I'd never recover. Guilty until proved innocent.

It was the beginning of five days' hard pounding, running, parading, polishing, scrubbing, digging, cleaning burnt soup cauldrons, from five in the morning to midnight. And it only stopped at five days because the colonel accepted, as well he might have, that there was no intention to go absent without leave or indeed to impersonate an officer. The five days were for abandoning valuable military equipment – to wit our belts and berets.

I was in Germany not for four months but for twice that. I found the in-barracks routine tedious with its emphasis on drill and equipment cleaning. I made serious efforts but must admit I was not a natural in-barracks soldier. My first five days 'Confined to Barracks', as the punishment was officially and euphemistically called (and known as Jankers to everyone), was therefore not my last spell of this particular torture.

Life outside the barracks on manoeuvres suited me much better. We rode half-track armoured vehicles and learnt to cooperate with our tank regiment, the 9th Lancers, in their huge Centurion tanks. The war of movement for which we were preparing meant that we were constantly, day and night, on the move. Later that summer we joined with other national contingents in vast manoeuvres, 'schemes' we called them, with up to 100,000 NATO troops involved. We would roam the woods and hills of Westphalia, living rough, sleeping rough, cooking in the open, fighting to stay awake on guard, digging trenches, and learning the British soldier's art of making himself comfortable whatever the conditions. It was a way of life I took to with ease. Indeed, it was surprisingly like my hitch-hiking days.

There were times when the only roof we slept under for two or three weeks on end would be the roof of an occasional German barn. Most times we were filthy but (as German ex-soldiers often remarked upon) always well-shaven and with newly cleaned boots. With luck we would come across an Army Mobile Shower Unit from time to time, but often not for several weeks. On a scheme there was no such thing as leave – another big difference between us and the barrack-based troops in the service units. I had just one weekend's leave in Germany in the whole eight months I was there. International tensions were still high. We didn't talk much about it but amid all the jokes, the lack of sleep, the aches and pains and the freezing conditions as the German winter approached, we were all well aware what we were preparing for. The opposing armies in these vast manoeuvres were usually titled something along the lines of Red Force and Blue Defender, so there was no doubt in anybody's mind about what we were anticipating – a sudden Russian attack (like the

North Korean assault of the previous year) across the dividing line
between East and West Germany.

During a long scheme I seldom knew which day of the week it was.
When a letter was delivered to me in a wood above the Rhine from
London County Council, threatening to remove my University
Maintenance grant if I didn't reply by the end of October, I had to
run around asking if anybody knew which month it was. It was
November already – but the LCC relented.

I found a particular enjoyment in this wild life in the woods. Most
of our activity was conducted at night. Mock attacks on the
'enemy' were fierce, hand-to-hand affairs. The Belgians and French,
I knew from listening to their radio messages, were surprised by the
seriousness with which we fought our allotted role. In turn I was
fascinated to discover how easily you could panic a hundred
exhausted men with loudspeaker broadcasts of approaching tanks,
flares, cat-calls and screams in the night – the techniques the
Japanese had initiated in Burma and which we were now developing
further in Germany.

Once in barracks it was a different story. One that, for me, very often
ended in another spell on jankers.

Then one evening, shortly before the whole battalion was
scheduled to depart on an Anglo-American-French scheme in
Southern Germany, I was just leaving our barrack block when the
company sergeant-major stopped me. 'Rifleman . . .' We had in fact
become good friends working together on manoeuvres, but he always
immediately resumed a very formal manner once in barracks. So, of
course, did I.

'Sir?'

He held some sheets of paper in his hand. 'List of the new draft
arriving Sennelager tomorrow night. Got a Rifleman Wheal, K.
22458791 here. I hope to God there's not two of you.'

I felt a surge of pleasure. 'My brother, sir. He's just finished at Bushfield.'

'You've got a brother, have you?' He shook his head at the prospect. 'I only hope he's quicker on the parade ground than you are. Does he like the Army?'

'Loves it, sir.'

'Yes, well, he volunteered to be in this hole. Why was that?'

'We've always looked out for each other.'

He grimaced. 'Be able to keep you out of trouble then, will he?'

'We can only hope, sir.'

'Strewth! That's one job I wouldn't take on,' he said as he went on his way.

I had of course known Kit was finishing his training at Bushfield but had lost track of exactly when. The next night I was loading, under arc lights, our section half-track on the main barrack square. There were forty other half-tracks, a dozen jeeps and a Bren gun carrier platoon all loading at the same time for the forthcoming scheme so it was not difficult to slip away now and again. It was of course exactly the sort of thing that earned me spells of jankers whenever I was in barracks.

I crossed to C company barrack block four or five times that evening. On the last visit the noise on the top training floor made me sure they'd arrived. It was nearly six months since I'd seen Kit. I walked into the first room and couldn't quite believe my eyes. I expected a raw-looking young recruit. Far from it. His kit was already unpacked and laid out on his bed in the regulation manner, ready for inspection later that evening.

I saw with astonishment that everything was in perfect condition. He had taken to heart my descriptions of life in the Green Jackets. He had, for instance, remembered that on your first day at Bushfield you were handed two pairs of oiled boots and expected to make them gleam like stars in the blackest night within an impossibly short time. To relieve the first week's pressure he had therefore bought two pairs of regulation ammunition boots at an Army surplus shop a month before he was due to arrive at Bushfield. He and my father, working together in the kitchen at White City, had then 'hot-spooned' them to draw out the oils in the leather and polished them to a glittering finish.

There was, of course, only one regiment for him to join and the Army always responds to requests to keep brothers together. It was pure pleasure to see him. He looked totally at home for someone who was straight out of Basic Training. He had grown in six months and we were now almost exactly the same size. For me this was nothing but good fortune. Every morning he would wake and listen for the clack-clack of my patented Wilkinson Sword razor, our B company bathroom windows being opposite his C company barrack room. If it was before 5.30 in the morning he would know I had collected another spell of Confined to Barracks the day before, and come racing over to my block with his perfectly pressed battle-dress and gleaming boots.

Help was a serious necessity. The jankers principle (executed ferociously by Regimental Police Sergeant Johnson) was that you were run off your feet. Every minute of the day, 5.30 a.m. to half-past midnight, was filled with near-impossible orders. Nobody could live through five days of jankers without friends dressing you, getting food for you, waking you as you cat-napped to recover lost sleep. Even with good friends and a brother in the next block, fourteen days could reduce you to a zombie-like state of exhaustion.

Fortunately, of my eight months in Germany I probably spent little more than two months in barracks. Most of my memories of Germany are of that summer into early winter (with occasional three or four days in barracks) out on manoeuvres, sleeping under the stars. One evening, near Luneberg Heath, the former German Army exercise area, we found ourselves camped ('leagered up' was our term for it) in a wood near the town of Bergen. On some errand I can no longer recall, I found myself walking alone through the wood. Ahead I saw a faded sign nailed to a tree. It read: *Bergen-Belsen – the site of the camp liberated by British troops in April 1945.*

All that horrifying news footage I had seen as a fourteen year old flooded back. There was no camp left, of course, just flat, cleared land. Birds sang and fluttered from tree to tree as they must have done in the years of unspeakable cruelty that had taken place here. I wondered if there were still bodies buried and remembered the terrible pits full of the emaciated dead I had seen in the newsreel. It would have been impossible to recover them all. If there weren't bodies, there were parts of bodies. Today, at a time when architects and governments scramble to put up complex symbolic monuments in steel and concrete, I wonder if something like this, birds fluttering around a bed of flat land and a simple board nailed to a tree, isn't the best, the most movingly appropriate, way of remembering the dead, and the brutality of the times.

As the manoeuvres began to involve more and more NATO forces we were dispatched in the autumn to South Germany, to join a scheme on the borders of the French and the American zones. The opening move was to rendezvous with a French brigade who would take our company of a hundred and fifty men under command to do a night retreat across a river. The name of the river now escapes me, as does the part of the French zone in which we were operating. The village where the French and British units were to meet was small and picturesque. Gabled roofs were adorned with storks' nests or archery targets (presumably because any hunting firearms were forbidden to German citizens). We waited for the French unit to arrive.

Some two hours later the French Army drifted down the village street in small groups, wrapped in rain-capes. They were hungry, miserable and lost. They pointed in various different directions as the possible location of their battalion or brigade headquarters. I spoke to some of the conscripts and they complained bitterly about their cigarette ration having arrived damp and their wine ration having turned up late. A cigarette ration! A daily wine ration! They were the saddest sacks I had ever seen in uniform. Later, in a dug-out in the woods, I spoke to a French Intelligence Officer. He said the morale of the French forces in Germany was dangerously low. Politics at home, he saw as the reason. A constant Communist Party propaganda barrage against NATO. Was it the same in the British Army?

This was not the view of most of the National Servicemen I served with and who spent weeks among the German villages of Westphalia. Out on manoeuvres, being helped by a German householder as you dug a slit trench in the middle of his lawn, or sitting in a farm kitchen chatting with a *hausfrau* as she cooked, and shared, your rations, it was impossible not to see the overwhelming majority of them as people like us. I am not, by any means, avoiding the issue of how members of the SS divisions and some of the German Army behaved in Russia. But in these periods of halting Anglo-German contact the sense of raw fear, especially among the women, of a Russian advance across the dividing line between East and West, went a long way towards providing us with our *raison d'être*. In 1951 a six-foot hole dug in the middle of your lawn was not a high price to pay if it meant the only forces between you and the Russians were better trained to defend you.

The sheer physical demands of life in an infantry regiment in Germany (even more so in Korea) at this time made nonsense of that jokey estimate, common enough in Britain then and even more so today, of the value of National Service. We were soon disabused of any smug civilian idea that we were 'just playing soldiers'. You can't move thousands of men at night in convoys of fifty-ton tanks mixed with vulnerable soft-skinned vehicles, all without lights, through forest paths and dust-clogged back lanes, without accidents. You can't learn to fire live ammunition without, somewhere, a mortar bomb exploding in the trees above someone's head or a grenade being dropped at the very moment the pin has been pulled. River crossings on pontoon bridges were particularly dangerous.

Converting civilians to well-trained infantry in less than a year is a hazardous business. There were, inevitably, not infrequent injuries and an annual death toll.

The British Army of the Rhine operated under a system of alerts. During my time in the 11th Armoured Division we were called out several times, most on Amber but one full Red Alert. When we were stood down the colonel ordered every company commander to address his men on the Soviet threat. Listening posts had detected a huge movement of Soviet armour up to the line just 100 kilometres from our position. Perhaps three hours away at an armoured rate of advance. After a few hours the Soviet armour had slowly pulled back. These were not games. The danger of an incident unwanted by either side, or of a planned attack across the line, was real.

There have not been many recent revelations from Moscow in the area of aggressive military intent in those years. It's probable that the Soviet Union was, throughout most of the Cold War, at least as concerned about NATO intentions as we were about theirs. But there were periods of real danger. The post-war Blockade of Berlin and the Cuban Missile Crisis in the sixties are obviously two. Another was when I was in Germany in the early fifties when Stalin's mental powers were daily becoming more erratic; when he could act with the cunning it took to launch the Korean War and yet, deep in paranoia, was daily seeing assassination plots all around him. And when, on at least one occasion, he called a military conference to discuss the feasibility of a Soviet lightning advance to the English Channel. (The Soviet generals counselled against it.)

Fortunately for the world he died, possibly murdered, in March 1953. He was deeply mourned, and not only in the Soviet Union.

But then so many Western journalists had for years spent their column inches on giving him an impossibly good press.

I returned to England in the winter of that year to retake the War Office Selection Board, WOSB. This time it was a walkover. My father briefed me on crosswords and my ten-minute lecture covered the militarily unimpeachable subject of this year's NATO manoeuvre in Germany. I don't know if the colonel remembered me, but he smiled as he read the report on my lecture. 'Good stuff,' he said. An hour later I learnt that I had passed.

Eaton Hall Officer Cadet School was no place to be in winter and I had managed once again to start a training period in January. The Hall itself was a louring Victorian Gothic mass, leased from the Duke of Westminster. Most cadets lived in the familiar long wooden barrack huts that nestled at the Hall's base like a medieval village round a cathedral. The regime was non-stop drill, military knowledge and manoeuvres. On the drill square I achieved the all-time Eaton Hall record of being charged fourteen times by a Welsh Guards sergeant-major who couldn't believe that my slow right and left turns were anything but dumb insolence. The fourteenth charge also saw me escorted to the Guardroom cells where I spent the night contemplating my future, if any, at Eaton Hall.

I could easily have been returned to my unit but was, I think, saved by the fact that I had showed keenness by taking part in the Eaton Hall Boxing Championship (which I won as a middle-weight, having lost a good number of pounds in Germany). I had also come top in three of the four military knowledge tests. The morning of my appearance on fourteen separate charges I was faced by the colonel commanding, a formidable red-haired Guards Officer named Colonel Basil Eugster. Had he (and I) possessed the ability to look into the future he would have known that his niece Diana Eugster would sometime become my wife and the mother of my twin daughters, Caroline and Elizabeth-Anne. Thank God he possessed no such powers! He mused about the fourteen charges, read my company commander's report, presumably looked at the military knowledge results and simply told me to try harder on the drill square in future. I was saved.

I knew that my birth certificate meant there was no chance of my going back to the Green Jackets as an officer so I applied for the Parachute Regiment. I had two reasons for doing so. The first and most important was that it was a regiment with the same prestige as the most elite formations in the British Army but there was no class discrimination there. Officers were plumbers' sons as often as they were Peers of the Realm. The other reason was important to me. It was the sense of challenge. I knew what I thought about jumping from a plane at a thousand feet. It was against nature. But I wanted to see how I would react to something that was so much against *my* nature.

I had in fact been encouraged to apply by my company commander at Eaton Hall Officer Cadet School, himself in the Parachute Regiment. He was a hard-faced man named Captain Fletcher, bored by the interminable drilling of our Welsh Guards sergeant-major and much more interested in work in the field. He recognised I was too.

With his favourable report I thought I was bound to be accepted – and I was. He had called me into his office to tell me this but, a grim-faced man at the best of times, remained as grim-faced as ever. There was a hitch. A certain minimum period of remaining service was required for transfer to the Parachute Regiment and, with my two-month early release for university, I lacked the necessary time. I would therefore be assigned to an infantry regiment somewhere in the world, do my parachute training before release and be posted to a reserve parachute battalion if I passed.

The day our postings were handed out on our last day at Eaton

Hall, the tension was evident as we paraded (under Sergeant-Major Evans) on the small stable drill square. Captain Fletcher came forward and began reading out the postings. I had had no time to state a regimental preference after he had told me that my lack of remaining time in the service precluded an immediate posting to the Parachute Regiment. My surname, as so often, took me to the bottom of the list. I had plenty of time to speculate about where I might be sent – and at that time it was almost anywhere in the world.

The company commander finally came to my name: Second Lieutenant Donald Wheal . . . to the 1st Battalion, The Loyal Regiment – currently stationed in Trieste.

I had been assigned what some thought of as one of the very best of postings, a spectacularly beautiful, Italian-speaking port on the sun-drenched coast of the Adriatic. I was pretty sure it was Captain Fletcher's doing. I feel, with no more than a touch of paranoia, that I've been plagued throughout my life by people who consider that I've had things too easy. Sergeant-Major Evans, Welsh Guards, glowering at me as Trieste was announced as my posting, was certainly one of them.

THIRTY FIVE
Trieste

Trieste as a city played a unique and largely unknown part in the Cold War. Tucked high in the corner of the Adriatic, bordering Yugoslavia, it was the object of territorial claims by both Tito and the new Italian Republic. In the middle, in the port itself and in the mountains around, sat three battalions of British infantry and a regiment of American troops. We had no supporting tanks, no heavy artillery. We would of course have been swept into the sea by a Soviet advance from Austria or Hungary, a fact acknowledged by the presence of a secret underground lorry park, the trucks kept filled with petrol and all engines tested twice a week by the battalion duty officer. In other words we were ready for anything – but only as long as it was a moonlight flit.

The Italian claim to Trieste was clearly enough stated by the Sunday demonstrations (sometimes turning to fairly minor riots) in the Piazza Unità, the main square. Indeed in my later months there I had an Italian girlfriend who used to riot against the British on Sunday morning and go dancing with me at the Bastione Fiorito club on a castle rampart in the evening.

The Yugoslav demands on what was then called the Free Territory of Trieste were even less subtly pursued by guerrilla attacks on ammunition dumps and aggressive patrolling of the border. This could amount, on occasion, to incursions into our territory to kidnap an Italian policeman for bartering against one of their deserters. This unique Cold War situation was presided over by a British general and it was therefore the British who were considered, by Italians and Yugoslavs alike, the villains of the piece. In Trieste itself if, during the more violent incidents in the Piazza Unità, a British unit was to be relieved by an American company, there would be missiles and cat-calls for us as we left and corresponding cheers for the arriving Americans, although I know, from talking to American senior officers, that they were prepared to be distinctly quicker on the trigger than we were permitted to be.

But mostly, as spring brought a Mediterranean warmth and it became possible to take a weekend leave in Venice, Trieste justified its reputation as one of the more agreeable postings. Demonstrations in the Piazza Unità seldom resulted in people being hurt although there was some shooting and a number of deaths (some on the British side) before the situation was finally resolved.

In the heights behind Trieste it was different. Yugoslav soldiers would risk their lives to come sliding down the British side of the mountain and desert to the West. The Loyals, along with the two other regiments in the brigade, regularly patrolled this rough, rocky mountain region. The political situation was complex beyond our understanding. By 1952 the break between Stalin and Tito had already taken place. I know for a fact (because my platoon was involved) that we were secretly supplying Tito with arms through the limestone caves which ran beneath the border. In the underground darkness we appeared to be friends; up above, in the bright sunlight bouncing off the rocky hills, still bitter enemies.

In such confusing situations soldiers of all nations fall back on their own instinct for survival. The first patrol I was to lead along the mountain border was to have, as was usual practice, a local guide, an Italian policeman who knew the mountains. He was nervous, very nervous, of a kidnap attempt. There had been two by the Yugoslavs, he told me, just a week earlier.

It was not a border along which you could string barbed wire. There was some soft earth where mines could be planted but it was mostly bare, inhospitable, sun-drenched yellow rock. Long before we reached the high point we were slick with sweat, fingers slipping off our weapons. It was no place for a Sunday afternoon stroll.

The Italian policeman asked me if he could stop on one side of a massive outcrop of rock while the patrol continued on climbing round the mountain as we followed the actual border. He would wait in safety next to one of the huge Demarcation Boards we had erected up there, saying on one side in English and Serbo-Croat: *Warning. You are now entering the British Zone*, and on the other side: *Warning. You are now entering the Yugoslav Zone*. Our guide's proposal was that he would meet us ten or fifteen minutes later as we emerged from the other side of the outcrop.

It was my first patrol. I was green. I knew the kidnap attempts were real. The system was that the Yugoslavs would claim the Italian policeman had infringed the border and try to barter him for three or four of their own deserters. I looked at the great rock rising sixty foot. I looked at the policeman. He was probably in his fifties. Old, to my eyes. I agreed.

My patrol was not small. It consisted of twenty-five men, all armed with rifles or Sten guns. We set off to follow the border which the guide had told me was a straightforward path around the massive outcrop. Within five minutes I discovered he had said nothing about the point at which the path appeared to split into three separate directions. I took the route closest to the rock, checking my compass. There was no map which could possibly help up here. I gave the signal to move on.

We marched and scrambled across scattered rocks, lost and refound the path, slid down screes and climbed slopes for about twenty minutes. The sun reflected white off the rocks. The temperature was in the nineties. I decided the guide could wait a little longer and put out sentries while the rest of the patrol broke for a smoke, weapons handy, in the shade.

The ground had not at all corresponded to the configuration the guide had described with such cheerful Italian certainty. I was still fairly sure we were in more or less the right position although I could feel the alarm mounting in my chest. I knew that if we strayed across the Demarcation Line, we would have to submit to being taken prisoner or fight our way back to our zone. Either course could lead to casualties and an international incident at the very least.

'Don't look much like the country walk our Eyetalian promised us, sir,' the patrol corporal said. 'Think he was just trying to save himself a few extra blisters.'

'I'm thinking the same thing,' I said. I could sense the uneasiness in the corporal's voice. 'Main thing now is that we stay on the right side of the line. Get the lads ready to move. I'm going to check the board.'

I climbed to the top of a mass of rock and tried to see the end of the outcrop where we were to meet up with the guide. No sign of him. No sign of the end of the outcrop either although there was a Demarcation Board about half a mile ahead, and fortunately its positioning seemed to show we were well within the British Zone.

When I got back the patrol was spaced out along the dusty track. I called on the corporal to get them moving, and with the usual groans they adjusted their ammunition belts and started off down the broken path which I hoped would curve round the rock back to the point where we were to meet the guide. I wasn't feeling too well disposed towards him at that moment.

Mountain walking is not easy. Maintaining direction in such broken terrain is even more difficult. I tried to keep the big board in my sights. I seemed to lose and re-find it constantly until, after five minutes or so in which it had totally disappeared, we rounded a rock and there it was a hundred and fifty yards in front of me. It read in

English and Serbo-Croat: *Warning. You are now entering the British Zone!*

The patrol had seen it too. It meant we were well inside Yugoslav territory. There was not only the chance of being shot at from the heights around us, but the existence of mines on this track was a real possibility.

We got off the earth path and on to the hard rock of the steep side of the mountain where mines were unlikely to be planted. Slipping, sliding, feeling the strain on the ankles every step of the way, I cursed the Italian guide. And myself. It was the longest hundred and fifty yards any of us had ever walked.

The boys in the patrol reacted well to what was obviously my error. Pouring with sweat, hands slipping on our weapons, we reached the last outcrop and had begun to round it when I stopped dead.

Six Yugoslav soldiers were sitting in the shade of an overhanging rock doing what we had just done: cooling down, drinking from their water bottles, smoking cigarettes. I could see the shock on their faces. We were a patrol twenty-five strong. We were well armed, carrying rifles and Sten guns at the ready. They were sprawled in the sun. Or had been. Now to a man they had jerked into a sitting position. I looked at the Yugoslav I took to be the sergeant in charge, the only man standing. He had had his back to me and was now half-turned, looking me in the eyes. We were only ten yards apart. His rifle, like most of his men's weapons, was leaning against the rock. I carried a loaded Sten gun. Among the stacked Yugoslav weapons was a light machine gun. He knew he could never have got to it in time.

I lifted my hand to him and he nodded with infinite slowness. One of his men moved behind him, towards the stacked weapons. The sergeant said something and the man stayed half-kneeling, ready to jump towards the rifles. The sergeant nodded again to me and I signalled for the patrol to pass, my corporal and myself walking slowly backwards, watching the Yugoslavs for any movement towards their rifles. Within a few minutes we had crossed under the Demarcation Board. This time the Yugoslav sergeant lifted *his* hand, as relieved as I was.

There was no Italian policeman waiting on the other side.

When we got back to Rossetti Barracks in the Via Michelangelo, I filled in the patrol report with trepidation. I reported that we had 'lost contact' with our Italian police guide for several minutes and had observed a Yugoslav patrol at rest. I was well aware I had risked the lives of twenty-four of my own men by my willingness to accommodate the Italian policeman; possibly even risked the lives of some Yugoslav border troops, too. There was no excuse. But it was the last patrol I ever did without a local guide.

These were heavy responsibilities, and hard lessons, for a twenty year old.

For some of the hottest days of summer we were camped on a rocky plateau high up above Trieste. Just before sunset one evening, after a day of exercises in baking heat around the mountain villages behind the town, I had carried out all the necessary junior officer's duties – checked that a meal was being prepared for the platoon as soon as they'd cleaned up, checked their rifles, checked the condition of their feet (vital in infantry battalions), checked that any who had suffered bad cuts or falls during the day reported to the medical tent . . . I was looking forward to a cold beer and a shower when a fellow subaltern said there was someone to see me at the guard tent of the encampment. A woman.

We were several miles up above Trieste. The roads were narrow dust tracks with screes and drops on either side. 'You serious? What sort of woman?'

My friend had only received the message from the guard tent. He hadn't seen her.

'Is she alone?'

'Apparently.'

I couldn't imagine my former Italian girlfriend, Marghareta, elegant and impeccably dressed, tottering her way alone up through these dust-covered Slovenian-speaking mountain villages. But I couldn't guess what other woman would have made it up here either. I should have.

As I approached I could hear a woman's voice speaking in English. As I reached the entrance she turned from the guard sergeant she was talking to. It was Marie.

Of course. Who else would have been able to sweet-talk her way up here to a militarised zone forbidden to civilians other than the few hundred inhabitants of the area? She jumped up. That smile. Those hooded eyes. She was tanned and certainly not dressed for these rough hills in a white shirt, blue summer skirt and sandals. The contrast between Marie standing there, a visitor from my other world, and the sheer roughness of Army life took my breath away. I stared at her, for the moment stunned, only slowly breaking into a smile.

'A young lady to see you, sir,' the Regimental Police sergeant was saying. *You lucky devil* was threaded rather obviously through his words. 'If the young lady was calling on other than an officer, sir, I would have had the pleasure of putting her under arrest.'

I barely heard him.

She was thinking of going to live in America. From the moment she told me that I was sure that meant she was going to get married. Had she come to Trieste to tell me that? It was nearly two years since we had seen each other, well over a year since we had ceased writing. Yet she was her normal, extraordinary self. Perhaps I was tempted to make too much of her arrival. Today, when the young back-pack the world, a journey from Vienna to Trieste is hardly an undertaking. In 1952 it was wrapped in military restrictions. Certainly I'd never met a single tourist since I'd been here. For me, with no more than the

occasional scent of freedom for the last twenty months, I suppose it
seemed Marie's arrival must have some significant intent. Why had
she come?

I got changed out of my dust-caked uniform and we went down to
Trieste. Darkness fell as we had dinner at a trattoria overlooking the
Adriatic. We talked, mostly I seem to remember, about Vienna. She
asked me what I had been doing in my spare time. Perhaps I told her
of my brief fling with Marghareta whose target was an officer who
would marry her and take her back to England, I don't remember.
What else was I to tell her? There was no spare time, or very little,
there was no wider experience than what we did every day . . .
marching, firing thousands of rifle and machine gun rounds at targets
on the hillsides in live ammunition practice, patrolling the squares of
Trieste or the hills and mountains between us and the Yugoslav
Army. This and the responsibility for looking after the health and
safety of 39 Lancashire lads the same age as myself had absorbed my
days since my arrival in March. So we talked mostly about Vienna.

We left the restaurant late. Trieste looked spectacular. We walked,
right through the few hours of darkness, the length and breadth of
the old city, through its cool narrow alleys and across its grand open
squares, past groups of uniformed Triestino policemen in cafés
singing opera. We walked with our arms round each other until dawn
broke over Hungary and Austria and the Yugoslav mountains.

At 4.30 we sat on a step near the train station. The sun was already
warm. I wanted to talk about her plans to live in America or about
really why she had come to Trieste but I found I couldn't. I had
convinced myself that she had come to tell me that she was going to
America to get married. But why would she come to Trieste to tell
me after two years apart?

We drank one final coffee in the station while her train was huffing
and spitting steam. We stood silently facing each other, glancing up
with every sip of hot espresso, smiling at each other a brief smile.
Whistles and shouts surrounded us. The guard waved his green flag

and Marie climbed aboard. I caught sight of her once or twice as she threaded her way to her seat. Should I have said something? What had she wanted me to say? Had she wanted me to say anything at all?

Moments later the train was pulling away. I stood on the platform, still speechless, not even waving her goodbye.

Of course, I do believe now she came on a spur of the moment decision, not to say anything, not to have anything said by me – but simply for the trip. But Army life is harsh; romance is notably lacking. I think I needed Marie's presence in Trieste to mean more than just a visit from Vienna.

I've often thought of that night. It has come to take time and space in my memory, and with it a distant, fadeless charm. A fantasy that happened.

THIRTY SIX

Cambridge

I left the Loyal Regiment without real regrets. The senior officers were not up to the standard of the Green Jackets and many of the private soldiers, amiable Lancashire country boys, scored higher on endurance than initiative. The battalion was held together by its NCOs, as indeed is any infantry battalion. But there too, with some real exceptions, the Loyals still had some way to go to match the levels demanded by the Green Jackets.

The Parachute Regiment entered my life again with a posting, when I arrived back in England, to Abingdon Parachute Training School. For weeks our squad of about twelve men of all ranks were hooked up to wire contraptions and invited to jump from high platforms or go swinging through the trees like orang-utans. At ground level we struggled through assault courses and practised the forward and backward rolls off the back of a moving truck.

For some reason all candidates found 'The Fan' the most disagreeable item in our initial training. It was simple, probably not dangerous, but it possessed that special quality of being compellingly against nature. You stood about forty foot up on a slender platform, wearing a parachute harness attached to what appeared to be a very thin wire cord. The cord was attached to the spindle of a small fan.

Obviously you were expected to jump to the ground below. So what stopped you plunging down to broken legs and pelvis? The fan. An apparatus with blades about the width of a medium-sized household appliance.

I checked with the sergeant instructor. 'Does this fan have some sort of electric braking mechanism?'

'No, sir.'

'I see.' Doubt in my voice. 'Does the fan have any more resistance than the simple movement of its blades through the air?'

Deadpan: 'Why would you need that, sir?'

Hmm.

I positioned myself on the edge of the platform and looked down. Forty foot is about the height of a three-storey building. Add six feet for your own eyeline and think about the *lack* of resistance provided by the flimsy blades of that fan . . . 'Go!'

I didn't jump. I stepped outwards, eyes not quite closed. Speed of descent depends on the bodyweight of the victim. I came down quickly enough but hit the ground with no more force than a seven- or eight-foot jump. Easy. Even so, we all felt the same about it when smilingly offered a chance by our instructor to do a few more.

Our first real jump was from a balloon, a barrage balloon, a great, grey, tattered, swaying elephantine thing with an enclosed basket swinging underneath. Held by a wire thread controlled from a winch truck on the ground, lifted by the gas-filled monster above us, our ascent was slow and silent. Only when we reached 800 feet could I hear the wind tugging at the torn pieces of the balloon's outer cover. At least, I hoped it was just the *outer* cover.

It was a clear day, with perhaps a few thin clouds above us. The ground, the RAF huts, the green DZ or Drop Zone, seemed strangely flat, like looking down from a skyscraper that had been built in the countryside. As the only officer in our 'stick', or group, I was to jump first. I positioned myself at the door, checked my static line which would pull the parachute out of the back-pack, checked it

again as instructed (this was before the days of reserve parachutes –
the first one *had* to work), and on the command, jumped.

There was no time to be terrified, though I suppose I was. The first
real sensation is an exhilarating lift through the air as the parachute
opens. Then a few moments of sheer wonder as you float down
before the ground tips crazily towards you as you attempt to execute
your still inexpert forward roll.

I was down, sprawling on the grass, being tugged forward by my
billowing parachute before I knew it. But feeling wonderful.

Jumping from an aircraft is of course very different. Jumping with a
heavy pack attached to your leg is more different still. Suddenly you
come to understand the instructor's maxim: a parachute is just to get
you there. The real work starts when you're about to touch the
ground.

After nine aircraft jumps we were awarded our wings. One man
had already left. At any time before the last jump it was quite
legitimate to refuse. You were treated courteously and discreetly.
After the last jump it was a court-martial offence.

I was in the Parachute Regiment but as yet unposted to a battalion.
It was only a matter of weeks now before I was released to take up my
place at Cambridge. I spent some time at Aldershot and met the man
who was to become my commanding officer in the reserve 13th
Battalion, The Parachute Regiment, Lt. Colonel Cleasby-
Thompson, one of the most distinguished members of the regiment.
Highlights of my time with the 13th included a cancelled (thank
God!) night water jump over Southport Bay, a brigade drop from
Bickeburg, Germany, from a cheerfully efficient US Air Transport
squadron, all wearing Stewart tam o'shanters they had picked up in
Edinburgh, and a windy battalion drop at Thetford when two men
tangled and were killed.

On that jump the man behind me in the stick fatally hesitated in the doorway while the number three moved round him and then jumped. As I floated clear I looked up at the aircraft to get my bearings and saw him, arms flailing, hanging from the tailplane with his static line strap wrapped round his neck. It seemed certain he would be strangled to death, but he was freed by the sergeant-dispatcher leaning far out of the plane and shaking violently on his static line. Suddenly his parachute blossomed and moments later he was on the ground with no more than raw strap burns from his near-hanging.

I had completed my National Service. I was demobilised from Preston and travelled down to London to spend two days with my parents at White City. My father kept nodding and smiling. My mother struggled to hold back the tears of relief that she had recovered at least one of her sons. Kit, of course, was still in Sennelager. He had just been selected for promotion to weapon-training full corporal. It's difficult to make it clear how significant, and indeed rare, that was in the Green Jackets. But Kit was developing fast under the responsibility he had been given. I only really understood how fast when he first came home on leave. My younger brother was a changed man, in most senses a younger brother no more.

It was a mist-laden October late afternoon when I reached Pembroke College. A carbon copy of the afternoon I had first arrived at the arched entrance to the porters' lodge two years ago. Only this time I was no longer a supplicant, I was an undergraduate.

I stood on the pavement opposite and watched young men unloading ancient trunks from taxis. Most of them had their names painted on the sides: 2nd/Lt. John Smith, 4th Hussars . . . 2nd/Lt. John Smythe, Royal Marines. I thanked my lucky stars that I had decided to do my National Service before coming up. I couldn't guess what it would be like for an eighteen year old, straight from grammar school, among the overwhelming majority of the college, all of whom were two to three years older, and bound together not only by accent and mannerisms but by using the same unknown references and language of military service.

I didn't go into the college immediately. I'm not sure why. I told myself I'd like to look at Cambridge one last time as an outsider but it was probably the knowledge that I was about to start a new life, one that would continue what the Army had started, one that would take me away from all I had previously known.

I walked on a few minutes. I had just one bag, the pigskin Gladstone of earlier days, having finally come to recognise its worth. There were lights in the shops along King's Parade. The pale stone pinnacles of King Henry's great chapel rose sharp against the receding grey background of evening. It was hardly possible not to try and guess what the next three years would bring. I think one simple question – would I have friends? – dominated all others. I remember reminding myself that I had thought the same at Bushfield, in Germany, at Eaton Hall and in Trieste, and on each occasion it had worked out well. I remember, as I passed the corner of Pembroke Street, promising myself that whatever happened I would not lose contact with my mother and father, with Kit, and with everything I thought of as the World's End.

I didn't really think about the work. Interested as I was in History, I knew I was not going to become an academic historian. I needed Cambridge for a whole set of other reasons of personal growth. But none of this would be achieved if I huddled in my rooms, excluded from the life of a college that was largely made up of public school entrants. I thought of the people I had met in the Green Jackets. My platoon commander Adam Butler, I imagined, would be beginning his second year here. I thought of Marlburians like John Mortimer who had tried to convert me to Christianity in a freezing 'spider' in Bushfield Camp. I thought of Richard Rougier who had offered to write to the Dean to get us adjoining sets of rooms. But all that was a long time ago. I had no idea what had happened to any of them in the last two years. One or two, friends from Eaton Hall, I already knew, had died in Korea.

The porter had told me where to find my room and I passed through the screens to the lighted windows of Ivy Court. New Court had been built two hundred and fifty years later in a Victorian classical style. I turned into it from the Fellows' Bowling Green and saw my staircase ahead. Painted white on a glossy black square beside the double doorway was a list of names. It was, strangely, with something like a shock of recognition that I saw, painted there on the stone, my own name: D. J. Wheal.

I stood looking at it with a tingle creeping up my spine. The examination seemed so long ago, so much had happened in between, half a lifetime in terms of experience. Yet somehow, with no communication at all between the college and myself for two whole years, it had all come to pass. With confidence enough to hand-paint our names in white on that black background, the college had awaited our arrival in Cambridge this evening in October 1952 from wherever in the world we'd all been for the last two years. But then it had done something similar without a break for the past six hundred years.

I stood, pigskin Gladstone bag in hand, one foot on the step to the entrance to my staircase, trying to get these things into perspective, when I heard singing coming from a window to my right which would be next to my new rooms. Singing that was less than tuneful. Less than tuneful – and in Latin. It was hard not to laugh:

> *Odi profanum vulgus*
> *et arceo . . .*

THIRTY SEVEN

For the Moment

The World's End never really left me. Many nights in those next three years I would leave the three people who became my closest friends at Pembroke, Richard Rougier, Robert Yeatman and South African Tommy Armour, and wander past the Wren Chapel into Old Court. An autumnal or wintry mist is a more or less permanent backdrop to Cambridge from November through to February or March. Late at night in Old Court I often summoned up the image of my madcap grandmother Eliza, dancing, large hat askew, past the medieval Old Library and through the screens into Ivy Court, trailing as she disappeared the musky odour of a twist of snuff and the last strains of '*Mademoiselle from Armenteers parlay-voo*'.

I never lost the sense of privilege I had from growing up in the World's End. Most of all I retained and still retain a strong sense of my good fortune in having had the parents I did. My brother Kit feels the same. He returned to England in my first year at Pembroke, mature for his age, a man given self-confidence and experience by the promotions and responsibilities the Green Jackets had heaped on him. World's End and the Army set him on his way to the chairmanship of Hallmark Cards and the several other companies he led in Britain and Europe.

There would be tragedies to come for all of us: for the whole family, the early death of my father; for me, the break-up of my first marriage, and the death of my French second wife. But there were triumphs too, such as the birth of my twin daughters, Caroline and Elizabeth-Anne, and the long, astonishingly contented widowhood of my mother.

But here we're reaching into the future. For the moment, as that first Cambridge summer arrived, the present was a punt on the Cam, a book, a girl for company (if you were lucky), a trailing bottle of white Mâcon cooling on a string, a wind-up gramophone playing Sidney Bechet or Humphrey Lyttleton, the sun-warmed brick of Queens' College above the timber shadows of Isaac Newton's Mathematical Bridge . . . And that sense that the world did, after all, belong to me.

For the moment.